Jesus's Identification with the Marginalized and the Liminal

The Messianic Identity in Mark

Bekele Deboch Anshiso

MONOGRAPHS

© 2018 Bekele Deboch Anshiso

Published 2018 by Langham Monographs
An imprint of Langham Publishing

Langham Partnership
PO Box 296, Carlisle, Cumbria CA3 9WZ, UK
www.langham.org

ISBNs:
978-1-78368-430-4 Print
978-1-78368-431-1 ePub
978-1-78368-432-8 Mobi
978-1-78368-433-5 PDF

Bekele Deboch Anshiso has asserted his right under the Copyright, Designs and Patents Act, 1988 to be identified as the Author of this work.

All rights reserved. No part of this publication may be reproduced, stored in a retrieval system or transmitted, in any form or by any means, electronic, mechanical, photocopying, recording or otherwise, without the prior written permission of the publisher or the Copyright Licensing Agency.

Unless otherwise stated, Scripture quotations are from the New Revised Standard Version Bible, copyright © 1989 National Council of the Churches of Christ in the United States of America. Used by permission. All rights reserved.

British Library Cataloguing-in-Publication Data
A catalogue record for this book is available from the British Library

ISBN: 978-178-368-430-4

Cover & Book Design: projectluz.com

Langham Partnership actively supports theological dialogue and an author's right to publish but does not necessarily endorse the views and opinions set forth here or in works referenced within this publication, nor can we guarantee technical and grammatical correctness. Langham Partnership does not accept any responsibility or liability to persons or property as a consequence of the reading, use or interpretation of its published content.

Dedication
This book is dedicated to
Uncle John Stott, Miss Moira McLure and
the saints at Speen Baptist Church.

Contents

Abstract xi
Acknowledgements xiii
Chapter 1 1
Introduction
    1.1. State of the Problem and the Research Question 4
    1.2. Preliminary Studies Already Undertaken on Messiahship 7
    1.3. Concluding Summary to the Previous Studies on the Subject 13
    1.4. The Nature of the Research and Research Hypothesis 15
    1.5. Research Procedure and Methodology 17
    1.6. Defining and Explaining the Terms "Margin" or "Marginality" and "Liminal" or "Liminality" 20
        1.6.1. Margin or Marginality 21
        1.6.2. Liminal or Liminality 22
    1.7. Social Status of Individuals and Groups of People in Mark's Gospel 24
        1.7.1. Jesus and the Elite 25
        1.7.2. Jesus and Retainers 26
        1.7.3. Jesus and the Common People 26
        1.7.4. Jesus and the Poor 29
        1.7.5. Jesus and the Outcasts 30
    1.8. Conclusion 32

Chapter 2 35
Jesus and the Marginalized and the Liminal in Mark
    2.1. The Spread of Jesus's Popularity 35
        2.1.1. Introduction 36
        2.1.2. Literary Context 36
        2.1.3. Jesus Changes His Venue to Teach and to Heal People 39
        2.1.4. Jesus Heals Many/All 42
        2.1.5. Jesus's Real Identity Was Recognized and Declared 43
    2.2. Jesus Exorcises the Gerasene Demoniac (Mark 5:1–20) 46
        2.2.1. Introduction 47
        2.2.2. Literary Context 47
        2.2.3. Jesus Comes to the Demon-Possessed Man in the Gentile Region 51

- 2.2.4. Demoniac Recognized and Proclaimed Jesus's Divine Identity..................52
- 2.2.5. The News of Jesus Spreads in the Whole Area..................56
- 2.2.6. Jesus Sends the Ex-Demoniac to Bear Witness among Gentiles..................57
- 2.2.7. Conclusion..................59
- 2.3. Jesus and the Blind Beggar (Mark 10:46–52)..................60
  - 2.3.1. Introduction..................60
  - 2.3.2. Literary Context..................61
  - 2.3.3. Jesus Comes to the Blind Beggar at Jericho (Mark 10:46–52)..................63
  - 2.3.4. A Blind Beggar Addresses Jesus, in His Royal Messianic Title..................64
  - 2.3.5. A Blind Beggar Receives Sight and Follows Jesus..................67
  - 2.3.6. Conclusion..................70
- 2.4. The Death of Jesus, the Son of God (Mark 15:33–41)..................70
  - 2.4.1. Introduction..................71
  - 2.4.2. Literary Context..................71
  - 2.4.3. The Reasons for Jesus's Abandonment and Death..................73
  - 2.4.4. Irony in Mark's Narrative..................74
  - 2.4.5. Death of Jesus, the Son of God in Mark's Narrative..................74
  - 2.4.6. Jesus and the Women..................86
  - 2.4.7. At the Conclusion of Mark's Crucifixion Narrative, Who Are These Women?..................90
  - 2.4.8. Conclusion..................91
- 2.5. Chapter Conclusion..................92

Chapter 3..................95
The Messianic Identity in Mark's Gospel
- 3.1. Introduction..................95
- 3.2. The Messiah..................97
  - 3.2.1. Definition and Introduction..................97
  - 3.2.2. The Messiah and the Messianic Hope and Expectations in the Old Testament..................98
  - 3.2.3. The Messianic Idea in Judaism..................101
  - 3.2.4. The Messianic Hope and Expectation in the Gospels..................105
  - 3.2.5. Conclusion..................108
- 3.3. The Son of David..................109
  - 3.3.1. Introduction..................109
  - 3.3.2. Jesus the Son of David (Mark 10:47–48)..................110

  3.3.3. Is Jesus Son of David or Lord of David?
    (Mark 12:35–37) 111
  3.3.4. Conclusion 116
 3.4. The Son of God...117
  3.4.1. Introduction 117
  3.4.2. Meaning of the Title "Son of God" 120
  3.4.3. Divine Man – θεῖoV ἀnήr – *Theos Aner* 120
  3.4.4. "Son of God" in the Gospels...132
  3.4.5. Jesus as the Son...134
  3.4.6. God as Abba as Father 135
  3.4.7. The Revelation of Jesus in Mark's Gospel 136
  3.4.8. Conclusion 142
 3.5. The Son of Man...143
  3.5.1. Introduction 143
  3.5.2. The Background of "Son of Man" 144
 3.6. Chapter Conclusion 174

Chapter 4 177
Jesus's Marginality and Liminality

 4.1. Introduction..177
 4.2. Jesus's Voluntarily Marginalization as Galilean Jew 178
  4.2.1. Jesus the Galilean Jew 178
  4.2.2. Jesus and Galilee 180
  4.2.3. The Significance of Jesus's Galilean Identity 182
  4.2.4. "Galilee of the Gentiles" 184
  4.2.5. Jesus of Nazareth 189
 4.3. Jesus's Marginalized Occupation 189
 4.4. Jesus Became Marginalized as Regards His Unique Style
   of Teaching 191
 4.5. Who Made Him Marginalized and Liminal? 193
 4.6. The Purpose of Jesus's Liminality and Marginalized Death............205
 4.7. Conclusion 206

Chapter 5 209
Conclusion

 5.1. Unified Work of Mark's Narrative...210
 5.2. Jesus's Self-Identification with the Marginalized and Liminal........211
 5.3. Jesus's Unique Death and the Revelation of Divine Identity..........216

Bibliography... 221

Abstract

This book aims to examine the idea of the messianic identity in the Gospel of Mark, emphasizing Jesus's self-identification with the marginalized and liminal people. In the whole gospel, particularly, in its decisive points, the Markan Jesus is revealed and announced as the divine Son of God by the heavenly voice, by demons and finally by the unsuspected humanity. Nevertheless, Mark recorded Jesus's messianic identity in less obvious ways which has caused ambiguity amongst New Testament scholars.

In order to discover Jesus's divine identity, preliminary studies undertaken in the past, are briefly discussed. This focuses on the "messianic secret" as the key point of discussion to which a satisfactory consensus has not been reached. Some Markan scholars, such as William Wrede and his supporters, believed that in the first half of Mark's record of the gospel, Jesus did not think that he was the Messiah. Theodore Weeden and his followers thought that Jesus was not the Son of God but, as described in Mark's second half, that he was the suffering Son of Man.

Therefore, in order to engage the narrative elements of the text and to interpret and understand the message in its own narrative context, narrative criticism is utilized. Its importance will be demonstrated as it investigates the meaning of the text as a completed work. Use is made of the probable sources Mark had available, of which the most important are the Old Testament traditions on which the Evangelist drew for his background to his text. In addition, some intertestamental writings such as Qumran literature and apocryphal and pseudepigraphical works will be discussed, not to build an alternative understanding of messiahship of Jesus, but rather to attempt to understand the contemporary Jewish thinking about the Messiah.

This book accepts that Mark's gospel is the unified work of the evangelist. It is demonstrated that Jesus is portrayed as having thought that he was the divine Messiah in a unique sense. Chapter 2 exegetes and interprets particular texts, in Mark's gospel, in which Jesus's divine Sonship and vindicated messiahship is shown. His divine identity is revealed and proclaimed not only as the messianic Son of God by his miraculous activities in Mark's first half, but also as the suffering and vindicated Son of Man in the second, yet associating himself with unsuspecting people who are marginalized and liminal at various levels.

Chapter 3 critically evaluates certain christological themes through which Jesus is understood and confessed as the unique figure whose divine messiahship is proclaimed by God self and by humanity, and redefined and reinterpreted by Jesus himself in terms of vindicated Messiahship.

This book ends with a brief chapter challenging and encouraging the readers and interpreters of Mark's gospel to understand not only Jesus's self-identification with the marginalized and liminal in and around Galilee but also his extreme marginality to the point of shameful death and glorious resurrection in Jerusalem to save humanity.

Acknowledgements

This book would not have been possible without the guidance and encouragement of numerous people. First of all, I would like to express my especial appreciation and thanks to Professor Jeremy Punt, my supervisor, at Stellenbosch University, for his careful and impeccable, and critical and excellent supervision as well as for his great concern for me and my family. I am also grateful to the leadership of George Whitefield College in Cape Town, particularly, Mark Dickson, Dr Benjamin Dean and his family, and Jonathan More and all the faculty and staff members for their Christ-like and sacrificial concern and support for me and my family.

I would also like to thank BEST-Crosslinks Trust, Bill and Juliet Woodmann, Ms Moira MacLure, Speen Baptist Church in England, James and Jayne Tetley, Andreas and Pieternel Baur, Jamie Wood and his family, Robert Joseph and his family, James and Sandy Entwistle, Andy and Carolyn Gower, and Dr Bernard and Rosy Palmer for their prayers and financial support throughout my academic years in the University.

I also appreciate and thank Dr Steve M. Bryan, my life long teacher and friend, for helping me to become a student of the New Testament and for his exemplary life in following the crucified and exalted Jesus. My thanks must go to Prof Richard Bauckham, Prof David Seccombe, Dr Steven Wright, Dr Susanne Henderson and Dr Peter Bolt for their helps in various ways during the writing of my dissertation regardless of their hectic programmes. I also extend my appreciation to my internal examiner, Prof Elna J. Mouton for paying especial attention to read my dissertation and for her valuable criticisms and constructive comments. I would also like to thank Dr Desta Heliso and his wife, Joanna Jeffry, for being behind me and showing concern, in every way, for me and my family.

My special appreciation and thanks go to my wife Tesfanesh and our children, Mihret, Endegena and Kibemo/Beimnet, to whom this study is dedicated, for their amazing patience and sharing my journey during my busy years of studies.

Finally, all thanks and glory must go to Yahweh-God who identified himself with me to help, to save and to make me a follower of his Son, Jesus!

CHAPTER 1

Introduction

As James R. Edwards said, "From start to finish, Jesus is the uncontested subject of the Gospel of Mark." Throughout his whole gospel, Mark persuades his readers and listeners to understand who Jesus was. However, Edwards rightly goes on to say, "Unlike the Gospel of John, for instance, where major themes are made explicit, Mark has much more *implicit* major themes, requiring readers to enter into the drama of the Gospel in order to understand its meaning."[1] In other words, Mark believes that the idea of Jesus's true/real or full identity,[2] as the Son of God and/or the divine King-Messiah, is the central theme of his gospel, but he writes it in a critical or less obvious way than the popular expectations of his time. The reason is that, according to the second evangelist, Jesus avoided the open use of messianic title, the "Messiah." Put simply, he did not explicitly claim to be the Messiah; rather, he silenced demons and ordered other people not to proclaim it openly. Nevertheless, even though the triumphal entry (Mark

---

1. Edwards, *Gospel According to Mark*, 12–13.
2. It is true that the gospels do not give us an account of the "full" or "real" identity of Jesus if, by that, is meant all that made Jesus a person in history. In one sense, what Mark is claiming implicitly is not to give us the full identity of Jesus due to our limited and partial understanding of God, but he seems to be aiming at an account of Jesus's identity that would be true and reliable. I believe that in Mark's understanding, Jesus's identity is to be understood only to the extent that God revealed God self "fully" in Jesus of Nazareth. However, nobody can grasp that awesome reality fully until we see him face to face and know God fully. Reliable understanding is commended even when it is partial, provisional and incomplete, and needing continuously to be filled out by revelation from God and grasped by faith. In that sense, what Mark is pressing his readers toward is not full understanding of Jesus's identity but sufficient understanding (i.e. understanding sufficient to participate in the saving purposes of God). Even if no one, including Mark, has access to the full identity of Jesus, the gospels give us portraits of Jesus in which we see glimpses of his character, his "true likeness" – a likeness sufficient to understand who he was and what he aimed to do.

11) and trial (Mark 14) at which Jesus declares his messiahship clearly shows his messianic role, the readers of the gospel understand that his full identity was revealed in a different way, unexpectedly,[3] through his suffering and death which indicates that his action[4] is more important than his teaching.[5] Therefore, as will be discussed below, in order to communicate to his readers about Jesus's divine identity, Mark underlines the idea of the glory and suffering of Jesus as clues to his full identity. One of the outstanding features in Mark's gospel, is the way he places alongside one another the powerful deeds of Jesus (which dominate chs. 1–8) and the suffering and death of Jesus (which dominate chs. 9–16).

Therefore, the purpose of this work is to carefully investigate the idea of Jesus's divine identity, in Mark's narrative, as the glorious Son of God and the suffering/rejected and vindicated Son of Man, who is revealed in a unique way proclaiming God's kingly rule in words and deeds. In doing so, unlike other so-called messiahs of the Old Testament and the first century, Jesus has identified himself with those who were marginalized and liminal[6] individuals and groups, and so unexpected ones in the eyes of the world. Finally, Jesus's real identity was made known to all, not through his miraculous deeds or fighting against the enemies of Israel on the battle fields but through his unique death on the cross, the shameful place.

---

3. Throughout this work the word "unexpectedly" or "unexpected" will serve the idea that although he was declared as the divine Son of God by God his Father as his beloved Son in 1:11 and 9:7, and by Peter as the Christ in 8:27–30, the divine identity of Jesus was not revealed to and declared by scholars from Jerusalem (Mark 3:22–30), Jesus's own family members and close disciples who were expected to know him better and proclaim his full identity. In other words, while his own family members misunderstood him, and so questioned his mental stability (Mark 3:20–21); his first close followers were confused as to who he really was (4:41) and people in his home town identified him as a carpenter and the son of Mary (6:3), but poor and outcasts such as the demon possessed (1:24; 3:11; 5:7), poor blind beggar (10:47–48) and a gentile soldier recognized and declared Jesus's divine identity as the divine Son of God (15:39). This idea will be explained, briefly, in "the Son of God" section in chapter 3 of this work below.

4. As will be discussed in details in sub-section "Death of Jesus, the Son of God, in Mark's Narrative" in chapter 2 of this work, the great action that Jesus took during his unique and victorious death was the significant event in which his real identity, as the Son of God, was revealed and proclaimed by humanity to all to hear.

5. See Edwards, *Gospel According to Mark*, 13.

6. The meaning of the term "liminal" or "liminality" will be defined below.

At the beginning of his gospel, Mark tells his readers and listeners that Jesus is the Son of God (1:1).[7] To make his point clear, he shares with the Old Testament writers regarding Jesus's unique divine identity. In 1:2–3, Mark begins his gospel with an Old Testament citation, "See I am sending my messenger ahead of you, who will prepare your way; the voice of one crying out in the wilderness: 'Prepare the way of the Lord, make his paths straight,'" which is attributed to Isaiah but actually conflates two texts; one from Isaiah 40 and one from Malachi 3:1. It is interesting that Mark has altered the pronoun in Malachi 3:1 to read "ahead of you" rather than "before me." This obviously has some christological significance for Mark in as much as the "me" of Malachi and "Lord" of Isaiah 40 refers to Yahweh which points to his unique divine identity. Mark the evangelist shows that John's ministry was the fulfilment of the voice in the wilderness of Isaiah and the Elijah-like messenger of Malachi who prepared the way for the coming of Yahweh himself, and that that coming is to be equated with the coming of Jesus.[8] Thus, for Mark, the coming of Jesus, the Son of God is indeed the coming of Yahweh, God self.

As will be briefly discussed later, Mark also affirms that, during Jesus's baptism and his transfiguration, the voice from heaven declared that Jesus is God's uniquely beloved Son (1:11–12; 9:7). Similarly, demons, supernatural beings, repeatedly (1:24–25, 34; 3:11; 5:7) and the Roman (gentile) centurion in (15:39) declared Jesus's divine Sonship.[9]

Likewise, Mark narrates not only Jesus's miraculous deeds in the first half of his gospel, but also as a crucial part of Jesus's divine identity, he pictures Jesus as the suffering Son of Man, and the crucified and raised or

---

7. The words, "Son of God" do not appear in some ancient MSS of Mark's gospel. For this reason, some critics omit them; however, most scholars are convinced that throughout his gospel, Mark attempts to persuade his readers by using similar expressions which indicate the importance of the title "Son of God" in the narrative – e.g. Jesus's baptism 1:11, transfiguration 9:7, the demons's confession 3:11; 5:7; at the Crucifixion 15:39; and additionally, in the question of the high priest 14:61. Therefore, the textual evidence, heavily favours authenticity, and the omission may have been accidental due to six consecutive words in the Greek text having the same ending. See Brooks, *The Death of the Messiah*, 39.

8. This idea was taken from Bryan, Class Lecture New Testament One.

9. For further understanding of this view on Jesus's divine Sonship which is affirmed and declared by God his Father, by demons and the Roman (gentile) centurion, read Kingsbury, *Christology*, 60–68, 86–89; Stein, *Mark*, 164–166; France, *Gospel of Mark*, 658–660; Hooker, *Gospel According to St. Mark*, 379 and Brooks, *Mark*, 263.

vindicated Son of Man in the second half of his gospel from 8:31 onwards. Thus, Mark's readers discover that Jesus's messianic identity is truly unique among all other messiahs of the day.[10] In short, Mark describes Jesus's divine identity not only as the glorious Son of God performing great miracles or works of power in the first half of his gospel but also Jesus's destiny as the suffering Son of Man who must die and rise again after his death on the cross in the second half.

Thus, the readers are to understand that if Jesus's identity can be properly understood by grasping the truths of both halves or sections of Mark's gospel, it is not the case that the two halves of Mark's gospel can simply be added together to yield an understanding of who Jesus really is. Rather, the power and authority spoken of in the first half of the gospel must be understood as defined in the second half of the gospel. In other words, the readers of Mark discover that the power of Jesus and his kingdom is so unique which was manifested to the readers and listeners in unexpected ways. Already this is evident in the first half of the gospel with the indication that the kingdom brought by Jesus comes in unexpected ways, such as the power of the growing seed, and with indications of early opposition to Jesus.

Throughout his gospel, Mark portrays Jesus as the unique Messiah who identifies himself with various sorts of people, particularly, with those who were marginalized and liminal from a wide range of people who differ, physically, culturally, sexually, spiritually and socially. Regardless of opposition from many directions, it is the second evangelist who introduces Jesus's divine identity as the one who brings liberation to their physical, spiritual and social plights as well as restoration to their whole being. Further, Mark teaches about Jesus as the one whose true identity was revealed by and declared to unexpected people, in unexpected ways.

1.1. State of the Problem and the Research Question

It is true that Mark in his narrative's decisive points recorded that Jesus is revealed and announced as the divine Son of God by both supernatural beings (God and demons) and finally by humanity. However, he recoded Jesus's

---

10. See Wright, *Challenge of Jesus*, 76–85.

divine messianic identity in less obvious ways which has caused ambiguity among New Testament scholars for a long time. In other words, it has been a problem of/to the NT scholars because the Gospel of Mark speaks about one Jesus, who is described as both the messianic Son of God in the first half of the gospel (Mark 1:1–8:26), and the suffering Son of Man in the second half of the gospel (8:27–16:8). Further, while Jesus was performing miracles or works of power, as the divine Messiah, in the first half of the gospel, on the surface it appears that he is guarding (keeping secret) his messianic identity and commanded people for whom he had done great things and even demons not to proclaim what he did for others. Further, he even commanded demons, supernatural beings, not to say anything on this issue. Therefore, as will be discussed shortly, some scholars think that Jesus did not think or recognize that he was the Messiah during his earthly life and ministry; but that this was acknowledged by the evangelist after his (Jesus's) resurrection.[11] Others believe that his messiahship did not originate with the resurrection but it was in Jesus's own consciousness[12] prior to Easter. Still others argue that Jesus's Sonship to God in Mark's first half is a wrong understanding of Jesus's first followers (disciples), but his real identity is the suffering Son of Man who died and rose again as described in the second half.[13] Therefore, this dissertation argues that even though Jesus rejected self-acclamation before the people for reasons, according to the second evangelist, he indeed claimed to be the Messiah though he redefined the meaning of his messiahship which was often revealed in unexpected ways.[14] I also argue that in Mark's narrative, Jesus was both revealed and proclaimed as being the divine Son of God and the unique Messiah – again often in surprising and unexpected ways, and proclaimed by socially marginalized people according to the socio-cultural values of the first-century Mediterranean world.

---

11. For further understanding of this view, read Cullmann, *Christology of the New Testament*, 2nd ed., 133–136; E. Schweitzer, *Jesus*, 13–15, 70–71, 91; Sanders, *Jesus and Judaism*, 307–308; de Jonge, "Historical Jesus' View of Himself," 21–37; and Borg, *Conflict, Holiness, and Politics*, 17–18.

12. For this idea, read particularly Schweitzer, *The Quest of the Historical Jesus*, 335, 338–348, 368–395.

13. See Weeden, *Tradition in Conflict*, 65–67; Perrin, "Christology of Mark," 108–121.

14. Manson, *Jesus the Messiah*, 216, 220–221; Wright, *Jesus and the Victory*, 477–539; Chester, *Messiah and Exaltation*, 307–324; and Bird, *Are You the One*, 29.

In doing so some questions need to be answered: what do the unexpected ways in which the identity of Jesus is revealed in Mark's gospel tell us about Mark's understanding of the ways of God and the nature of witness? Why, for instance, does the climactic revelation of Jesus to be the Son of God come through a Gentile? Unlike other so-called sons of God in the tradition, in Mark's gospel, Jesus was proclaimed by God as God's uniquely beloved Son (Mark 1:11 and 9:7), not by any human being.[15] He was also, unexpectedly, proclaimed as God's Son by demons, supernatural beings (Mark 3:7–12; 5:1–20), by Bartimaeus, a poor blind beggar (Mark 10:46–52), and finally, by a gentile centurion (15:33–41). Furthermore, if it is appropriate to think that, as Matera said, "the real secret, however, concerns Jesus' Sonship rather than his messiahship," Jesus is to be understood as the uniquely beloved Son of God, and so the unique Messiah.[16] Richard Bauckham is also right by arguing that Mark's identification of Jesus as the Son of God is not merely messianic, but rather reveals Jesus's divine identity, as the divine Son of God.[17]

If that is the case, then why does Mark reveal that identity in such unexpected ways, for instance, through demons, a poor blind beggar and a Gentile, rather than his Jewish family and close friends, the disciples? Why are they able to see Jesus's "God-ness" while others are not? What ultimately does this reveal about God? Why do these sudden penetrating insights come the way they do?

In other words, since God his Father in Mark 1:11; 9:7 and even demons, the supernatural beings, in 3:11; 5:7 proclaimed that he is the Son of God (divine Messiah) and since Mark recorded that unexpectedly this Jesus was recognized and proclaimed as the Son of God by none other than a Roman/gentile centurion (Mark 15:39), why is it that his divine identity was revealed in many powerful ways in the first half of the gospel but yet suppressed in other ways? This has been an ongoing subject of discussion among NT scholars to which a satisfactory consensus has not been reached. Therefore, it is appropriate to discuss and evaluate previous studies undertaken on the subject by the scholars with a view arguing that Mark's gospel speaks of Jesus's unique divine messiahship (his divine Sonship to God).

---

15. See Hengel, *Son of God*, 21–24, 30.
16. Matera, *What Are They Saying about Mark?*, 21.
17. See Bauckham, *God of Israel*, 264–266.

1.2. Preliminary Studies Already Undertaken on Messiahship

Regarding the identity of Jesus in Mark's gospel, New Testament scholars have had different views for a long time, and still, it has been an ongoing subject of discussion among scholars to which a satisfactory consensus has not been reached.[18] One of the key points of discussion in the study of Mark's gospel has been the messianic Secret, due to the significance of the fact that for Mark much more than for the other gospels, Jesus guards his identity as the Messiah. In Mark's gospel outsiders are forbidden an insight into the mystery of the kingdom (Mark 4:10–12). Demons, who by virtue of their supernatural nature understand who Jesus was, are rebuked when they attempt to declare his identity (Mark 1:25, 34; 3:12). People for whom Jesus did miracles were forbidden to report what Jesus has done for them (Mark 1:44; 5:43) and Peter and the disciples were silenced without any of the praise mentioned in Matthew's gospel as soon as he confessed Jesus's identity to the disciples.

In the light of the above, New Testament scholars have understood the identity of Jesus in Mark's gospel in different ways over many years. For instance, first, William Wrede, who originally brought the discussion of this feature of Mark's gospel into the open, argued that it was Mark's way of justifying his belief that Jesus was the divine Messiah though Jesus never mentioned it. In other words, Wrede believed that Jesus did not think that he was the Messiah, nor did he identify himself as the Messiah. Furthermore, he argues that Mark, in his gospel, presents Jesus as the Messiah while, in reality, he (Jesus) is not the Messiah. For Wrede, it was only after the resurrection that Jesus was acknowledged as the Messiah.[19] Moreover, Wrede did not think that the Gospel of Mark was a reliable source about the life of Jesus. Finally, according to Wrede, the idea of the messianic secret was a transitional concept which began after the resurrection of Jesus when the church believed that Jesus was the Messiah, even though Jesus did not. So, for him, the messianic secret was an invention of Mark intended to resolve

---

18. See Johansson, "Identity of Jesus," 388.
19. See Wrede, *Messianic Secret*, 216–218, 230.

a contradiction between the early church who regarded Jesus as the Messiah and the historical Jesus who made no such claim.[20]

Rudolf Bultmann was a strong supporter of Wrede's theory of "the messianic secret." He demonstrated his total acceptance of Wrede's theory saying that, "indeed it must remain questionable whether Jesus held himself as the Messiah at all and did not rather first become Messiah because of the faith of the community."[21] He thinks that Mark's major role in writing the gospel was only the connecting unity between each narrative, because Bultmann wanted to say that, "Jesus' messianic claims cannot be traced to Jesus' own lips," but rather to the imaginative work of the evangelist. In other words, Bultmann affirms that the main reason for Mark to use this theme "messianic secret" is just to combine the church tradition and the historical information, which he knew about Jesus.[22] Both Wrede and Bultmann believe that, in Mark's gospel, the life and ministry of Jesus is not historical fact, but the result of the faith of the believing community in the early church beginning with the resurrection. Similarly to Bultmann, Grant used form criticism to interpret Wrede's theory of messianic secret. Indicating his agreement with Wrede's theory of messianic secret, Grant concludes that in Wrede's thesis, ". . . enough has been said to indicate that in principle the thesis must be accepted."[23] Nevertheless, whereas Wrede proposed that the messianic secret was the product or invention of the Christian community, Grant chose to emphasize more Mark's creative use of the theme "the messianic secret."

Burton Mack, who agrees with Wrede's theory, thinks that pre-Christian myths played a significant role in contributing to Jesus's claims to Messiahship. In other words, Mack argues that Mark purposefully blended Greek myths with the stories he knew about Jesus in order to create his narrative of the life of Jesus.[24] He thinks that Mark was not only a creative editor of his gospel, but also that he had special ability and literary skills to select narratives and to put them together. It is evident, having shown their

---

20. For further understanding of Wrede's insufficient view on messianic secret, read an excellent description by Wright, *New Testament*, 104.
21. Bultmann and Kundin, *Form Criticism*, 71.
22. See Bultmann, *Theology of the New Testament*, 22, 32.
23. Grant, *Gospel of the Kingdom*, 161.
24. Mack *A Myth of Innocence*, 289–290.

own account of presuppositions and emphasis[25] on the present subject, all these scholars whose works are discussed above concluded that the historical Jesus never claimed to be the Messiah.

However, some scholars began to attack Wrede's view of Jesus's messiahship. For instance, William Sanday, a contemporary of Wrede, strongly attacked Wrede's theory as steeped in error.[26] He argued that if Jesus's messiahship is not prior to the resurrection, it would be unthinkable to assume that the believing community of the first century created it as the product of their Easter faith. Even though Albert Schweitzer seemed to be in agreement with Wrede in some points,[27] later he began to criticize Wrede's view. A fundamental difference between both scholars was their disagreement about the historicity of the Gospels. For example, whereas Schweitzer believes in the historicity of the Gospels, Wrede does not. Thus, Schwietzer concludes that "either the Marcan text as it stands is historical, and therefore to be retained, or it is not, and then it should be given up."[28] In other words, Schweitzer rejects Wrede's view precisely because he believes that the Gospel of Mark should be read and interpreted as genuine history rather than just the theology of the evangelist and of the early church.

In addition, for Schweitzer, if Jesus is not really the Messiah, and if he did not claim to be so, the early church would not have desired to make him the Messiah.[29] In other words, for Schweitzer, the second evangelist and the early church claimed that Jesus was the Messiah because Jesus himself

---

25. Although, basically, they agree with Wrede's view in which he argues that Jesus never claimed to be the Messiah, but it was an invention of the early church and the second evangelist, his supporters have their own emphasizes on the subject. For example, while Bultmann believes that Jesus did not claim to be the Messiah; it is only an imaginative or editorial work of the second evangelist combining the church tradition and historical information he heard about Jesus (Bultmann, *Theology of the New Testament*, 22), Grant believes that Mark himself, not the early Christian community, created the theme (messianic secret) in order to meet the needs of the early church's theological agenda. Burton also emphasizes more on Mark's special ability with literary skills to combine Christian myths which were written in the form of Greek Myths, before the New Testament, with the stories he heard of Jesus in order to create the life of Jesus. In other words, for Burton, these writings rather than the historical facts of the gospels, contributed to describe about Jesus's identity.

26. Sanday, *Life of Christ*, 70–75.

27. For the similarity of both scholars' views, read Joy and Arnold, *Africa of Albert Schweitzer*, 330–331.

28. Schweitzer, *Quest of the Historical Jesus*, 336.

29. See Schweitzer, 343–344.

claimed to be the Messiah; additionally, Jesus did awaken in his followers the belief that he was the Messiah they had been hoping for.[30] However, in my opinion, even though Schweitzer is correct in thinking that Jesus possessed the idea of his messiahship, in his conscious thoughts, the problem with Schweitzer and his supporters' view at this point is they believe that Jesus thought that he would bring the end of the world through his own death, which is, according to Schweitzer, his glory. Therefore, he argued that his messianic claims did not originate with the resurrection appearances, but in Jesus's own self-consciousness.[31] Put simply, Schweitzer, unlike many of his contemporaries, thought that the pre-Easter Jesus believed himself to be the messiah and thought that he was dying as Israel's messiah.

Schweitzer thinks that Jesus is the frustrated eschatological Messiah who was defeated when he died on the cross. In other words, Schweitzer is one of those modern scholars who think that Jesus died an abject failure. However, as will be discussed in detail in the exegetical part of this work in Mark 15:33–39, I argue that, having demonstrated Jesus's divine authority over sin through forgiveness, over illness through healing, over demons through exorcism, and over natural chaos and physical death which are seen as manifestations of ultimate death, this Jesus, the unique Messiah, has revealed his supreme power and authority over death itself through his own death.[32] Therefore, the reader understands that the death of Jesus is not a sign or symbol of his failure or defeat on the cross, but rather the

---

30. Bornkamm, *Jesus von Nazareth*, 172. For further understanding of this matter/issue read Kingsbury, *Christology*, 5–7, and Käsemann, "The Problem of the Historical Jesus," 37–38.

31. Schweitzer, *Quest of the Historical Jesus*, 335, 338–348, 368–395. Though we do not hear many scholars who hold this view today, in Schweitzer's time quite a few believed that the resurrection was the event which led the early disciples to conclude that Jesus must have been the messiah. According to this view, the disciples did not think that he was the messiah before Easter because Jesus did not claim to be the messiah and did not believe that he was the messiah. The weakness of this view includes the fact that it has to disregard the gospels' evidence of Jesus's own messianic consciousness. Thus, this is somewhat different from saying that resurrection is unique to the messiah and therefore proof of his messiahship. Resurrection was something most Jews expected for everyone in due course (see Wright, "Christ Is Risen").

32. See Bolt, *Jesus' Defeat of Death*, 10–11, 271, 278–279.

ultimate victory of God over death itself, and Mark's "Jesus is the crucified but victorious King-Messiah."³³

Moreover, contrary to Wrede and his subsequent supporters, N. T. Wright rightly rejects Wrede's view on Jesus's messianic identity, explaining that Wrede's theory is baseless, impotent or insufficient. He also points out that,

> Wrede paid dearly for the simplicity of his basic (and simple) idea – that Jesus did not think himself as Messiah – at the cost of ultra-complexity everywhere else, and even then there was a lot of data which still refused to fit. It is no good cleaning out under the bed if the result is a pile of junk under the wardrobe.³⁴

Put simply, whereas Wrede thinks that the first followers of Jesus, not Jesus himself, believed him to be Messiah, Wright's point, surely, is that Jesus himself thought he was Messiah; thus, the first followers of Jesus indeed understood him to be the Messiah (Mark 8:29–30). As mentioned above, the question is that since Jesus was the Messiah and his followers understood him to be so, and since it is declared by them, why did Jesus keep it secret? And what is the main point of Wright's argument with this regard? As will be explained more in the exegetical section of this work in Mark 3, Wright correctly points out that there were some political connotations related to the title "Messiah" in the first century. To make this point clear, Wright says:

> Herod had already heard about Jesus, and reckoned he was a prophet of sorts. If he had known more, he might not have been content with merely "hoping to see him." We have already seen that Jesus spoke about Herod, and about John and himself in relation to Herod, in ways which implied an awareness that he was making a claim which Herod would find threatening.³⁵

Furthermore, there is no doubt that Jesus accepted the title "Messiah" but the point, according to Wright, is that Jesus redefined the real concept and significance of this title. Finally, contrary to Wrede's theory, Wright

---

33. Wright, *Jesus and the Victory*, 609–610; Seccombe, *God's Kingdom*, 577–578, 601.
34. Wright, *New Testament*, 104.
35. Wright, *Jesus and the Victory*, 529–530, see also 495–497.

correctly and powerfully explains the messianic nature of Jesus's life and ministry saying that:

> It was a claim to a messiahship which redefined itself around Jesus' own kingdom-agenda, picking up several strands available within popular messianic expectation but weaving them into a striking new pattern, corresponding to none of the options canvassed by others at the time. Jesus' style of messiahship was sufficiently similar to those in the public mind to get him executed, and for his first followers to see his resurrection as a reaffirmation of him as Messiah, not as something quite different. But it was sufficiently dissimilar to mean that everyone, from his closest followers through to the chief priests, misinterpreted at least to some extent what he was really getting at; and that the movement which did come to birth after his resurrection, though calling itself messianic, cherished agendas and adopted lifestyles quite unlike those of other movements with the same label. If Jesus was a Messiah, he was a Messiah with great difference. But Messiah was what he claimed to be.[36]

Finally, as referred by Kingsbury, some interpreters such as Theodor Weeden, Norman Perrin and their followers emphasize mainly the suffering messiahship of Jesus in Mark's gospel. For them, Mark's Jesus is only the Son of Man or suffering servant rather than the messianic Son of God. As it has been discussed under the "Corrective Christology" in some books,[37] these scholars think that, in Mark's gospel, the ultimate title in which Jesus identified himself must be "the Son of Man who must suffer and die but who will also rise and come again at the end of time."[38] Furthermore, they think that what Jesus said and taught in the second half of Mark's gospel beginning at 8:31, by describing himself as the Son of Man, is to correct Peter's and other disciples' wrong belief and confession of Jesus as the Son of God or the Messiah because, for them, Mark is correcting the title "Son of God"

---

36. Wright, 539.
37. See for example, Matera, *What Are They Saying about Mark?*, 22 and Kingsbury, *Christology*, 33.
38. Kingsbury, *Christology*, 41.

in the first half of Mark with the "Son of Man" in the second. Moreover, like Weeden, Perrin argues that the title "Son of God" came to the evangelist (Mark) from the tradition.[39] According to these scholars, in utilizing this title (Son of God), the evangelist tried to establish a close relationship with his readers and finally, moving through the gospel story, he corrected it with the "Son of Man." In other words, these scholars think that Jesus's identity as the "Son of God" in the first half of Mark's gospel is a wrong belief of Jesus's first disciples which needed Jesus's correction, in the second half, to be the "Son of Man." However, I argue that it is impossible to split or divide Mark's gospel into two parts as though its first half speaks about Jesus's divinity and divine acts, and the second part about Jesus's humanity since both sections speak of Jesus's divine identity as the divine Son of God and the suffering and the vindicated Son of Man who identified himself with the marginalized and liminal humanity. Furthermore, this study, from the beginning to end, argues that "the identity Jesus bears in Mark's story is unified: Jesus of Nazareth is the Davidic Messiah-King, the Son of God."[40]

1.3. Concluding Summary to the Previous Studies on the Subject

In conclusion, for a long time the argument over the theory of the messianic secret rested on Wrede's view which summarized that Jesus did not claim to be Messiah, but that the second evangelist and the early church had invented it for their own theological agenda. Furthermore, even though they have their own interests on the subject, other scholars who supported Wrede's view concluded that Jesus did not recognize to be the Messiah prior to the resurrection.

Contrary to Wrede and his subsequent followers, others rejected his view by arguing that Jesus revealed his divine identity to his followers as Messiah prior to the resurrection. Hence, without compromising the historicity or the message of the gospel, describing the life and ministry of Jesus, they argue that Jesus's messiahship is not an invention or product of either Mark or of the early church.

---

39. See Perin, "Christology of Mark," 104–121; Kingsbury, *Christology*, 41.
40. Kingsbury, *Christology*, 175.

Nevertheless, from his words, "Towards Passover, therefore, Jesus sets out to Jerusalem, solely in order to die there," one can understand that Schweitzer indicates that Jesus is the disappointed eschatological Messiah who was going to bring the kingdom due to his own death.[41] Generally, it is possible to think that even though Sanday, Schweitzer and other scholars played significant roles in shaping Markan Christology as well as the theme "messianic secret," their reactions did not stop Wrede's influence in the subsequent years.

What will be argued next, and in the rest of this study is that, according to Mark, Jesus claimed to be the Messiah. Hence, I argue that one of the fundamental problems with Wrede's view when he emphasized the hiddenness of Jesus's messianic identity prior to the resurrection, is the command of Jesus to the healed leper to "show yourself to the priest" in Mark 1:44. Further, the readers discover that Jesus's divine messiahship and his divine acts were publicly declared in the early chapters of Mark's gospel (e.g. 5:7; 7:36–37). In other words, since Jesus himself commanded people to show his divine acts to others and since those divine acts were openly declared among people, it is unlikely to think that his messianic identity was hidden before the resurrection. In addition, the readers are to understand that to make a dividing line between pre-and post-Easter Christology (Mark 9:9), as Wrede supposed, is a false dichotomy since his divine acts continue to be demonstrated even in the second half of Mark's gospel when Jesus rids a boy of an evil spirit (Mark 9:14–29), heals blind Bartimaeus (10:46–52) and curses a fig tree by his divine authority (Mark 11:12–14, 20–22).[42] Hence, unlike Wrede who made a dividing line between the pre- and post-Easter Christology and Weeden and his followers who thought that the real and ultimate identity of Jesus is the "Son of Man" in the second half of Mark rather than the "Son of God" in the first half, I argue that the Gospel of Mark is a unified work of the second evangelist. Hence in his gospel, his readers discover the real and unique identity of Jesus as the miraculous and divine Son of God and the suffering and vindicated Son of Man whose shameful death on the cross has become the victory of God.

---

41. Schweitzer, *Quest of the Historical Jesus*, 391.

42. Wrede, *Messianic Secret*, 72. For further understanding of this view, read Henderson, *Christology and Discipleship in the Gospel of Mark*, 9–13.

Therefore, the readers are also to know that even though his style of messiahship was similar in some ways to others,[43] it was also unique in significant ways since it was redefined by Jesus himself through his shameful death rather than any other way of becoming a messiah of those days.[44]

1.4. The Nature of the Research and Research Hypothesis

According to the whole gospel in general, and in the passages mentioned above in particular, I want to argue that Mark did think that Jesus was the uniquely divine Messiah, so he wrote his gospel to show why Jesus's messianic identity was not explicitly revealed by Jesus, but Mark shows that Jesus deliberately suppressed his identity. The question is, since he is the glorious Son of God with extraordinary power and authority, why did Jesus suppress his identity as the divine Messiah, recorded in the first half of Mark?

First, I argue that it was precisely because he did not want his ministry to be disturbed by revealing his identity (divine Messiahship), apart from his suffering, because his full identity, as the divine Son of God and the suffering Messiah, should have been understood by Mark's listeners and readers as it was intended by Jesus himself (Mark 9:9; 15:39; 16:6–7). Put another way, Jesus is cautious about revealing his full identity as the Messiah precisely because of the danger that it would not be understood as he intended it to be and would thus actually hinder his ministry.[45] In other words, I suggest

---

43. See Wright, *Jesus and the Victory*, 539.

44. Finally, this book's interaction with other scholars and publications primarily includes discussions of work undertaken until the 1990s. However where later relevant publications have become available, these are reflected in the book. The first chapter, written in Ethiopia, used available literature which seldom included material from after the 1990s. Chapter 1 is intended to draw the broader framework of the discussion, and indicates the representative interpretative positions with which the dissertation interacts. One of the most influential books used to discuss the subject is William Wrede's work published (translated) in 1971, and much of the subsequent literature were produced by scholars to argue for and against Wrede's view. The disagreement and discussion between scholars of course did not stop in the 1990's but has been an ongoing subject to which a satisfactory consensus has not been reached until the present day. The initial focus on the pre-1990's discussion in chapter 1, which sets the scene for the larger argument of the dissertation, is therefore elaborated in the ensuing chapters in order to reflect the finer nuances in the scholarly debate.

45. This idea will be further explained later in the exegetical part of this work in Mark 3:11–12.

that Jesus realized that his divine identity would only be understandable after the resurrection. Furthermore, from the opening verses of the gospel (Mark 1:1, 11), the readers know that Jesus is the Spirit-anointed Son of God; and in the middle of the gospel, Jesus is the Christ (Mark 8:29), but as will be discussed later, the full significance of this title was not recognized or declared by anyone until the gentile soldier declares him to be the Son of God in Mark 15:39.

Second, unlike other miracle workers and the traditional expectations of the day, Jesus refused to acclaim or proclaim himself as the Messiah so that his disciples were able to understand not only his identity as the man with unique power, but also his coming destiny, taking the path of the cross, on the basis of which, the ultimate victory of God is proclaimed to all to hear. The reason for this is that he is the unique Messiah whose kingdom-of-God agenda on earth and its goal is so different from other messiahs of those days. Thus, the readers of the second evangelist are to learn that Jesus is the uniquely divine Messiah whose real identity was recognized by and through unexpected outcasts.

Third, in his narrative, Mark wanted to tell his readers and listeners that as the unique Messiah who is revealed in unexpected ways, Jesus is proclaimed as the Son of God by the marginalized – including unexpected people such as a man named as blind Bartimaeus – rather than his inner circle of friends, who were Peter, John and James, and other disciples.

Finally, the climactic revelation of Jesus as the Son of God came through a gentile centurion, Mark 15:39, again not through his Jewish friends or close disciples. I will also discuss whether or not the gentile centurion had become a believer at the moment or even after his declaration of Jesus as God's Son, and will conclude that either wittingly or unwittingly, at the climactic moment of Jesus's death, he confessed that Jesus was the Son of God. In other words, the death of Jesus on the cross, paradoxically, revealed Jesus's divine Sonship. This happened not on the battle field or the political arena as with other messiahs of the day, but on the cross while he was dying a shameful death. In either case, in that of the demons' declaration and the confession of the gentile centurion,[46] Mark senses the sovereignty of God

---

46. The gentile centurion can be considered as marginalized from the Jewish perspective, or in relation to the Jewish majority in predominately Jewish areas or regions.

who intended to reveal God's Son, Jesus, in such unexpected ways, to identify himself with those who are marginalized and liminal in various ways. He did so to save and atone all humanity who confess Jesus as the Son of God (Mark 15:34–39). So, Bauckham rightly states "Jesus' divine identity is revealed not only in his deeds of divine authority, nor merely in his coming participation in God's cosmic rule, but also in his godforsaken death."[47]

Furthermore, as indicated above, one can argue that Jesus is the unique, divine Messiah who is able to reveal himself to all humanity in various ways using some unexpected people who were marginalized and liminal, and identified himself with them in unexpected ways. His messiahship was not through fighting against the enemies of Israel to liberate them as true people of the creator God, and building visible temples as many others did in those days,[48] but by dying on the cross. Moreover, as noted earlier and will be discussed briefly later, Jesus did not want to identify himself with the political expectation of those days, because he did not want to reveal himself in a political, merely religious or nationalistic sense. The reason is that he did not want his messiahship to cause conflict with political and religious groups until his right time had come to die and rise again (Mark 9:9; 15:39; 16:6–7). Therefore, while people had been expecting a victorious Messiah, he was revealed as the crucified one.

Hence, in conclusion, a need exists for a study that thoroughly investigates not only Jesus's divine messianic identity shown in the Gospel of Mark as the miraculous figure but also, as the suffering Messiah whose agenda on earth is so unique, his self-identification with the outcasts was in order to liberate them; in other words, the whole of humanity is touched through his unique death.

1.5. Research Procedure and Methodology

This study of the revelation of the divine messianic identity of Jesus in Mark's gospel is undertaken primarily by means of a narrative approach that

---

47. Bauckham, *God of Israel*, 266

48. Regarding the means through which a messiah of the first century was expected to accomplish his mission in order to become a messiah and the uniqueness of the Messiahship of Jesus, see Wright, *Challenge of Jesus*, 76, 85, and *New Testament*, 320.

is narrative criticism. Narrative criticism is the art of reading scriptures as story. In Mark's gospel the central character is Jesus who identified himself unexpectedly with people such as the poor and outcast by entering into their situation in the first-century Mediterranean culture where honor and shame were valued.[49] Mark's Jesus associated himself with the poor and outcast by giving them physical and emotional help both in Jewish and gentile territories. He also uplifted them through his own shameful death on a Roman cross and subsequent honourable resurrection. In other words, Jesus entered into the shame of humanity and experienced its horror through crucifixion, but finally won victory over its power through resurrection.

According to Allan Powell, the goal of narrative criticism is to read the textual story as the implied reader,[50] who is assumed by the narrative, and to interpret the meaning of the text in its own context, focusing on the story, events, actions, character and settings as a coherent narrative unit.[51] Focusing on the particular theological or christological themes and passages mentioned below which speak of the revelation of Jesus's unique identity, found in Mark's gospel in unexpected ways, my work will be mainly an exegetical, interpretive and evaluative in nature. Since my work is based on biblical studies, I believe that to exegete the text in its context is a proper way to understand the message in the gospel. Likewise, depending on the texts (e.g. 3:7–12; 5:1–20; 10:46–52; and 15:33–41),[52] I would like to argue

---

49. For further understanding of this idea, read Malina, *New Testament World*, 27–52.

50. Mark's readers or "the reader implied in the text" (Fowler, "Who Is 'the Reader' of Mark's Gospel?," 15) would be both historical (in imagining Mark's original audience) and ahistorical (in imagining his subsequent readers across place and time). As I tend to think, Mark deliberately ended his narrative at 16:8. So, I think that as an active messianic community, he wanted to draw his readers into the narrative as participants. In other words, Mark recorded the story as a paradoxical gospel, a riddle or irony that provokes its readers' participation, as a narrative that contains ambiguous and puzzling character (e.g. Jesus the suffering and vindicated Son of Man). Thus, readers are expected not simply to read Mark's story but enter into it – live in and live out of it. Just as Jesus did, Mark intended to leave his readers with a puzzle precisely so that they would keep puzzling over it by asking questions – probing a bit more, finding their curiosity rise and then re-engaging with the story again.

51. Powell, *What Is Narrative Criticism?*, 20

52. Even though there are many similar stories in Mark's narrative, these passages are selected precisely because, regardless of his supernatural authority in the whole gospel, they speak of the Marcan Jesus who is revealed and proclaimed by both supernatural sources and human beings as the one who identified himself with the marginalized and liminal people at various levels to liberate.

that while Jesus is the uniquely divine Messiah and Son of God, he identified himself with those around him who were in a marginalized and liminal state of life, and so were really in the greatest need of liberation and atonement for sins (14:24; 15:38; 10:45).[53] In order to make the message of these texts clear, various exegetical tools and strategies will be used.

As noted above, the primary exegetical methodology will be narrative criticism whose aim is to engage the narrative elements of a literary text, and to interpret and get meaning of biblical passages in light of their own narrative context. It focuses on what the content of the text itself says to the believing community and how it works out as a unified whole.[54] In other words, narrative criticism investigates the meaning of the text as a completed, self-contained unit.[55] In addition, I suggest that, first, Mark's theology is evident primarily in the gospel as a finished work. Second, we have only very limited access to Mark's sources. Third, the most important of these are the Old Testament traditions on which Mark draws for background in his text and which he develops. This is part of the analysis of the Gospel of Mark as a literary work.

Additionally, some historical background will be considered in order to elucidate the theological intent in Mark's gospel. In other words, the interpretation of this work requires that we consider not only the literary context in Mark's narrative, but also the theological and historical context, in which the evangelist wrote.

Therefore, I assume that the literary portrait of Jesus need not be brought into conflict with the presentation of Jesus as an historical figure. So, I believe that the traditional view that Mark's portrait of Jesus corresponds in some manner to the figure of the historical Jesus. In other words, I also assume that the traditional historical position that the Gospel of Mark is saying something about the historical figure Jesus of Nazareth is correct. Because Mark writes well, he is able to shape the literary portrayal of Jesus so that he writes a compelling story of him. But there is no need to separate these two pictures on postmodern ideological ground, as this would be an imperialistic

---

53. Bauckham, *God of Israel*, 266–268.
54. See Powell, *What Is Narrative Criticism?*, 85–91.
55. See Resseguie, *Narrative Criticism of the New Testament*, 18–19.

imposition[56] on the ancient text. There is in fact heuristic value in assuming, with the long standing traditional reading, that Mark's portrayal of Jesus correlated with the historical figure as the one who walked and worked among people in and around Galilee and in its first-century cultural context. Thus this claim is not with regard to the historical accuracy of Mark's presentations but rather a heuristic choice regarding such presentations.

Likewise, in order to interpret the text and its main idea as well as its tradition in Mark, I shall include both biblical and extra-biblical texts, such as Jewish scripture (Old Testament passages) and intertestamental writings such as the Qumran literature, and some apocryphal and pseudepigraphical works.

1.6. Defining and Explaining the Terms "Margin" or "Marginality" and "Liminal" or "Liminality"

Before going further, it will be appropriate to clarify the meaning of the terms "margin" and "marginality," and "liminal" and "liminality," as used in this study. As a number of cultural manifestations of *communitas*, Victor Turner mentions marginality and liminality in relation to the social structure of the time as will be explained shortly. Whereas marginality indicates that a person is on the edge of something or the social structure of the day, liminality indicates that he or she is in between or in midpoint of transition. In other words, marginality is living on the outside or the periphery and liminality is living in between two positions.[57] Put simply, while marginal individuals are found on the one corner of social status (e.g. the demoniac of Mark 5 and blind Bartimaeus of Mark 10), liminal individuals are found to be "neither here nor there; they are betwixt and between the positions assigned and arrayed by the law, custom, convention, and ceremony" (e.g.

---

56. It is an imposition on the text, from a later age, the twentieth to twenty-first century, because it is not native to the first century. It is imperialistic, because usually interpreters who wish to do this seem to be absolutely convinced that they and their framework of thought are superior to that of the first-century text. In other words, it is to force to explain or interpret the text from outsider perspective rather than from the point of view of those inside the culture. This can be the same for exegesis, that is, I explain the text on its own terms, within its own times and cultures, not from the vantage point of a later and foreign outsider perspective.

57. See Punt, "Biblical Hermeneutics," 12.

Jesus himself).[58] We can also discuss further, what we mean by the terms "Margin or Marginality" and "Liminal or Liminality."

1.6.1. Margin or Marginality

It is true that explaining the concept of these terms "margin" and "marginality" in several aspects is beyond the scope of this study, but defining of terms is not, particularly since our concern is with its use as a noun form "margin" or "marginality," and its use as a verb in the form of "to marginalize." It also fits well to describe the situation or condition of the marginalized people with whom Jesus identified himself in the Gospel of Mark.

Generally, the term "margin" means "edge, border, of surface, whence . . . condition near the limit below or beyond which a thing ceases to be possible, etc."[59] Thus, one can think that the person who is marginalized has been separated from the rest of society; forced to occupy the fringes and edges, not to be at the centre of things. Marginalized people are treated by others as though they are not important, being out of any position of power or influence. In other words, marginalization is the social process of becoming or being made marginal and relegated or confine to a lower social standing[60] or outer limit or edge, of the normal social standing.

In social terms, Shure discusses marginality in relation to inferiority in which the only difference is the extent by which they are excluded: the inferior figure is almost always economically inferior, whereas the marginal figure is generally pushed to the edges for social reason (race, creed, etc.). Finally, he rightly concludes that both marginality and inferiority refer to a position of powerlessness, and that those in this position have no choice as to where they are placed in the marginal or liminal scale.[61] While discussing the relationship between hermeneutics and marginality, in that the twofold nature of marginality, as Jeremy Punt points out on the one hand, the term marginality can be enforced by oppressive forces from outside, it has a negative connotation which indicates persons are powerless in their relegation to

---

58. Turner, *Ritual Process*, 95.
59. Fowler and Fowler, *Concise Oxford Dictionary*, 744.
60. For further information, consult "Marginalization," http://thefreedictionary.com.
61. Shure, "About: What Is Liminality," 5.

an unwanted state by oppression meted out to them by others from outside.[62] The reason is that this decisive force is exercised by the powerful, in assigning marginality and this creates alienation, estrangement and marginalization of people, serves the interest of the powerful who establish themselves at the centre. On the other hand, with reference to Roetzel, Punt rightly goes on to say that those who are marginalized at the periphery can utilize their marginality as an opportunity for radical possibility – what is considered as given, as reality can be re-imagined, and a new reality can be envisaged, construed and lived.[63] Put differently, to be marginalized is to be excluded by others from outside, away, from the center of important things, and to be forced to outer edge of the society. Nevertheless, as will be noticed throughout this study in Mark's gospel, it is also possible to see that liminality may become an opportunity and envisage something new and important.[64]

People both as individuals and group members may become marginalized for different reasons in various areas of their lives, such as economic, political, cultural, sexual, religious, and social as well as spiritual by something else or by pressure from other individuals or groups of people. For instance, some may be born marginalized due to their family or tribal position in the cultures in which they were born. Others may be marginalized due to poor health at birth or deterioration in health as they grew up. Still others may be marginalized, due to their national, personal or economic poverty. Finally, some people may be marginalized because they are possessed by evil or unclean spirits. In certain religions and cultures in which they live, there is the possibility that they may be forced to separate from the society and become totally outcast in their social lives.

1.6.2. Liminal or Liminality

As it was noted above in the case of explanation the full concept of the terms "margin" and "marginality," it is also beyond the scope of this study to elucidate the full concept of the terms "liminal" or "liminality," but it is possible to define it since it fits the subject at hand. So, I will raise them

---

62. Punt, "Biblical Hermeneutics," 12.
63. Roetzel, *Paul a Jew on the Margins*, 2; see Punt, "Biblical Hermeneutics," 12.
64. See also Lee, *From a Liminal Place*, 4–9.

shortly since Mark's Jesus identified himself with those who were liminal at several stages of their social lives.

The term "liminality" which was first used by Arnold Van Gennep is a difficult concept to define even in many dictionaries or to define it clearly. Both liminal and liminality are derived from the Latin "*limen*," which means "threshold" or the bottom part of a doorway that must be crossed when entering a building.[65] Liminality is the quality of ambiguity when individuals are in the middle stage of something when they are separated from the social status they obtained before, but have not yet begun the transition to the status they are aiming or looking for. In short, it is their status which is socially and structurally ambiguous. In other words, during a liminal stage or position, individuals stand at the threshold between their previous way of life and a new way.[66]

With reference to Mary Douglas's *Purity and Danger*, Turner points out that liminal individuals are polluting, and thus dangerous, to those who have not gone through the liminal period [and thus they] have nothing: no status, insignia, secular clothing, rank, kinship position, nothing to demarcate them structurally from their fellows.[67] Put simply, liminality is the exact opposite of structure, in society, in which there is no social hierarchy but all within the group of people seem to be equal. For example, one can understand that thousands of Ethiopian illegal immigrants and stateless Somalis who live and work in South Africa can be regarded as liminal because they are "betwixt and between home and host," part of society, but sometimes never fully integrated.[68] It is also true that although these illegal stateless immigrants are socially equal as outsiders in the foreign land, but economically there is a vast difference between them on many levels. It is also important to notice that, on the positive side, liminality allows freedom to move from place to place. This has a negative effect since there is a lack of stability, because in

---

65. Further, consult Shure, "About: What Is Liminality?"; see also Van Gennep, *Rites of Passage*, 95.

66. For instance, Lee explains Moxnes's idea that "this liminal space entered by Jesus and his disciples as 'a location that not yet defined,' 'no-place,' an 'in-between position,' a space of the 'dislocation of identity,' and a 'zone of possibilities'." Lee, *From a Liminal Place*, 63; cf. Moxnes, *Putting Jesus in His Place*, 55, 68, 70.

67. Turner, *Ritual Process*, 98.

68. Thomassen, "Uses and Meanings of Liminality," 19.

this position, individuals do not belong anywhere, but they are in between the old and the new.

Additionally, Van Gennep describes the term "liminality" and its concept as a threefold structure: first, the preliminal state in which the person is first stripped of the social status which he/she possessed before his change in status. Second, a liminal state in which he/she is admitted into the middle stage of transition, and third, a post-liminal state in which the individual is reincorporated into society with a new identity as a new being.[69] As indicated above, even though the group of liminal individuals do not have a typical social hierarchy there are a communal group in which all are equal.[70] There are degrees or steps of liminality in which the social status of individuals or groups is stratified in which they experience liminality.[71]

When one comes to the New Testament, what do the four Gospels in general, and the gospel of Mark in particular, teach us about the social status of individuals and groups, and Jesus's identification with those who are marginalized and in a liminal state?

1.7. Social Status of Individuals and Groups of People in Mark's Gospel

Before saying something about marginalized and liminal people and Jesus's self-identification with them in Mark's gospel, it is important first to say something about the whole social status of all sorts of people in his narrative. The reason is that, according to the second evangelist, Jesus touches or covers the whole social spectrum on many levels, even though predominantly he walked and worked here on earth with marginalized and liminal people. In other words, Mark does not exclude some elite who were in the top of the social scale and were known as political rulers as well as the landed aristocracy and their retainers who gained their living from the elite, but his gospel was written mostly about ordinary people who were not in the category of the social elite. It is also true that unlike many ancient biographies written about the highest category of elite, Mark's gospel was written not only about

---

69. See Van Gennep, *Rites of Passage*, 21.
70. See Shure, "About: What Is Liminality?," 2.
71. See Thomassen, "Uses and Meanings of Liminality," 16–18.

common people, but also it was about the poor and destitute along with the outcast in the lowest category of society. So, the reader discovers that Jesus himself was born into the common or lower end of the social scale. He was born and served as a man of common people starting his life as a village artisan.[72]

1.7.1. Jesus and the Elite

Some commentators rightly categorize the social status of individuals at various levels in Mark's gospel. For example, regarding the urban elite, Rohrbaugh mentions a few elite persons, a tiny minority, perhaps 2 percent, ruling over the vast majority of the people.[73] It consists not only of the highest ranking political rulers (such as the Roman emperor in 12:17, the Herodian family [e.g. Herod Antipas, 6:14–22, Philip 6:17, and Herodias and her daughter 6:17, 22], rulers of the Gentiles in 10:42, governors in 13:9, and the governor Pontius Pilate in 15:2), but also high-ranking priestly families in Jerusalem (such as those listed Mark 14:53, Joseph of Arimathea, member of council in 15:43, and the high priest 2:26; 14:47, 53–54, 60–66) as well as other landed aristocratic families (such as the owner of a house with a large guest room in 14:14, and the woman with expensive ointment 14:3). And finally, there was Jarius from the small Galilean village who was a local elite and a "ruler of the synagogue," along with his family (his wife and daughter in Mark 5:22–23, 40), the rich man in 10:17, the wealthy (10:23, 25); the vineyard owner and son in 12:1, 6, and rich people in 12:41, who were parts of the local village elite and were also mentioned. Many of these elite lived in the most secured and luxurious parts of the cities, far away from ordinary people, and enclosed in separate walls, drawing their incomes from their large landed areas in the countryside (rural areas) because, during the first century, the larger parts of the land belonged to the Herodians and other powerful families.

Especially important in lower Galilee, was the land controlled by the Herodian family, which included tens of thousands of acres.[74] In other words, this family lived totally isolated from the rest of the society and considered

---

72. See Witherington, *Gospel of Mark*, 32.
73. Rohrbaugh, *New Testament*, 141–145.
74. See Fiensy, *Social History of Palestine*, 60.

themselves as though they had very little, physically, politically and culturally, to do with the common or ordinary people in the lower classes of society. Thus, the reader may consider these people to be on the upper extreme edge or margin on the periphery of the social status of the time.

1.7.2. Jesus and Retainers

The retainers were the ones through whom the control of the elite over other people was exercised. They gained their living from serving the elite. The retainers comprise lower-level military officers such as courtiers, officers (6:21), bodyguard to Herod (6:27), soldiers (15:16), the Roman/gentile centurion (15:39), as well as officials and bureaucrats, personal retainers (Levi, toll collectors 2:14), household servants/slaves (14:13, 47, 66), lower-level lay aristocracy and scribes or scholars (12:28). This group of people did not have much power or independence, but in order to exercise it over others, they depended for their position on their relation to the urban elite.[75] They are in a liminal position since they were neither elite on the higher scale of society, nor outcastes at the lowest social scale.

Although most of the elite and their retainers were opponents of Jesus and his agenda on earth, some of them such as Joseph of Arimathea, the woman with expensive ointment, and Jairus's family, among the elite, and Levi the tax collector and the Roman centurion, among the retainers, had positive relationships with Jesus. In other words, the readers of Mark's narrative recognize that Jesus's movement does not exclude people of high-rank due to their position or wealth, whatever it is, but according to Mark, it includes all sorts of people depending on Jesus's willingness to come to them and their positive response to the message of God's kingdom.

1.7.3. Jesus and the Common People

Concerning the common people who are the majority of the people mentioned in Mark's gospel, they are common ordinary people. In the first place, there were peasants who got their livelihood by working their own land or the land of the wealthy elite to survive. It was not only for their own survival, but also they were expected to support the temple, priesthood,

---

75. See Rohbraugh, "Social Location: Jesus' World," 145–148.

Herodian regime and Roman tribute through heavy taxation which took their economic viability to the brink.[76]

In other words, on the one hand, the peasants could not be considered as poor since they lived and worked in Galilee, a rich and fertile region, and so they were the only real source or means of the wealth of the land; however, on the other hand, they can be seen as poor because they never used or utilized it for themselves since the stronger ruling elite and their retainers took their wealth away either by plunder or by taxes. Put simply, the "state took the surplus from the peasants and gave them nothing in return."[77]

Second, alongside with peasants, there were tenants who were basically peasants who had lost their independence through indebtedness; many of them and their families fell hopelessly in debt and abandoned their ancestral lands altogether. "In some extreme cases . . . an entire village worked as tenants for a single landlord."[78] Third, day labourers, some of whom were landless, were marginalized and at the bottom of the socio-economic scale. These are mostly peasants who had lost their land through indebtedness and were caused to work by the hour, day, month, year, three or seven years for their landlords. In some cases they may have drifted to the cities and towns seeking new jobs, due to extremely high death rates of the urban non-elite.[79] Fourth, there were also some slaves who occupied different social positions (e.g. some might have been retainers, others peasants), and small traders who were in the same social scale as the new arrivals.

Mark also records some farm workers or peasants such as the sower (4:3) or the one who scattered seed (4:26), tenant farmers, (12:21) and Simon (15:21). Most of the artisans who were regarded as a small minority, including Jesus the wood worker (Mark 6:3), were in this section or category. They were considered to be below even the peasants on the socio-economic scale, and so were marginalized at the bottom of the social scale.[80] Likewise, the first followers of Jesus, the disciples (1:16, 19, 20), especially, four of

---

76. Oakman, *Jesus and the Economics*, 52–72; see also Josephus, *War* 5, 405
77. For further information, consult Neyrey, "Who Is Poor in the New Testament?," and Borg, "A Portrait of Jesus."
78. Rohrbaugh, *New Testament*, 27.
79. See Fiensy, *Social History of Palestine*, 84–85.
80. See Rohrbaugh, "Social Location: Jesus' World," 156.

the Twelve including Peter and Andrew who were known as net casters (1:16–18) and James and John who fished from a boat (1:19), were known as fishermen who had been considered as common people or people of low-ranking.[81] The reason is because the Galilean fishermen were despised by all just because an elite Roman like Cicero categorizes them thus. However, in the system of commercialization of the first century, it is true that the fishermen were on a contract with the elite to supply specified amounts of fish to be delivered, to gain their meagre income. Thus one can guess that it is highly profitable arrangement for the elite who were in the Roman governors and their troops giving the fishermen very little. Additionally, although they earned a small amount from fishing, the taxation system was also a heavy burden on them as they were expected to pay not only the agreed amount of the catch, but also an extra amount in taxes to the regional governing body.[82] In other words, although the group of Jesus's inner circle, the disciples, appeared to represent all of the followers of Jesus, socially and economically their status was below even that of peasant farmers and they had less long-term security.[83] Thus they are categorized in the lower social scale since they were from such a poor social level even though they were not at the bottom as the outcast were.

In 2:4 Mark also introduces the term "crowd," (or in Greek, ὄχλος, *ochlos*) thirty-eight times in his gospel. The term "crowd," or *ochlos*, according to Byung-mu, appears to refer to a confused majority, or to the ordinary soldiers in a combat unit, but not to the officers.[84] It also refers to non-combatants who followed the army and performed menial duties. Byung-mu goes on to explain that the term *ochlos*, after the time of Ezra, came to mean specifically

---

81. Regarding the position of the disciples with regard to the marginalized, one can think that they called from marginality simply because they were from among common ordinary Galileans, and their former occupation (fishing) was considered as despised job by some Roman elite such as Cicero. However, it is difficult to categorize them as though they were entirely marginal before they were called by Jesus. Besides, not all disciples were fishers (just the four are identified as such). Levi, for instance, was a tax collector, which again meant he had a steady income. Therefore, I believe rather that they were called toward marginality. The reason is that to take up the cross and follow the crucified Messiah is to locate oneself among the most despised, humiliated, and disempowered group one can imagine.

82. See Witherington, *Acts of Apostles*, 20.

83. See Rohrbaugh, "Social Location: Jesus' World," 155.

84. Byung-mu, "Jesus and the Minjung," 139, 149.

the lower class or poor uneducated peasants, and those ignorant of the law. Thus, we conclude that in Mark's gospel, both the crowd among whom the followers of Jesus came out of, and the disciples, considered themselves to be in a similar lower social background and they shared the same responses to Jesus.

According to Byung-mu, thus, in Mark's narrative the crowd are also identified as sinners and social outcasts, however, they are welcomed as part of Jesus's community (3:32).[85] Even though they are neglected and rejected by the Jewish leadership, the crowd were supporters of the Jesus movement. Furthermore, the rabbis taught that the observant Jews should neither share meals with, nor travel together with, the crowd *ochlos*, but according to Mark, Jesus openly identified himself with them regardless of their lower and often unpleasant social status.

Others who were on the same social level, such as Peter's mother-in-law (1:30), Mary the mother of Jesus and his brothers (6:3), the friends of the paralytic (2:3) and the epileptic boy and his father (9:17), as well as a young man at Gethsemane (14:51), were all from the strata of the common people. Most of these mentioned here were people who lived near or close to subsistence level. Thus, when economic hardship happened, they easily lost their relatively secure livelihood and were reduced to the tasks of bandits and begging.[86]

1.7.4. Jesus and the Poor

Mark shows throughout his gospel, that Jesus was surrounded by various kinds of poor people who needed his help for their afflictions in many ways. Here we see his willingness to help or liberate them. There were some individual beggars and others from among the crowd, for example a poor widow (12:42), a woman with hemorrhage, the impoverished (5:25), and the disabled or sick and a poor beggar (e.g. the paralytic man 2:3), a man with withered hand (3:1), the deaf and dumb (7:32), the blind man (8:22) and Bartimaeus, the blind beggar (10: 46). They can be considered not merely to be poor, but also, according to the Gospels, they were destitute because

---

85. Byung-mu, 149–150.

86. For further information, consult, Bauckham, "The Gospels as Histories: What Sorts of History Are They?"

they lived below the social scale on the margins, at a meagre existence level. It was also possible to put them, in this category, because they were physically unable to work, and they became beggars. Thus, one can think that even though giving to the poor was a well-recognized Jewish religious duty, it was shameful to be reduced to begging.

1.7.5. Jesus and the Outcasts

Mark records incidents from the lives of outcasts who lived at the lowest social level and were marginalized and excluded from Jewish society. According to Jewish purity law, certain people, places and things were considered holy, unholy, or common. For instance, people with skin diseases (Mark 1:40) were considered unclean or impure and were made to live on the boundaries of the community, becoming in effect outcast. Likewise, a woman during her menstrual cycle, and also chronically ill people, were temporarily unclean. Furthermore, in this religious culture, sickness and sin were normally associated (e.g. John 9:2).

However, Mark's Jesus, in whom the newness of God's perfect dominion was brought and declared, redefines the whole idea of purity and impurity arguing that only the impurity which comes from the human heart makes people unclean (Mark 7:20–23). Moreover, he also demonstrated these radical new values by allowing sinners, tax collectors and other marginalized people to join in the table fellowship with him thus demonstrating the purity of the new system.[87]

Likewise, bandits could be seen not only as unimportant people, but also as ones who attack or hurt others in various ways. They were regarded as thieves, robbers and rebels who fight, particularly against the ruling of the state or local elite. Nevertheless, the goal of their activities is not to overthrow the regime of the elite, but to attack it in order to use it as the source of livelihood by any means possible. According to Hobsbawm's definition, the term "banditry" (social banditry) "consists essentially of a relatively small group, usually of men living on the margins of peasant society, whose activities are considered criminal by the prevailing official power-structure and value system of the day, but not . . . by the peasantry themselves precisely because peasants supported them, expecting that bandits are the ones who will stand

---

87. See Witherington, *Acts of Apostles*, 34–35.

against injustice."[88] However, they are regarded as threats to the community as they attack estates, cities, tax collectors, government officials, travellers, and so on, as well as committing other forms of disruption. As suggested by some thinkers, the state (Hasmonean, Herodian, Roman) handled social bandits either by killing them in battle, executing them, or deporting them.[89]

In the tradition of Mark's Jesus as well, bandits were regarded and categorized as the armed social group who hurt or set out to rob others, usually violently (Mark 14:48; see also Matt 26:55; Luke 22:52). For instance, Barabbas was a bandit among other rebels in custody because he was known to have committed murder (Mark 15:7; see also John 18:40; Luke 23:18–19). Likewise, there were two bandits between whom Jesus was crucified as a criminal which reminds Mark's readers that it happened as the fulfilment of the prophecy of the Scripture in Isaiah 53:12 (Mark 15:27–28). The two bandits crucified, "one on the right, one on the left," remind Mark's readers of the request made by James and John to sit on his right and left side in his glory (Mark 10:37). Even though it was Jesus who was willing to be identified with the bandits on the cross, the irony of this is the bandits, not his own disciples, who were to be crucified with Jesus at the hands of the state (10:39). The disciples simply ran away, not being prepared to be counted with the transgressors.[90] In other words, amazingly, this was a result which confirmed and fulfilled much earlier Scriptures (e.g. Isa 53:12), indicating that Mark's Jesus identifies himself with such unexpected outcasts who were crucified with him as rebels rather than his close followers/friends.

The Gerasene demoniac (5:2) was also an outcast, not simply because he was under the control of evil spirits and hurting himself regularly, but also because he was from among Gentiles who were considered as unclean by the average Jews.[91] Likewise, the Syro-Phoenician woman, with her daughter, was regarded as despised and thus a neglected person, not only because of her sex as a woman, but also because she was a Gentile (7:25). The reason being that the social values of Jesus's day like the rest of the Mediterranean world, was an androcentric society which viewed life from a man's point of

---

88. Hobsbawm, "Peasants and Politics," 143.
89. See Stegemann, Malina, and Theissen, *Social Setting of Jesus*, 296.
90. Myers, *Binding the Strong Man*, 387.
91. See Elwell and Yarbrough, *First-Century World*, 70–72.

view. In such a society, although the women were not totally abandoned or forgotten in the community, decisions made on property purchased, and marriages contracts, were drawn up in ways that promoted the interests of men and their ideals and views of the society in which they lived. It was in almost every respect a "man's world."[92]

Finally, Mark tells his readers of Jesus's self-identification with unexpected people who were on the margin or the periphery, of the social scale, and so were regarded as unimportant in society, and Jesus unexpectedly brought to them liberation from their plight and afflictions. He also revealed his divine identity to them and was declared by them as the divine Son of God as well as made them part of his kingdom-of-God's mission on earth. Therefore, as indicated above, it is true that the extreme marginality of these marginalized people and the liminality of the liminal people has received new opportunity of possibility, given by Jesus through whom the newness of kingdom-of-God's value has come.

1.8. Conclusion

This opening chapter has explored the idea of Jesus's divine identity as the Son of God even though it was not explicitly stated but implicitly narrated from the outset of Mark's gospel. The readers understand that Mark records Jesus's divine messianic identity not only in his narrative account (Mark's gospel) but also he quoted it from the Old Testament indicating Jesus's glorious, Yahweh-like coming[93] (e.g. see Mark 1:2–3; 4:35–41) as the Saviour and Elijah-like messenger as the Judge.

It is true that Jesus's full identity is not clear to many, including some NT (Markan) scholars who argue that Jesus could not understand or claim to be the divine Messiah either pre- or post-resurrection, or to those who made a dichotomy between Mark's first and second halves thinking that

---

92. See Witherington, *Acts of Apostles*, 32–33.

93. It is true that the OT does not refer to Jesus, but the NT authors identify him in various ways with OT figures and with Yahweh himself. One of the peculiarities about the NT authors is that they understand OT texts which speak about the coming of the Yahweh as fulfilled in the coming of Jesus. In addition, since John the Baptist is regarded as the forerunner of the Messiah, it would be appropriate to say that John is associated with Elijah whose role it was to prepare for the coming of Yahweh.

Jesus's Sonship in the first half of Mark's gospel as the Son of God, was corrected to be the Son of Man in the second half. Nevertheless, I argue that the evidence of Jesus's divine identity as the divine Messiah can be found not merely in the first or the second half of Mark's gospel but also throughout the gospel narrative.

As discussed previously, the problem was that Mark's gospel is about one Jesus who was understood as the miraculous Son of God, but who guarded his divine identity and commanded demons and people not to proclaim this divine Sonship openly to others in the first half of Mark's gospel. However, one can argue that Mark's readers and hearers knew that Jesus, the unique Messiah, was so different from all other messiahs of the OT and of Israel in the first century, because his style of messiahship is totally unique as redefined by Jesus himself, who revealed his true identity through his unique death – not on the battle field, but on the cross, the shameful place.

Jesus's unique messiahship is also seen in Mark's narrative through his self-identification with various people touching the whole social spectrum at many levels. He did this, not only with those who were on the top or in a liminal state, but also with those who were outcast and so marginalized at the bottom of the social scale, on the periphery, in order to set them free from their various plights, both physical and social.

Finally, Mark's readers understand that Jesus identified himself not only with those who were physically and socially in liminal states, or marginalized on the lower social scale of society, but also with those who felt spiritually abandoned by God and were crying in his absence due to their sins. He did so to save or atone the whole of humanity, without any discrimination between people, since they recognized and proclaimed that Jesus was God's divine Son.

In the next chapter, I shall consider four passages from the gospel (Mark 3:7–12; 5:1–20; 10:46–52 and 15:33–41), where Jesus's unique divine identity is revealed to and declared by some unexpected marginalized and liminal individuals. Indeed, a close exegesis and exposition of these episodes that describe Jesus's divine messianic identity as well as his self-identification with those who were poor and outcast will be discussed. This provides the basis for the continued assessment of his unique divine identity, which was ultimately declared in his death on the cross, as a result of which the victory of God's transforming power to all humanity is revealed and proclaimed.

CHAPTER 2

Jesus and the Marginalized and the Liminal in Mark

2.1. The Spread of Jesus's Popularity

In the previous chapter, we examined the unique identity of Jesus, as the divine Son of God and the suffering and vindicated Messiah who identified himself with different people from various backgrounds, particularly, with those who were known as poor or destitute, and outcast, on the margin or the lowest scale of society. This chapter seeks to explore and carefully examine the God-like activities of Jesus and, regardless of opposition from different directions, the spread of his popularity as he liberates the poor and outcasts from various sorts of afflictions as well as their unexpected recognition and declaration of Jesus's divine identity as the Son of God.

To do so, certain passages from Mark's gospel, particularly, Mark 3:7–12; 5:1–20; 10:46–52 and 15:39–41, will be attended to, because the readers of these particular passages can clearly see that Jesus's divine identity as the Son of God was recognized and declared by two unexpected marginalized demoniacs, and by two marginalized and liminal individuals.

The first of these passages is about the spread of Jesus's popularity in Mark 3:7–12. It reads,

> Jesus departed with his disciples to the sea, and a great multitude from Galilee followed him; hearing all that he was doing, they came to him in great numbers from Judea, Jerusalem, Idumea, beyond the Jordan, and the region around Tyre and Sidon. He told his disciples to have a boat ready for him because

of the crowd, so that they would not crush him; for he had cured many, so that all who had diseases pressed upon him to touch him. Whenever the unclean spirits saw him, they fell down before him and shouted, "You are the Son of God!" But he sternly ordered them not to make him known.

2.1.1. Introduction

Mark tells his readers from the beginning of his gospel that God's kingship has already arrived in the presence of Jesus among them. The result was that opposition and conflicts arose from various directions. Also, Mark told some stories which indicate the inadequacy of the old categories of tradition and the law to express the new sort of conduct brought by Jesus. In the next sections, Mark portrays that, regardless of all oppositions and conflict, Jesus was a great figure progressing in his mission of God's kingly rule on earth, liberating many people in need and revealing his divine identity to unexpected people such as the outcasts.

2.1.2. Literary Context

In the first part of the early chapters of the gospel (1:14–3:6), Mark presents Jesus proclaiming his message of the kingdom of God which was the major subject of Jesus's teaching mission. In Mark 1:14–15, he affirms a programmatic statement for the whole of his gospel: that the time of God's dominion has been fulfilled. The perfect tense "has come" ἤγγικεν, suggests that the sense in which the kingdom has drawn near was more than just a reality about to dawn, but a reality that has already arrived through his words (in teaching and preaching) and powerful deeds.[1] Mark's readers were to understand that it is Jesus who played the prominent role in demonstrating the rule of God on earth through various activities among them. For instance,

---

1. The meaning of the term "has come" of God's kingdom in Mark1:15 has been much debated. Whereas some scholars contend that it indicates the arrival of God's kingdom in the presence of Jesus and his ministry (see Dodd, *Interpretation of the Fourth Gospel*, 28–30; Beasley-Murray, *Jesus and the Kingdom*, 72–73), by contrast, others argue that it denotes the nearness of God's kingdom rather than its arrival (see Kummel, *Promise*, 19–25; Campbell, "Kingdom of God," 91–94; Marxsen, *Mark the Evangelist*, 132–134). However, it is rightly argued that for Markan Jesus, the kingdom of God was not simply nearer because it was already near with the coming of John, who fulfilled the role of the promised Elijah in Mark 9:11–13; cf. Mal 4:5 and the prophetic promises (Mark 1:2–3), but it had come at work Mark 14:41; Luke 11:20 (see Stein, *Mark*, 73).

Mark records some stories as a result of which God's dominion was seen when Jesus exorcized demons in Capernaum (Mark 1:21–28), healed Peter's mother-in-Law from a fever (1:29–31), and cleansed a man from a skin disease (1:40–45). As he did so Jesus faced increasing challenges on many fronts from the religious authorities of the day (2:1–3:6). Regardless of all these conflicts Jesus is seen moving forward as the great figure through whose life and active ministry the reign of God reaches out to affect the lives of all the people he meets from different backgrounds. It is in Jesus's words and deeds that the power of the evil One is destroyed and Jesus's divine Sonship is recognized and declared (Mark 1:24, 34; 3:11). Put differently, after Jesus's announcement of the arrival of God's rule, it becomes immediately clear that the nearness of the kingdom generates opposition and conflict. This conflict is with the forces of nature, demons and illness; and conflict with the Jewish authorities. In 2:18–22 Jesus responds to a question in a way that illumines all five episodes[2] – the arrival of the bridegroom creates a new situation and calls for a new sort of conduct; the old categories of tradition and law are inadequate to express and judge the newness brought by Jesus.[3]

Therefore, as a result of this newness brought by Jesus, in the next section (3:7–12),[4] which is regarded as the summary of his ministry Jesus is seen, with his first followers, moving from Capernaum to the sea of Galilee, teaching the crowd, healing the sick and helping needy people in miraculous ways. However, regarding this section (3:7–12), Markan scholars hold differing views. For instance, while some see it is as the conclusion of the preceding stories, others argue that it must be an introduction to the section which follows (3:13–6:6). Both sides present a strong case. For example, those who see it as a conclusion regard themes such as Jesus's withdrawal from the

---

2. In these episodes, the readers know that there is the contrast between Jesus's authority and that of the Jewish leaders. There is a correspondence between the first episode (Mark 2:1–12) and the fifth (Mark 3:1–6) which involve healings and unspoken accusations against Jesus but also between the second episode (Mark 2:13–17) and the fourth (Mark 2:23–28) which have to do with eating in a way that apparently violates the law. In the centre (Mark 2:18–22) is a response of Jesus to the question which reveals these episodes and their significance regarding Jesus's self-association with the outcasts and marginalized people in various way (see also Hooker, *According to St. Mark*, 83–108).

3. This idea was taken from Bryan, Class Lecture New Testament One.

4. Many Markan scholars see this section as an editorial summary rather than a part of tradition that Mark passed on with or without editing. Nevertheless others rightly argue that it is a piece of tradition that Mark developed.

crowds (3:7–8).⁵ In contrast, others argue that it is an introduction of the next section preparing the reader to the things which would happen as Jesus's ministry progresses forward.⁶ Still others think that Mark 3:7–12 seems to serve as a bridge between what comes before (1:14–3:6) with what comes after (3:13–6:6a); because it is true that the exorcism story of 3:7–12 recalls 1:1:21–28, 34, 39 and prepares the reader for 3:23–30 and 5:1–20. Likewise, the healing ministry of Jesus in 3:10 looks backward in which he healed many (1:29–31, 40–45; 2:1–12, 17; 3:1–6) as well as forward to 5:21–43.⁷

As indicated above, these positions provide evidences for their views in these sections. However, the second position is more convincing for the following reasons. For instance, first, although there are some similar themes found in both the preceding section (1:14–3:6) and the next section (3:13–6:6a), there is no clue about the opposition from religious leaders to Jesus's mission in 3:7–12. Second, Jesus's move from Capernaum in Galilee, going to other further regions rather than back to Galilee indicates as though this section to be understood as an introduction to the next stories (3:13–6:6a). Even though 3:7 reminds the reader of the disciples of Jesus in 1:16–20, 29–30, 36; 2:15–16, 18–20, 23–26, it fits better the call and anticipated activities of Jesus's followers, as his companions, during his ministry in 3:13–19, 4:11–13, 34–41; 5:31, 37, 40; 6:1 and even beyond. Moreover, since the boat prepared in 3:9 is not mentioned in the previous section (1:14–3:6, even until 4:1), this section must be understood as preparing the reader for what is to come. This does not look back to 1:16–20 but forward to 4:1, 35–43; 5:1–2, 21 for in 1:16 the boat does not involve Jesus and is left behind.⁸ Thus, the readers understand Jesus's glorious move forward with his kingdom-of-God message identifying himself with those

---

5. This recalls Mark 1:35 and anticipates 3:13; 4:10; 4:34; likewise, the press of the crowds upon Jesus in 3:7–8, recalls 1:32–34, 37, 45, his healing power (3:10) recalls 1:29–31, 34, 40–45 and 2:1–10; the exorcism of demons and their recognition of Jesus's true identity as the Son of God (3:10–11) recall 1:24, 34 and the command to silence in 3:12 with 1:25, 34, 44 as though they have some similarity with the preceding stories, beginning at Mark 1:16, and thus this section functions as a conclusion. Keck, "Introduction to Mark's Gospel," 352–370.

6. Brooks, *Mark*, 69; Lane, *Gospel of Mark*, 12.

7. For example Witherington, *Gospel of Mark*, 141. For other sources for discussions on this topic, see Donahue and Harrington, *Gospel of Mark*, 120–121.

8. See Stein, *Mark*, 159.

who were marginalized and liminal people, not only in Galilee and Nazareth, his hometown but also in the neighbouring regions liberating them from various kinds of afflictions.

In this particular transitional section (3:7–12), how does Mark introduce Jesus to his readers? How does he present Jesus who was proclaimed as God's Son by demonic, supernatural beings in Mark 3:7–12? And what was the response of others to Jesus's true identity?

2.1.3. Jesus Changes His Venue to Teach and to Heal People

Having left the town of Capernaum due to his knowledge of the plotting of the religious authorities against his life in 3:6, Mark tells his readers that Jesus, with his earliest followers changed venue and departed from the crowds either for privacy or to avoid the crush.[9] He was regarded by the crowds as a great teacher and miracle worker whose fame was spreading throughout the surrounding regions. The phrase "withdraw to the sea" was neither for the purpose of retreat nor fleeing from the persecution caused by the religious authorities (3:6); because Mark, in his gospel did not at any time suggest that Jesus fled from his opponents in fear. Rather, according to Mark, the Greek verb ἀνεχώρησεν or "withdrew" indicates that Jesus's withdrawal or change of place is to create a good atmosphere in which to teach the crowds and to prepare his followers who were the essential part of his ministry in readiness for the further ministry detailed in Mark 4:1. In doing so, Jesus's desire was to move forward for the purpose of extending God's sovereign rule in the towns and synagogues at that time in Palestine and beyond. For instance, Mark tells his readers that it was not only in Galilee, the northern district of Palestine or Judea, or in Jerusalem, the holy and the chief city of Palestine but also Jesus was heading forward to Idumaea, in southern Judea, which the Edomite occupied in the fifth and fourth centuries BC. Likewise, many people were coming to Jesus from these areas and elsewhere because first Jesus took an initiative to come to them to do great things for them. Also, Mark mentions the regions beyond the Jordan which were occupied by Jews, as well as Tyre and Sidon, originally Phoenician sea ports which are regarded as predominantly gentile cities though some Jews lived

---

9. Stein, 161.

in them. Thus, the mention of these three areas and Jesus's progress toward them and beyond,[10] may suggest to Mark's readers that they should know that non-Jewish or Gentiles were coming to see Jesus to benefit from his proclamation about the kingdom of God (7:24–31). In other words, Jesus's change of venue, to the "sea" (θάλασσαν), was not for the purpose of retreat or fleeing from the religious leaders of Judaism but it was to teach his followers regarding his God's kingdom mission in and around Galilee. Thus, Mark's readers may understand these people who are coming to Jesus "as the initial Gentiles who foreshadowed the later reception of the Christian gospel by Gentiles in the church."[11]

In contrast to the rejection of religious authorities to Jesus's mission, Mark makes much of the great success of Jesus's ministry and the eager response of the huge numbers of people who followed Jesus. As discussed above, these people were not only from Galilee "where he attracted a crowd who simply 'followed' him to the sea," but also they came from a vast geographical region of Palestine.[12] These were principally "Jewish territories . . . mixed Jewish-Gentiles regions . . . [and] . . . largely if not entirely Gentile regions."[13] So, Mark's readers can realize the ethnic diversity of the crowd even during Jesus's early ministry while he was proclaiming God's sovereign reign on earth through his words and mighty deeds among all people. France also says this geographical list "excludes, . . . the area of Samaria and Decapolis, which were regarded as off limits for Patriotic Jews but includes along with recognized areas of Jewish population not only Idumaea . . . but also the officially non-Jewish territory of Phoenicia."[14] Therefore, as Myers rightly adds, the point of this geographical reference seems to be to make clear that the people were coming from north, east, south and west to reach Jesus.[15] It is possible to think that in 3:7–8 Mark presents Jesus as the one who came to gather and help all sorts of people without ethnic or geographical

---

10. Mark speaks of many people coming to Jesus from several areas precisely because, first, Jesus took initiative to come to them doing great things and associating himself with them.

11. Hurtado, *Mark*, 61; Brooks, *Mark*, 69–70.

12. Guelich, *Mark 1–8*, 145.

13. Edwards, *Gospel According to Mark*, 103.

14. France, *Gospel of Mark*, 154.

15. Myers, *Binding the Strong Man*, 163.

limitations, depending on their needs whatever they were. This may be the reason for Mark to emphasize the size of the crowds or numbers of people who followed Jesus as a "great multitude" (3:7). This "great multitude" had already been with Jesus since the beginnings of his ministry in Galilee. The term "followed," in 3:7 indicates that these people had been with him since 1:28, 33, 37, 45; 2:2, 13, attending his impressive ministry for a long time, until 3:6. Many of them might have been following him as a great teacher and healer and would continue to listen to him and expected him to heal them. However, the use of "came" (ἦλθον), in verse 8, instead of "followed" (ἠκολούθησεν), seems to describe those who joined him and his disciples from outside Galilee by hearing about him from distant areas, first of all as a great healer and miracle worker (v. 8). Thus, France is correct in saying, "the difference of verb reflects their geographical location rather than any distinction in the degree of their commitment."[16] In other words, these people who followed him from Galilee, as well as those who came from distant areas, did not have a clear understanding of Jesus's true identity nor did they say anything concerning who Jesus really was. Nevertheless, the readers knew that "though official Judaism had already rejected Jesus, all Israel gathers to him" precisely because "Jesus' reputation and ministry far exceeded that of his predecessor, or John the Baptist (cf. 1:5, Judea and Jerusalem)."[17]

Mark also tells his readers and hearers that Jesus, with his followers, wanted a boat made ready for him in order to move to a new venue, and for its continual usage in 4:1–2 and in the following similar stories in the gospel. The reason for such a boat to be ready was the necessity of it (3:9) to keep Jesus safe from the pressing crowds who were pushing forward even to the point of falling on him. Jesus also could use it as an effective floating stage or platform from which to teach his followers and the crowd that had been around him. Moreover, according to 4:1–35, this sort of teaching method of Jesus indicates not simply his fleeing from the press of the crowd seeking comfort or security for himself but rather it was to show that his primary concern is on teaching and preaching of the kingdom of God rather than healing and doing more miraculous acts.

---

16. France, *Gospel of Mark*, 153.
17. Hooker, *According to St. Mark*, 110; Guelich, *Mark 1–8*, 146.

Regarding the phrase "so that they would not crush him," some think that it refers to Jesus's forthcoming suffering and death but this is unlikely, because as Stein says, "the terms 'crush' and 'press' (ἐπιπίπτειν) serve not as hostile threats to Jesus's well-being but as examples of his greatness and fame."[18] The press of the people was hoping to get something helpful from him due to his unique ability. Also, as Witherington points out, "the press of the crowd seeking healing was so overwhelming that Jesus required the disciples to ready a boat to escape in as a safety valve."[19] Thus, the reason is that if Jesus were to teach them from a boat on the water, the people could not crowd him or reach him easily and therefore, not to disturb him while he was teaching.

2.1.4. Jesus Heals Many/All

Regardless of what their motive or intentions were, when they flocked to Jesus and pressed him, he did not leave them un-healed, but he helped all who came to him. So, Stein rightly says "the clause, 'for he healed many' should not be interpreted to mean that some who came for healing went away without healing as though Jesus was able to heal 'many' but not 'all'," because as he goes on to say, the term "many" in a semantic context means "all."[20] Thus, the idea that Jesus healed many who had diseases (μάστιγας) indicates that "scourges were understood to be divinely imposed afflictions or punishments against sin, but by now had become a general term for ailments . . .," which caused the people to flock to Jesus and to fall upon him for healing.[21]

On the question of touching Jesus or being touched by him for healing, it seems that the people who were trying to touch him thought that he had magical power and believed that if they touched him they would be healed. However, since Jesus healed some by touching them (1:40–45; 7:31–37; 8:22–26), and others by being touched by them (3:10; 5:27–28, 6:56), it must be a matter of faith in Jesus's unique supernatural power which healed them. Further, Mark's readers know that "healing is directly ascribed to Jesus'

---

18. Stein, *Mark*, 163.
19. Witherington, *Gospel of Mark*, 143.
20. Stein, *Mark*, 143
21. France, *Gospel of Mark*, 155.

action . . . as in 5:34 Jesus describes the woman's desire to touch his robe as an act of faith that 'saved' her."[22]

2.1.5. Jesus's Real Identity Was Recognized and Declared

Mark goes on to tell his readers about Jesus's interaction with the marginalized person who was under control of the evil spirits or demons, not only to demonstrate who Jesus really is as in 1:24, but also, unexpectedly, to proclaim him as God's Son, which was not yet understood even by Jesus's close followers. Thus, Stein correctly states "the act of submission by demons was manifested by the actions of those who were possessed by them."[23] In other words, their action of falling down at Jesus's feet indicated that those people who were under control of the evil spirits, and their actions also should be interpreted as the demons paying homage and their submission to Jesus's supreme authority.[24] However, with regard to the confessions of demons, some scholars suggest that the confessions made by the demons that Jesus was the Son of God was not for the sake of confession, but just to escape his authority over them, even to rob him of his strength.[25] Nevertheless, since there is no hint in the text, this is unlikely, as Jesus's divine Sonship has already been fully declared by God himself in 1:10–11 and is affirmed in 9:7 and again in the words of the gentile centurion in 15:39. Therefore, demons' humble submission to Jesus and their declaration to his divine identity reveals the "identity of the one whom they instinctively recognize as their superior."[26] It is also important to know that the confession of both the demons and the centurions could be taken as Markan irony; they both speak a truth that (perhaps) they do not understand. Thus, the readers realize that Jesus's divine messianic identity is declared by God himself, by the demons, and finally by humanity, yet this Jesus is able to identify himself with the oppressed or marginalized ones in order to help them in their needs.

Unlike the exorcising of the demons in 1:25, Mark's readers know that in 3:12, Jesus subdued or forbade them to speak about what happened. It

---

22. Guelich, *Mark 1–8*, 148.
23. Stein, *Mark*, 164.
24. See Hooker, *According to St. Mark*, 110.
25. See Edwards, *Gospel According to Mark*, 104.
26. France, *Gospel of Mark*, 155.

is not because in proclaiming Jesus's divine Sonship they were not correct, because it has already been declared as mentioned above. In this regard, Markan scholars hold various views. For instance, some think that it was because the time for such explicit declaration of Jesus's divine title had not yet come. This was to be understood only after Jesus's death on the cross and resurrection Mark 9:9.[27] Likewise, Hurtado thinks that Jesus's avoidance of the confession of his messianic or divine title was not intended to be openly proclaimed until after the decisive events of his death and resurrection had taken place.[28] Nonetheless, since, even in the early chapters of the gospel, the miracle secret in 1:45; 7:36 was disobeyed and demons in 1:24; 3:11; 5:7 kept on declaring Jesus as the Son of God, it is improbable that his divine identity must be fully revealed only after his death and resurrection. Instead, it is appropriate to think that for now Jesus must remain, from the point of view of the general public, incognito because he insists that his identity as the divine Messiah not be considered apart from his suffering; because for him, his identity is inseparable from his destiny.[29] So, as briefly indicated above and would be discussed later in the exegetical section of chapter 15:33–39, the readers of Mark are to discover that Jesus's divine identity becomes clear only as his destiny emerges. Put differently, in Mark's gospel, the two elements of glory and suffering had to be held together. The fact that Jesus immediately responds to Peter's confession of his messiahship with the first of a series of predictions of suffering and death reveals the central importance of this motif. Peter's refusal to accept the prediction of suffering reveals why the command to silence was essential. Similarly, the transfiguration which follows is a dramatic preview of the glory of Jesus; but this is glory which cannot be fully understood until after Jesus had died and risen (9:9).

As noted previously concerning the "messianic secret," Jesus wanted to avoid a confrontation with Rome by avoiding inflammatory titles and teachings because he had no political agenda in this matter. Further, Jesus's proclamation of the arrival of God's sovereign rule and his call to receive it (1:15) could, in the revolutionary atmosphere of first-century Palestine, be easily misunderstood as a call to arms. Thus, it was wise to teach the crowds

---

27. See Guelich, *Mark 1–8*, 149; Brooks, *Mark*, 70.
28. See Hurtardo, *Mark*, 57.
29. See France, *Gospel of Mark*, 155.

concerning its arrival in parables (4:10–12, 33–34) instead of publicly using titles, such as the Son of God, the King of Jews, Son of David, the Messiah or the Christ, which would cause misunderstanding of Jesus's mission by the Roman government, and so hinder Jesus's ministry. Hence Jesus preferred to use the title "Son of Man" as a more manageable designation, and through this he was able to teach that his ministry involved not political revolution but rather giving his life as a ransom for many (10:45).[30] Moreover, the readers understand that Jesus's own view of his messiahship which must involve his rejection and suffering is so different from that of the crowds and even the views of his own close followers or disciples. So for this reason Mark focused on Jesus's authoritative command to silence the mouths of demons from continuing to speak about his divine messianic identity, although what they said was perfectly correct.

It is also possible to suggest that even though Jesus's motivation for concealing his identity seems to be political, it is not political in the sense that he is worried about recrimination from Rome, but rather that he seeks to avoid the politicized distortion of his identity which come from Jewish perceptions of what messiah would do. Those distortions are not a concern in gentile territory where the demoniac's equating of what the Lord had done for him with what Jesus had done for him serve Mark's aim of clarifying the divine identity through gentile perceptions of Jesus.

Then Mark continues narrating Jesus's teachings and mighty acts of authority over demons in 3:20–35 and 5:1–20, over sickness, and his extended power over nature (4:35–41) and even over death (5:41–43), in not only Jewish but also gentile territories. However, instead of recognizing Jesus's real divine identity, Mark concludes this section by recording the unbelief of people even those who came from Jesus's home town, Nazareth (6:1–6; cf. Mark 10:47). In other words, regardless of all these great things that Jesus did, no human being could recognize who Jesus really was. So, in the following section, Mark presses on with narrative of other stories about Jesus's identity, including that of a marginalized person from the gentile area that was terribly oppressed by unclean spirits. This man lived in a gentile region which was regarded as unclean land.

---

30. See Stein, *Mark*, 25.

2.2. Jesus Exorcises the Gerasene Demoniac (Mark 5:1–20)

They came to the other side of the lake, to the country of the Gerasenes. And when he had stepped out of the boat, immediately a man out of the tombs with an unclean spirit met him. He lived among the tombs; and no one could restrain him anymore, even with a chain; for he had often been restrained with the shackles and chains, but chains he wrenched apart, and the shackles he broke in pieces; and no one had the strength to subdue him. Night and day among the tombs and on the mountains he was always howling and bruising himself with stones. When he saw Jesus from a distance, he ran and bowed down before him; and he shouted at the top of his voice, "What have you to do with me, Jesus, Son of the Most High God? I adjure you by God, do not torment me." For he had said to him, "Come out of the man, you unclean spirit!" Then Jesus asked him, "What is your name?" He replied, "My name is Legion; for we are many." He begged him earnestly not to send them out of the country. Now there on the hillside a great herd of swine was feeding; and the unclean spirits begged him, "Send us into the swine; let us enter them." So he gave them permission. And the unclean spirits came out and entered the swine; and the herd, numbering about two thousand, rushed down the steep bank into the sea, and were downed in the sea.

The swineherds ran off and told it in the city and in the country. Then people came to see what it was that had happened. They came to Jesus and saw the demoniac sitting there, clothed and in his right mind, the very man who had had the legion; and they were afraid. Those who had seen what had happened to the demoniac and to the swine reported it. Then they began to beg Jesus to leave their neighbourhood. As he was getting into the boat, the man who had been possessed by demons begged him that he might be with him. But Jesus refused, and said to him, "Go home to your friends, and tell them how much the Lord has done for you, and what mercy he has shown you." And he went away and began to proclaim in the Decapolis how much Jesus had done for him; and everyone was amazed.

2.2.1. Introduction

Mark has told his readers about Jesus's unique identity as the Son of God, declared by God himself and through supernatural beings, respectively, and his unique authority over demons (1:1, 11, 24; 3:11). He also narrates the authority of Jesus over sin through forgiveness (2:10) and over old ritual elements such as fasting and the Sabbath (2:18–28). Mark continues to tell his readers that, having revealed his supreme authority over nature in 4:35–41, Jesus, with his close but confused followers, came to a marginalized[31] man in a different location. Jesus did so, not only to destroy the power and strength of Satan and to deliver the demoniac from his plight, but also to reveal himself as the divine Son of God to the ex-demoniac and to send him back as a living witness of what he had done for him, to his family and friends in the gentile world. The readers should learn that before he met Jesus, this man was terribly oppressed by the evil spirits, rendering his life, physically, emotionally and socially almost untenable, but after he met Jesus, he became a healthy and important person even in the kingdom-of-God's mission of Jesus to Gentiles.

2.2.2. Literary Context

Beginning in the early chapters of Mark's narrative, as a result of the Yahweh-like coming of Jesus (1:2–3) and his proclamation of God's kingly rule (1:14–15), Mark records several stories about Jesus and his powerful activities through his words and deeds. One of the powerful activities of Jesus, according to the second evangelist, is exorcising or casting out demons as a result of which Jesus's universal authority and divine Sonship are revealed to those victims who were possessed by demons, and he is unexpectedly proclaimed to be the Son of God.

---

31. This man is a much marginalized person because he had been suffering many things physically, emotionally, socially and spiritually, by the unclean spirits, in a cemetery or tomb which is regarded as an unclean place in the gentile land.

Mark in 5:1–20 gives us the second miraculous exorcism story in his narrative. Compared to other exorcism stories in the gospel this is the longest and most detailed story which reaffirms the authority of Jesus over demons or evil spirits. Mark places it not in Palestine or Capernaum as he did it in 1:21–28, but in the further gentile regions of Decapolis. Thus, Mark's mention of the herds of pigs reminds the reader that the inhabitants of the area were predominantly Gentiles who were living an unclean life as pagans. Further, according to Matthew 7:6, Luke 15:15–16, and 2 Peter 2:22, pigs were regarded as symbols of paganism.

The Torah in the OT classified a pig as an unclean animal and so it was prohibited to be used for food (Lev 11:7–8; Deut 14:8; Isa 65:4; 66:17). Thus, according to the Jewish law, although one of these exorcism stories occurred in sacred soil, on sacred land, in a sacred place at the Synagogue in Capernaum (Mark 1:21–28), the present story occurred in the unclean land, in the unclean place, the tomb, on gentile land.

Therefore, in this narrative, Mark portrays Jesus as the protagonist in the drama of the whole gospel. The reader can see the progress of Jesus's kingdom-of-God proclamation moving forward from Palestine to the gentiles' territories, destroying the power of evil and identifying himself with the marginalized people. He does so going right into the locations where they are, and using some for the expansion of the kingly rule of God on earth (5:19–20). Thus, readers may understand that this story anticipates Jesus's mission to all nations (Mark 13:10). This will become clearer when Jesus, from afar, exorcised the demon from the daughter of a gentile woman who had faith in him (Mark 7:24–8:10).

Throughout Mark 4, using several parables, Mark teaches about Jesus and the gradual growth of the dominion of God on earth. Put simply, before the miracle of exorcism in Mark 5 in the gentiles' land, the readers see that Mark mentions a sea crossing miracle story where Jesus came into contact with a marginalized person, possessed by demons.

As these stories unfold, what confronts Mark's readers in his telling of the parables most acutely is the troubling fact that though it is said that the mystery is revealed to those inside, the first followers of Jesus do not understand who Jesus is and remain uncomprehending throughout the gospel. If there is a challenge to be like the fourth soil (4:20), it is not a challenge which the disciples apparently meet. Nor is it a challenge which anyone is even capable of meeting. Nevertheless, the parable does hold promise. For it suggests that whatever the slenderness of the results in the context of Jesus's own history, the promise that his gospel will yet yield a harvest is firm. If Mark's readers were only to look at Mark 4, there would be no way of knowing that the disciples differ at all from the understanding of others. In fact, later on in the gospel, Mark's readers are told that the disciples' hearts were hardened (6:51–52) and Jesus questions the disciples: "Do you still not see or understand? Are your hearts hardened? Do you have eyes but fail to see, and ears but fail to hear?" According to Mark, here the disciples are portrayed as no more discerning than those outside. But if the disciples did not see, even after private explanation was given to them, the promise remains that they will see in the future.[32] Although for them it was impossible it would not be so for God (10:26–27). Throughout the gospel of Mark, what is asserted in the most uncompromising way, was that the right to determine who sees and understands or who does not see and understand, belongs entirely to God.

For instance, despite Jesus's clear teaching in many ways such as in the parables about himself and the mystery of the growing dominion of God on earth in Mark 4, Mark reports the lack of faith or trust of Jesus's close companions, whose confidence in his Yahweh-like authority was paralyzed in the face of the raging wind and waves on the sea. Overlooking God's sovereign authority over natural chaos (Gen 8:1; Ps 74:13–14; 104:4–9; 107:25–30), and thinking that Jesus was indifferent toward them, they were terrified and asked him, "Teacher, do you not care that we are perishing?" (4:38). In contrast to their terror-filled question to Jesus during the full face of the storm, Mark's readers understand that Jesus's peaceful sleeping in the

---

32. It is true that this book reveals mainly the darker side of Jesus's first disciples who do not understand Jesus's full identity and the major focus of his mission. Thus, Mark portrayed them as the ignorant and failed people struggling for their own personal benefits or high position over others rather than humble service to others, and eventually they abandoned Jesus at his arrest in Mark 14. However, the readers understand that regardless of their poor background and former job as fishers among marginalized and liminal Galileans, Jesus identified himself with them by making them the beneficiaries of his especial appointment, and by teaching and empowering them with authority as the agents of God's kingly rule on earth. Finally, in spite of their failure in various ways, Jesus wanted to reveal himself to them as the divine Messiah and Son of God throughout the gospel; and in the end, he forgave their failure and promised to meet them again in Galilee and to continue to use them for his new mission after the resurrection (Mark 6:7).

stern, indicates his confidence and full reliance on God's domination even over the sea. In other words, although Jesus teaches them away from the crowd, privately, his main companions were paralyzed even to the point of not understanding who Jesus was. Put differently, even though they were expected to participate in the proclamation of the impending dominion of God, Mark's Jesus found his friends unable even to know who Jesus really was. Finally, from the whole context of the episode and the christological question of the disciples "who then is this . . . ?" in 4:41, the reader may understand that the refusal of Jesus's close followers to trust the victory Jesus won and proclaimed is the refusal of the kingdom authority he conferred upon them (3:15). Further, Mark 4:41 suggests that even after their deliverance the disciples did not have trust in him because they still did not understand who he really was. Put differently, it is possible to suggest that for one thing, Jesus's friends have just stirred him from a nap presumably because they do understand his power over the sea. For another thing, though, they do show amazement over his access to the divine power they have nudged him toward using. As noted above, in the passage that precedes, Jesus's faithful repose (his sleeping in the midst of the storm) contrasts with their frenetic panic, which he attributes to their lack of faith. There does seem to be some connection then between the question about his identity ("who then is this?") and his power to subdue natural chaos ("the wind and the sea"). In other words, even though they do understand Jesus's power to do miracles and extraordinary things, in this context, his divine identity as the divine Son of God was not fully clear to his first followers. This will continue to be so until Jesus's death and resurrection.

Mark, in the next chapter (Mark 5), tells his readers and listeners that his Jesus is seen moving forward with the same agenda of God's impending reign in further areas of gentile land. In this part of the gospel story (5:1–20), Mark tells his readers that Jesus comes to the most helpless and miserable person, the demoniac, not only to set him free from the power of evil spirits, by destroying the power of the whole army of Satan, but also by revealing his divine identity, as the Son of the Most-High God to the victim, thus expanding the mighty act of Jesus's, the Lord, among Gentiles.

In the next section of his gospel (5:21–43), Mark narrates two more miracle stories to further remind his readers of Jesus's authority to heal other marginalized people, and their full trust in his divine ability to heal as the agent of God's power. In both stories, that of the haemorrhaging woman and Jairus with his daughter, Mark's readers understand that those who were healed by Jesus in the gentile regions seemed to have the faith that Jesus closest friends have lacked (5:34, 36).

2.2.3. Jesus Comes to the Demon-Possessed Man in the Gentile Region

Mark tells his readers that Jesus, by his own initiative, and with his most intimate followers, came to this isolated man and met him in an alien location. "'And when he came out of the boat' (καὶ ἐξελθόντος αὐτοῦ ἐκ τοῦ πλοίου), introduces Mark's readers to Jesus's ministry to the Gentiles in Decapolis (5:1–20)."[33] Markan scholars are not in agreement about the location of this incident. Although "Gergesa" (El-Kursi) fits the geographical description on the eastern side of the Sea of Galilee, and though there is a historical record which supports this from the church fathers (Origen and Eusebius), it lacks textual support.[34] So, the most important thing is the significance of the mention that the place is in the area which was inhabited predominantly by Gentiles during Jesus's earthly ministry. It is possible to think that the man was a very miserable person, not only because he was connected with the dead as he lived among the tombs in a what was considered unclean gentile land,[35] but also because he was possessed by the evil spirit. In other words, Jesus came to this outcast person who was crying out in agony and identified himself with the man as his hope and helper because Jesus was moving beyond the Jewish territories towards that of Gentiles.

Additionally, as it was said, "by frequenting the tombs, since corpses and cemeteries were considered unclean, especially gentile ones," the tombs and mountains, in verses 2–3 and 5 show the uncleanness of the place as a "death-filled residence" due to the presence of demons.[36] The word "tomb" (τὰ μνημεῖα) is described as an unclean place as though it is "a place where

---

33. Stein, *Mark*, 251.

34. See Edwards, *Gospel According to Mark*, 153–154.

35. The gentile land itself was considered as unclean in Jewish perspective (see Edwards, *Gospel According to Mark*, 155).

36. Witherington, *Gospel of Mark*, 181; Stein, *Mark*, 252.

no one would want to go for any reason," except Jesus.[37] Thus, Lane correctly notes that the purpose of demoniac possession is to distort and destroy the divine likeness of man according to creation.[38] In doing so, according to Lane, the evil spirit attempted to reduce the man to animal status.

Also, "night and day" in verse 5 indicates the unending tragic situation of the victim because he was crying in agony attempting with his enormous strength, to destroy himself, because "he is possessed not only just by one demon . . . but by many."[39] In other words, Mark emphasized the futility of human efforts to control the destructive power of demons and to help this victim because all human attempts to control him repeatedly failed (vv. 4–5).[40] Nevertheless, Mark points out Jesus, the mightier one who "has already bound the strong man Satan . . . (3:26–27); Jesus is therefore able to subdue him without needing to bind him with a chain."[41] Thus, I argue that Jesus, the divine Son of God, has associated and/or identified himself with this helpless and outcast to liberate him as his only saviour from his afflictions.

2.2.4. Demoniac Recognized and Proclaimed Jesus's Divine Identity

In verses 6–13, the readers discover that seeing Jesus from afar, the demoniac was unable to do anything, but unwittingly prostrated himself before the superior power of Jesus, indicating his submission and homage to him (v. 6). Recognizing Jesus's universal authority above all else, the demoniac also proclaimed Jesus's unique divine identity as "the Son of the Most High God" (υἱὲ τοῦ θεοῦ τοῦ ὑψίστου) (v. 7) which indicates his unique position as the one true God.[42] This declaration of Jesus's real identity by the marginalized demoniac, may answer the question "who then is this man . . .?" asked by the close followers of Jesus who were confused in their understanding of who

---

37. Edwards, *Gospel According to Mark*, 155.
38. See Lane, *Gospel of Mark*, 182; Witherington, *Gospel of Mark*, 181.
39. France, *Gospel of Mark*, 227.
40. Furthermore, see 9:22, 26 for similar self-detractive incident caused by demons.
41. Hooker, *According to St. Mark*, 142.
42. On Jesus's unique identity as the Son of the one true God, his unique position in relation to God and his universal supreme authority over all other gods and goddesses, see Edwards, *Gospel According to Mark*, 156.

he really was in 4:41. The demons pleaded with Jesus, "in God's name" (v. 7), and tried to resist the power of Jesus because they wanted to escape the agony of exorcism in verses 6–7.

Burkill thinks that Mark portrays the words of the demoniac in 5:7, "What have you to do with me, Son of the Most High God?" as an attempt by the demons to gain power over Jesus; however, in doing so, Mark's aim is to make Jesus's unique identity and authority clear to his readers in a way that the Gentiles understand Jesus's divine Sonship to God.[43] For instance, from the very beginning, he knows that Jesus is the Son of God (1:1). Second, God from heaven declared that Jesus is his uniquely beloved Son (1:11). Third, the demons themselves recognized and declared that Jesus is "the Holy One of God" (1:24–25) and "the Son of God" (3:11). In other words, their confession and acknowledgment of Jesus under the title "God's Son" found in verse 5:7 is not a new idea by demons to gain power over him, but it is already known and would be repeated by God (9:7) and finally by the gentile centurion (15:39).

Already in Scripture the phrase "Most High God" indicates the transcendence and victory of the God of Israel over pagan gods and goddesses.[44] Likewise, Jesus has demonstrated his unique strengths by destroying a whole army of Satan in the gentile region on the east side of the lake (v. 13). Therefore, rather than simply "the Holy One of God" (1:24) and "the Son of God" (3:11), "Son of the Most High God" (5:7) reinforces that Mark's readers understand Jesus's unique ability and rank in relation to the God of the whole universe and his cosmic authority which is above all else. In addition, recognizing Jesus's divine Sonship, the demoniac's plea not to be "tortured" or "tormented" indicates his superiority over them and their submission to his unique authority. Particularly, the term "torture" reminds Mark's readers that Jesus has unique authority to punish or to judge evil spirits not only at the present but also in the future as the final Judge. Matthew's parallel "before our time" in Matthew 8:29 denotes the present punishment of the evil spirit; and the readers may anticipate the final judgement will be brought about by the same Jesus against all demons. Therefore, since Jesus is

---

43. Burkill, *Mysterious Revelation*, 86, 89, 94; see also Gundry, *Mark*, 250.

44. For example, Gen 14:18; Num 24:16; Dan 3:26; 4:2; and in the intertestamental literature, e.g. 2 Macc 3:31; 3 Macc 7:9; 1 Esd 2:3.

the one who is able to bind the evil spirit, Satan (3:26–27), there must not be any difference between the present and the final binding and destruction of demons by the same authority, that of Jesus.

Bultmann thinks that the demons' self-identification and their number "many" (v. 9) is a boast, in that they thought they could conquer Jesus by their power because they were many.[45] However, the reader knows that demons' "begging him earnestly" (παρεκάλει αὐτὸν πολλὰ) in verse 10 indicates "rather, their total submission and subservience to Jesus' universal authority."[46] In addition, the reader knows that the demons simply appear ridiculous because their boast, if that is what it is, is futile. Thus, I argue that there is nothing to support Bultmann's idea either in the dialogue between Jesus and the demoniac nor in the whole context. Also, in the whole gospel, even though Bultmann was not clearly implying that Jesus was afraid of anything, Mark does not indicate Jesus's fear toward any military force or their great number. Rather, Jesus, with his authoritative words expelled the whole army of Satan from the victim. In other words, there was not any challenge or resistance from the demons' side except in pleading for Jesus's mercy. Likewise, recognizing that their fate and destiny lay with Jesus alone, they begged him for permission to enter into pigs.[47] Additionally, unlike Burkill's and Bultmann's speculations, in the whole context, Mark's readers know that opponents of Jesus, whether religious authorities or family members or demons cannot deny the unique power of Jesus.

It is true that the statement "My name is Legion; for we are many," (Λεγιὼν ὄνομά μοι, ὅτι πολλοί ἐσμεν, v. 9), and the herd, numbering about two thousand, rushing down . . . into the lake; . . . (v. 13) have military overtones since "a legion" was a Roman military term. It is also possible that the rushing down into the lake and the destruction of the possessed pigs is meant to remind the readers of a military charge. Thus, some have commented on the political symbolism of this exorcism seeing Jesus's expulsion

---

45. Bultman, *History of the Synoptic Tradition*, 210; see also Edwards, *Gospel According to Mark*, 157.

46. France, *Gospel of Mark*, 253.

47. Pigs were regarded as unclean animals from the Jewish point of view in the Old Testament law of purity (see Edwards, *Gospel According to Mark*, 155).

of "Legion" as constituting a repudiation of Roman occupation.[48] In other words, some regard the name "legion" as an allusion to the Roman brutal occupation of the Holy Land and Jesus's action as a defence of the Jews.

This is unconvincing because, first, in the whole context Mark does not say anything related to the imperial occupation of Palestine and Jesus's defence of the Jews against the Romans. Second, when the incident took place, Jesus was not in Jewish territory, but rather in the gentile territory of Decapolis, "on the other side" of the Jordan. So third, Jesus was liberating a Gentile, not a Jew, from his satanic plight. In my opinion, understanding that the ultimate oppressor of all human beings is the devil, Mark's concern is Jesus fighting against the power of Satan, not that of the Roman Empire.[49] Therefore, by using a military metaphor, Mark's intention was not just to make clear the strength of the demons, but the more powerful presence and action of Jesus to defeat the whole army of Satan as his superior, and to bind Satan and plunder his kingdom. In addition, as Hooker pointed out, Mark probably intends his readers to see in the destruction of the swine the destruction of demons as well. Jesus permitted what the demons requested and, finally, he destroyed them, or he left them homeless.[50] Therefore, Mark's readers understand that Jesus is the one who crushes the kingdom of Satan and plunders his house (3:27).

Likewise, this story seems to be upsetting to some thinkers due to the destruction of many innocent animals belonging to someone else in the area, so they think that this is an economic catastrophe.[51] It is not only a loss of thousands of animals, but also, they think, that Jesus was destroying the food supply of the Roman army staying in their region.[52] However, in contrast to the imaginations of these thinkers, Mark explains the impression and amusement of the townspeople in what Jesus has done to this hopeless and helpless outcast (v. 15). In other words, instead of complaining about the destroyed pigs or loss of property, the townspeople were eager to see

---

48. See Watts, *Isaiah's New Exodus*, 163; Theissen, *Miracle Stories*, 255–259; Myers, *Binding the Strong Man*, 190–194.
49. Watts, *Isaiah's New Exodus*, 163.
50. Hooker, *According to St. Mark*, 144.
51. Witherington, *Gospel of Mark*, 182–183.
52. See Waetjen, *Reordering of Power*, 118.

what the Lord Jesus had done for the marginalized victim by coming to him to restore his whole being.

Therefore, according to Witherington, the reader understands that "it is a matter of priorities. A human life is seen as more important than a herd of pigs."[53] In other words, Jesus must be understood as the one who has the greatest concern to help the marginalized return to normal life (see Mark 5:13). It is true that in his eyes, "the rescue and restoration of one person is more important than vast capital assets."[54]

2.2.5. The News of Jesus Spreads in the Whole Area

Having seen what Jesus had done for the marginalized man by destroying the power of evil, the herdsmen spread the news of what Jesus did for the demoniac. Then the inhabitants came to see, not the dead pigs in the sea, but primarily to see Jesus who had done this great thing to the man by restoring him to a totally healthy state of life. As a result of this the inhabitants were full of fear caused by Jesus's extraordinary powerful presence. With regard to the term "fear," Guelich thinks that it indicates the financial loss of the swine saying, "what may initially have been 'awe' (5:15) turned to 'fear' of what Jesus might do next."[55] But, since Mark in 5:14–17 does not associate the request of the inhabitants with any mention of financial loss, and since the request to depart comes not from the herdsmen who suffered the loss of the swine, but from the townspeople (or inhabitants) those who had seen it (i.e. the exorcism v. 16), Stein rightly argues that the term "fear" must refer to the supernatural presence of God in Jesus rather than worries of the herdsmen for what happened to their pigs.[56] So, this is the supernatural power of Jesus which was revealed by destroying the demons and liberating the helpless victim which symbolizes the power of the kingdom of God greater than any worldly and/or spiritual forces. Thus, as Edwards suggests, for Mark the main purpose of the account is christological.[57] Thus, the reader knows

---

53. Witherington, *Gospel of Mark*, 183.
54. Edwards, *Gospel According to Mark*, 159.
55. Guelich, *Mark 1–8*, 284.
56. See Stein, *Mark*, 258.
57. See Edwards, *Gospel According to Mark*, 257.

that Mark is telling the story of the healed man as the result of this amazing event in which Jesus's divine identity and supernatural authority is revealed.

2.2.6. Jesus Sends the Ex-Demoniac to Bear Witness among Gentiles

In Mark 5:18–20, in contrast to the inhabitants (predominantly Gentiles) who requested Jesus to leave their territory, the healed man, in his gratitude and admiration, wishes to stay with Jesus.[58] His request to join Jesus or to "be with him" (μετ' αὐτοῦ ᾖ in v. 18), and the idea of discipleship (to "be with him" in 3:13–19), seems to be identical. Furthermore, since he experienced the powerful presence of Jesus practically, as well as received a revelation of Jesus's divine identity from Jesus himself, this man has already become the follower of Jesus. Additionally, Mark tells his readers that many other individuals (Mark 2:14–15; 10:52) and groups of people followed Jesus without being necessarily listed among the group of the twelve disciples, because discipleship means following Jesus and doing the will of God (3:34–35), rather than just walking behind him. Further, since Jesus's close disciples who were called and appointed by himself could not recognize his real divine identity, but this cured man could, the matter of seeing and hearing him and becoming his true disciple belongs to Jesus's willingness to reveal himself. Some commentators think that, similar to 1:44; 5:43; 7:36; and 8:26, Jesus's words in 5:19 reflect the secrecy motif (the messianic Secret in Mark) so that the man keeps it in his immediate family circle alone, but he disobeyed it in verse 20, because according to these commentators, "house" in Mark 5:38–43; 7:17, 24; 8:26; 9:28; and 10:10, serves as a place of secrecy.[59] "House" also "serves in Mark as a place of proclamation (cf. 1:29–34; 2:1–2, 15–16; 3:20–35; 14:3)" and since the Greek term καὶ ("and") at the beginning of verse 20 rather than ἀλλά ("but") connects it with verse 19, it should be interpreted as though the man's action in verse 20 is an act of obedience to fulfil Jesus's command to go home and proclaim his news. In Mark 5:19, Jesus refused the request of the healed man to stay with him in Mark 5:18; instead he gave him a missionary task to bear witness to what

---

58. See Moule, *Gospel According to Mark*, 42.
59. Wrede, *Messianic Secret*, 140–141; Gnilka, *Das Evangeliumnach*,207.

Jesus (ὁ κύριός, "the Lord," v. 19),[60] had done for him or to proclaim it among his family[61] and friends at home. Although the Greek term σούς, could refer just to family, "5:20 indicates that the broader meaning of 'friends'[62] is best here."[63] The reason why Jesus commissioned a cured man, unlike the leper in 1:44 and other similar passages in Mark, seems to be that publicity among the Jews posed a risk, but "in gentile territory this risk did not exist, since it was far from the scene of Jesus' regular ministry, and there was no ready-made messianic expectation to contend with."[64] Therefore, as Edwards rightly says, "remarkably, he is a Gentile sent to Gentiles."[65] Mark's readers detect that since Jesus himself had not proclaimed or preached in gentile territory before, this man seems to be the first missionary or Apostle to the Gentiles to preach the good news of Jesus, the Lord, to Gentiles in the Decapolis.[66] Thus, his proclamation can be seen as an anticipation of Mark 13:10 and 14:9 as the good news that would be proclaimed to all nations in the whole world. Further, the readers of the gospel may imagine that it is as a result of this ex-demoniac's witness among his friends and family that a gentile woman (Greek, of Syro-Phoenician origin) comes to Jesus with a request for help, even though these two incidents are distant from each other (Mark 7:26).

This marginalized man had received the revelation of Jesus's divine messianic identity as "the Son of the Most High God" (v. 7), and as "the Lord" (v. 19). He also received an amazing healing for his whole life – physically, emotionally and socially – and was commissioned by Jesus himself to share what God, in Jesus the Lord, had done for him because for Mark "the Lord of 5:19 is Jesus of Nazareth!"[67] In other words, the victim has recognized

---

60. The word "Jesus" or "the Lord" in 5:19 is to be understood as "God" in Luke's parallel (see Luke 8:39), because Luke used ὁ θεός rather than ὁ κύριός in Jesus's words.

61. The term "home" indicates "'his own people,'" Gentiles, see Hooker, *According to St. Mark*, 145.

62. Because the terms "your friends" in 'v.19 implies a wider circle than just the man's family (see Nineham, *Gospel of St. Mark*, 155).

63. Stein, *Mark*, 259; cf. Taylor, *Gospel According to St. Mark*, 284.

64. France, *Gospel of Mark*, 232–233.

65. Edwards, *Gospel According to Mark*, 160.

66. See Wright, *Mark for Everyone*, 57. Decapolis was a confederation of ten Greek cities or towns whose population were mainly Gentiles in the south and east of the Sea of Galilee, and the people in it were highly influenced by Greek culture.

67. Stein, *Mark*, 260.

Jesus's unique divine identity as the Son of the Most-High God (v. 7) or as the Lord (v. 19), and Jesus restored his whole life and sent him to others in his locality because Jesus's act of power inspired him to exceed the commission that Jesus gave him.[68]

As indicated above, in the next section, 5:21–43, Mark proceeds to narrate that this Jesus, the most powerful Son of God, will continue to identify himself with other marginalized people who were regarded as unclean in the community. He does so, focusing on the stories of other victims who were isolated as hopeless and helpless and in darkness. For example, in 5:21–34, Jesus was touched by a woman who was isolated from among others due to some sort of menstrual disorder which caused her to be unclean according to Jewish purity law. The next story in 5:35–43 is about a dead girl who was touched by Jesus regardless of the fact that her dead body made him (and of course others who touch them) unclean. However, in doing so, Hurtado correctly says, "in all these cases of the 'unclean,' Jesus is shown in triumph, liberating the people from their enslaving conditions."[69] Furthermore, Mark's readers know that "this recognition that the Jewish Messiah has a ministry, which must ultimately extend outside Jewish circles will become more central to Mark's plot towards the end of Act One (7:24 onward)."[70]

2.2.7. Conclusion

In conclusion, it is the second evangelist who describes Jesus as the one who moves forward with supreme authority over demons, sicknesses and all the natural elements, not only around Palestine but also in further regions of Gentiles. According to Mark, Jesus's universal authority is seen not only by destroying the power of the whole army of the evil spirits but also by delivering the victim from his hopeless situation. In contrast to Jesus's first disciples who were with him but confused about Jesus's real identity, Jesus revealed himself to the marginalized person not only to liberate him from his miserable condition but also to make him a part of his mission of God's dominion in gentile areas.

---

68. See Gundry, *Mark*, 255.
69. Hurtado, *Mark*, 84.
70. France, *Gospel of Mark*, 226.

In the next section which is the climax of the healing stories in the gospel, the readers of Mark discover Jesus's progress toward the goal with the message of God's dominion not only to give physical sight to the blind but also to offer spiritual insight for him to see his royal messianic identity. In other words, Mark records this story to show the spiritual blindness of Jesus's first followers who were expected to understand more about Jesus and his mission but failed to do so, and to explain about the spiritual insight which comes from Jesus's self-identification with outcasts. Finally, Mark does not place this story in the Synagogue or in any religious institution, but on the way to Jerusalem, the place of Jesus's death.

2.3. Jesus and the Blind Beggar (Mark 10:46–52)

They came to Jericho. As he and his disciples and a large crowd were leaving Jericho, Bartimaues son of Timaeus, a blind beggar, was sitting by the roadside. When he heard that it was Jesus of Nazareth, he began to shout out and say, "Jesus, Son of David, have mercy on me!" Many sternly ordered him to be quiet, but he cried out even more loudly, "Son of David, have mercy on me!" Jesus stood still and said, "Call him here." And they called the blind man, saying to him, "Take heart; get up, he is calling you." So throwing his cloak, he sprang up and came to Jesus. Then Jesus said to him, "What do you want me to do for you?" The blind man said to him, "My teacher, let me see again." Jesus said to him, "Go; your faith has made you well." Immediately he regained his sight and followed him on the way.

2.3.1. Introduction

Unlike the first followers of Jesus who could not grasp who Jesus really was, nor his mission on earth in the previous stories – and they therefore worried about their personal glory and high position over others – in this section, Mark introduces Jesus's Yahweh-like coming to a person who was poor and blind, not only to give him physical sight to see things around him but also to give him spiritual insight to recognize and confess Jesus's royal messianic identity. Thus, the readers of the gospel are to discover that the recognition of Jesus's true identity depends not on someone's physical, social or material conditions, but on Jesus's willingness to come and to reveal himself to them. So, the readers can see Jesus identifying himself with unexpected people in the society to make them his followers while on the way to his destiny in Jerusalem, the place of his execution.

2.3.2. Literary Context

As discussed above, regardless of the clear proclamation of the gospel of God through Jesus's words and deeds in the first half of Mark's gospel (1:1–8:26), Mark repeatedly indicates the failure of Jesus's first followers to understand who Jesus was. One way he does this is through narrating the story of the first blind man of Bethsaida in 8:22–26 which illustrates the spiritual blindness of Jesus's close followers, and the story of the blind beggar, Bartimaeus in Mark 10:46–52. Mark carefully constructed this section in which Jesus repeatedly instructs his followers, telling them about the nature of his own ministry as a suffering Messiah and the nature of discipleship, which must also have this characteristic. In other words, in this section, Mark presents disciples not only as models for how others come to faith, but rather he affirms that the meaning of discipleship to Jesus cannot be grasped without the element of suffering. It is important to understand that Mark's teaching about discipleship is intended to show that the failure in discipleship comes out of their inability to understand who Jesus is, because his identity as the divine Messiah is always bound up with his destiny (suffering vocation and resurrection). Furthermore, one can see not only disciples' incomprehension of Jesus's identity even as the suffering Messiah but also they failed to understand their own role as the main participants in proclaiming God's coming kingly rule.[71]

Mark not only demonstrates physical healing as seen in Mark 8 above, but he also demonstrates the power of Jesus to heal and give sight and inner insight in the story about Bartimaeus who was a blind beggar but was healed and followed Jesus (10:46–52). To teach this great lesson and provide a clear understanding of Jesus's divine identity, in the section 8:27–10:45, Mark teaches his readers about true discipleship, shaped by the cross, which requires the renunciation of status in the eyes of the world, together with

---

71. Henderson, *Christology and Discipleship*, 2.

an understanding Jesus's true identity and his mission on earth (Mark 8:27—9:1). Next, he continues to teach that clear understanding of who Jesus is entails a renunciation of status and accepting or treating of those who are marginalized and liminal in the community (particularly little children and an unnamed exorcist in 9:33—41); as well as the renunciation of status in the eyes of other disciples or fellow ministers (10:32—45). Finally, Mark reaches the climax of his teaching about discipleship setting himself (Jesus) forth as a model of self-sacrifice for the sake of others (10:45).

Furthermore, the previous story is about a wealthy respected person who was welcomed by others around him but who could not understand who Jesus was nor his mission on earth; as such, he was not welcomed by Jesus to follow him on the way to the cross. However, in the present story, Mark's readers "meet a man at the quite the other end of scale of social acceptability, a blind beggar . . . who will end up following Jesus ἐν τῇ ὁδῷ, with his sight restored."[72] In other words, having indicated what true discipleship entails, Mark moves on to the story of another marginalized person, a socially neglected beggar, called Bartimaeus and tells his readers that while Jesus was passing by, Bartimaeus called to Jesus. Then hearing the cry of this marginalized beggar, Jesus came to the man and healed him while he was doing his daily task by the road. Once the man got his sight, he not only saw things around himself as many others do, but also recognized Jesus's unique identity, addressing him with his royal messianic title the "Son of David" and following Jesus on the way to Jerusalem where he was going to die.

So, in the present story, Mark's readers may understand that, in contrast to the first followers who failed to see Jesus and his mission, and therefore had been struggling for glory and personal position rather than humble service to others, Mark presents the final healing story of a blind man who was marginalized in the society but recognized Jesus's royal messianic identity and followed him to Jerusalem.

Thus, in his final healing story of the blind beggar, Bartimaeus (10:46–52), what does Mark want to tell his readers about Jesus's true identity?

---

72. France, *Gospel of Mark*, 422; see also Mark 10:52.

2.3.3. Jesus Comes to the Blind Beggar at Jericho (Mark 10:46–52)

In this section, Mark reports that unlike Jesus's concern to conceal his identity in the first half of his gospel, except for warning not to speak of his transfiguration in Mark 9:9, his readers know that from 10:1, Jesus enters into Judea and from 10:32, he is headed to Jerusalem and his interest in concealing his identity has gone completely. Put another way, once the focus falls by means of passion predictions and related saying on the suffering vocation of the Messiah, the injunction to silence is lifted and the healing of Bartimaeus was instructive because although everyone tried to silence Bartimaeus, Jesus did not.

Thus, Mark affirms that the journey of Jesus which began in 10:1, with his first followers and a growing number of pilgrims[73] (see 10:32, 15:41) is now reaching its end. In 10:46, Mark introduces a blind beggar by his specific name as Bartimaeus whom Jesus met in a specific city called Jericho. Whereas Luke places this healing story as taking place while Jesus, with others, was approaching the city[74] of Jericho (Luke 18:35), Matthew in 20:29 and Mark in the present story agree that it happened on Jesus's way out of the city. Thus, according to the second evangelist (Mark), Jesus met and healed this socially neglected beggar in Jericho which is "the last major city in the east before the steep road to Jerusalem."[75] So, Mark's readers understand that since Jericho is so near Jerusalem, the goal of Jesus's journey is almost within sight.[76] Furthermore, Mark's readers know the nearness or finality of Jesus's destiny to accomplish his greatest mission in Jerusalem. In other words, while Jesus was heading towards the goal of his mission, Mark introduces

---

73. The Greek terms ὄχλοV ἱκανὸV, a "large crowd," in Mark 10:46 indicates a sizeable group of people and probably consisted of a large pilgrim group who were going up to Jerusalem to celebrate the Passover (see France, *Gospel of Mark*, 422; Stein, *Mark*, 493–494; Lane, *Gospel of Mark*, 386–387.)

74. The reason why Luke placed the story of the blind beggar before Jesus's entrance to the city (Jericho), seems to be that it allows him to bring this incident as the conclusion of salvation story which makes it the climax of his presentation of the message of individual salvation, since Luke's emphasis is on salvation of all men (see Marshall, *Luke*, 116).

75. Stein, *Mark*, 493.

76. Hooker, *According to St. Mark*, 252.

this miserable man not only by his specific and full name[77] but also in his real condition as a beggar sitting beside the road expecting something from pilgrims to Jerusalem, thereby trying "to take advantage of the occasion."[78]

While Mark gave his full name as the son of Timaeus, Bartimaeus, Luke omits the name of a blind beggar in Luke 18:35. Whereas Luke is concerned to give a greater emphasis to the name Zacchaeus[79] rather than the blind beggar, Mark's readers understand that for Mark, the name of this poor blind man has a great significance. Therefore, it is possible to think that the explanation of the name Bartimaeus makes sense to Mark's readers since he wrote his gospel for Romans who lived in Rome; and identifying the man as "the son of Timaeus" suggests that Timaeus was known to some of his gentile readers in Rome. Further, Mark's readers may have understood that the road on which the blind Bartimaeus was sitting is the road through which Jesus was speedily making his way to Jerusalem to give his life as a ransom for many (10:45). Therefore, one can suggest that "on the way" to Jerusalem in Mark 10:52 is more than "the side of the road" of Mark 10:46. As will be discussed shortly, I argue that it is a path of the cross or suffering, or the way of discipleship since the blind beggar did not simply receives physical healing but also became a follower of Jesus to Jerusalem, the place of Jesus's shameful death in order to save the marginalized and liminal humanity with whom he identified himself.

2.3.4. A Blind Beggar Addresses Jesus, in His Royal Messianic Title

Although the Davidic descent of the Messiah is mentioned in 12:35–37, Mark introduces Bartimaeus addressing Jesus with the specific title "Son of David" which indicates his royal Messiaship (vv. 47–48). Even though demons in Mark 3:11–12, 5:7, and Peter in 8:30 declared his messianic identity

---

77. Unlike Matthew and Luke, Mark introduces a blind beggar Barthimaeus in his name which is a bit unusual, because "*bar*" is the Aramaic word for "*son*" and "*Timaeus*" (ΤιμαίοV) is a translation of the name which makes sense in the mixed culture of Mark's readers used by this beggar's father.

78. France, *Gospel of Mark*, 423.

79. Having omitted the name of the blind beggar, Luke's mention of the name Zacchaeus seems to have a great significance to his readers in order to indicate that salvation is available even to materially rich people as well since they believe in Jesus, whereas for Mark, Jesus is seen identifying himself with a marginalized beggar.

as the Son of God and the Christ, this is the first time in Mark's gospel that Jesus is addressed by this title, "Son of David." Also, unlike in the NIV where "Jesus of Nazareth" indicates the name of Jesus's hometown, the Greek term Ναζαρηνός, (e.g. 1:24 and 10:47) denotes not the place of Jesus's origin, but of his powerful anointing by God as the one who had descended through the Davidic line or who was the offspring of David according to the prophesy in 2 Samuel 7:11–14. In other words, even though Mark describes Jesus as the one from Nazareth to distinguish him from others with the same name (e.g. Mark 1:14, 14:67; 16:6), Mark's primary concern was not to explain Jesus's historical situation or original place but it was to affirm Jesus's divine origin as "the one who is to inherit and fulfil the promises made to David long ago," yet identifying himself with the poor and outcasts.[80]

It is suggested that by the middle of the first century BC this title "Son of David" in *Psalms of Solomon* 17:21 "refers to a warrior king who will punish sinners, whereas here it refers to one who will have mercy on them."[81] Even though it is not inappropriate to understand Jesus as a warrior king, it is inadequate because according to Mark Jesus is "this and more."[82] So, as will be discussed later, unlike other Messiahs of the first century, Bartimaeus recognized Jesus in this title "Son of David," which "carried explicit messianic overtones and shows that he looked to Jesus as the Messiah who could bring healing and wholeness."[83]

Whereas some suggest that Mark indicates by his blindness that Bartimaeus's confession was wrong because he is blind,[84] others rightly argue that though it was true that in Mark's eyes "Son of David" is not an adequate title for Jesus (12:35–37), yet "it is typical of Mark's irony that the blind should see more than those with sight."[85] This idea will appear throughout this work as I argue that Jesus's divine identity was revealed to

---

80. Stein, *Mark*, 494; France, *Gospel of Mark*, 423; Brooks, *Mark*, 173; also, 2 Sam 7:12–16; 1 Chr 17:11–14; and Ps 89:29–37.

81. See Edwards, *Gospel According to Mark*, 330.

82. Stein, *Mark*, 495.

83. Edwards, *Gospel According to Mark*, 330; cf. Hofius, "1ˢᵗ Jesus der Messias? Thesen," 107.

84. Via, *Ethics of Mark's Gospel*, 162; Kelber, *Kingdom in Mark*, 95.

85. Hooker, *According to St. Mark*, 253; Kingsbury, *Christology*, 102–107.

and declared by the unexpected marginalized and liminal people rather than the expected ones.

Others think that this title refers to Solomon because he is David's son and his great ability to heal and exorcise is mentioned in the intertestamental literature, nevertheless a connection here with Solomon is extremely tenuous.[86] Rather, for Mark's readers, "'Son of David' would have been seen as a reference to the promised royal descendant of Israel's greatest king, Jesus Christ, the long-awaited Son of David."[87] In addition, since the title Υἱὲ Δαυὶδ is further emphasized by repetition in the narrative,[88] rather than preventing him from shouting "Son of David," Bartimaeus's repeated cries and his twofold repetition of "son of David" "indicates that Mark wants to emphasize that Jesus is indeed the Son of David."[89]

Further, Marcus argues that Mark's words in the introduction (1:1), Peter's confession[90] in 8:30, the following story in Jerusalem and the temple (11:1–11) and the inscription on Jesus's cross "the King of the Jews" in 15:26 all point to this understanding of the title.[91]

Unlike Jesus's motive in silencing those who make false or premature confessions in the first half of the gospel, this is the attempt of the crowd, not only of the disciples[92] (see Mark 10:13) to prevent "someone of no status who wants to gain access to Jesus."[93]

Mark does not explain the term "many," who they were, and why they admonished Bartimaeus to keep quiet, because it seems in Mark's story such information is not very essential. However, some suggest that whoever they were, the "many" "thought Jesus had more important things to do than to

---

86. See Gundry, *Mark*, 600.
87. Olekamma, *Healing of Blind*, 69–81.
88. See France, *Gospel of Mark*, 424.
89. Stein, *Mark*, 495; also see Eckstein, Marcus 10, 50.
90. Although Peter's confession of Jesus as the Christ was correct, it is not sufficient because he could not understand the real identity of Jesus as the Son of God and the suffering and vindicated Son of man.
91. See Marcus, *Way of the Lord*, 137–139.
92. One can see a bit difference between the motives of the crowd and the disciples as they try to silence someone because whereas the crowd tried to silence the beggar to prevent him not to disturb Jesus (see Brooks, *Mark*, 173), the disciples tried to silence Bartimaeus not because he was annoying but because it was dangerous to proclaim Jesus as son of David in and around Jerusalem.
93. France, *Gospel of Mark*, 424.

spend time with a blind beggar looking any real status,"[94] or they wanted Jesus to set up his messianic kingdom in Jerusalem rather than spending his precious time with this powerless beggar by the road. As noted above, the "many," including the disciples, try to silence Bartimaeus because his acclamation of Jesus as the Son of David is dangerous in the vicinity of Jerusalem. However, Bartimaeus joins the throng who then hail Jesus in the same Davidic terms precisely because Jesus had paid attention to his case.

Further, it reminds Mark's readers of the story in 10:13 in which Jesus's close followers attempted to prevent little ones who were socially neglected from coming to Jesus. However, the attempt of the crowd to prevent Bartimaeus from coming to Jesus was unsuccessful because the call to this marginalized person was from Jesus himself; even on his way to Jerusalem to die, Jesus had time for the marginalized individual who needed his help.[95]

2.3.5. A Blind Beggar Receives Sight and Follows Jesus

Edwards comments, "how remarkable that the Son of Man allows the cries of a poor and powerless person to stop him in his track."[96] The cries of this miserable beggar which offended the crowd and also probably the disciples, causing them to rebuke him, were rewarded by Jesus and so caused him to stop (v. 49). The repeated cries of this marginalized beggar to the Davidic Messiah to have mercy on him was welcomed by Jesus as a doorway to faith in him.[97] Then the "many" of verse 48 who attempted to discourage the blind beggar changed their minds and instead of discouraging him, they encouraged him to come to Jesus precisely because the origin of this call is Jesus, the Son of David himself. Having stopped to rebuke him, they began now to serve him as Jesus's messengers on behalf of this desperate beggar. That is the reason why Bartimaeus pushed his outer garment aside and abandoned everything he had in eagerness to come to Jesus.[98]

Some Markan scholars think that Bartimaeus was not totally blind because there is no mention of anyone, either from among the crowd or among

---

94. France, 424.
95. Cranfield, *Gospel According to St Mark*, 345.
96. Edwards, *Gospel According to Mark*, 330.
97. Hooker, *According to St. Mark*, 252–253.
98. See also Mark 1:18, 20; 2:14; 10:21, 28.

the disciples, helping him to approach Jesus.[99] However, such an inference is uncalled for, since Mark says nothing about whether the man was helped or not. Rather, it is important to think that "his throwing it [his outer garment] away suggests that he believed that he would need it no more."[100] Furthermore, Lane suggests that the blind beggar "cast aside his outer garment, which he has spread on the ground in front of him to receive alms, sprang up, and came to Jesus."[101]

Further, in contrast to the poor and selfish request of the sons of Zebedee (John and James) for glory and power over others (Mark 10:35–45), Mark reports that Bartimaeus asks Jesus a proper and acceptable question regarding healing, recognizing Jesus's universal authority to make the blind to see.[102] So, Bartimaeus's understanding of Jesus's real identity seems to be deeper than that of Jesus's close followers because their selfish ambition for power made them foolish in the eyes of God, due to their ignorance toward the self-sacrificial service of Jesus to others.

Thus, the readers understand that Bartimaeus's honourable request was accepted and rewarded by Jesus as a result of which he received not only physical healing for his eyes but also spiritual insight to see and recognize Jesus's royal messianic identity (vv. 47–48), to acknowledge Jesus as his Master,[103] and to follow him in the way. This is true because as Stein correctly said, "the term 'saved' can refer to both physical healing 3:4; 5:23, 28, 34; 6:56 cf. also Mark 13:20; 15:30–31 and spiritual healing . . . 8:35; 10:26; 13:13."[104] Thus, Mark's readers understand that soon after he gained his sight, Bartimaeus "followed Jesus in the way" (v. 52) rather than being sent away as others had been.

With regard to the phrase ἠκολούθει αὐτῷ ἐν τῇ ὁδῷ (he "began to follow him in the way" in v. 52), whereas some think that it is not all about

---

99. Taylor, *Gospel According to St. Mark*, 603.
100. Hurtado, *Mark*, 178.
101. Lane, *Gospel of Mark*, 338.
102. See also Mark 8:22–26; Isa 35:5.
103. As many others who were called by Jesus did in 1:18, 20; 2:14; 10:21, 28, having abandoned everything he had, Bartimaeus came to Jesus and addressed him in a more reverential form as his Master, Ραββουνι which means "my rabbi" rather than a common form "rabbi" (see also Hooker, *According to St. Mark*, 253).
104. Stein, *Mark*, 497.

Christian discipleship to follow Jesus,[105] others argue that since Bartimaeus was not only healed and able to walk around, and was not sent home as many others (1:43–44; 5:19), but since he immediately followed Jesus, he thus became a follower or disciple of Jesus.[106] Furthermore, France rightly explains that since the Greek term Ραββουνι (cf. 'Ραββί, in 9:5; 11:21; 14:45) indicates that in each of those cases the speaker is a disciple, it is the "privileged status which Mark has given to Bartimaeus" which allows him not only to address him as the royal Davidic Messiah or his Master but also to do what a true follower is expected to do.[107] Likewise, Hooker adds, "Bartimaeus' faith in Jesus' power, his confession of his authority, and his willingness to follow him all mark him out as a disciple . . . [in] contrast to the poor showing of the Twelve in the previous story."[108]

Finally, having compared this story to the story of the sons of Zebedee (John and James) in 10:32–45, Painter concludes that the story is full of irony, for it is the blind man in this crowd who can see Jesus for who he is, and not the disciples.[109] In other words, unlike the first close followers of Jesus who were expected to know Jesus and his mission on earth but could not understand it, Mark shows that although he was not found in the list of the twelve followers, this marginalized beggar does become a follower of Jesus. It was not during Jesus's miraculous activities around Galilee that he achieves full insight and recognition of Jesus's royal messianic identity but on the way to Jerusalem, the place of Jesus's execution. Nevertheless, the question here is how the blind Bartimaeus was able to see Jesus's divine messianic identity whereas the first followers of Jesus were not, even though they remained with him for a long time and were involved in many activities with him? In short, Mark tells his readers that the divine messianic identity of Jesus, the unexpected Messiah, is to be recognized only by the revealing power of God rather than people's expectations (Mark 4:11).

---

105. See Kingsbury, *Christology*, 104–105.
106. See Evans, *Mark 8*, 134; Best, *Following Jesus*, 143.
107. See France, *Gospel of Mark*, 424.
108. Hooker, *According to St. Mark*, 253; see also Witherington, *Gospel of Mark*, 202.
109. See, Painter, *Mark's Gospel*, 152–153.

2.3.6. Conclusion

At the climax of his healing story, Mark portrays Jesus as the one who identifies himself with the marginalized person, a blind beggar, not only to give him physical sight to see things around himself but also to restore both his physical and spiritual sight to recognize Jesus's royal messianic identity and to declare it. Despite discouragements from other people around him and in contrast to Jesus first and close followers, the blind poor beggar was rewarded the restoration of his whole being to follow Jesus with clear understanding of his identity. It occurred on the road from Jericho as Jesus was approaching his destiny to die, not to perform other miraculous stories among the crowds.

In the next section, Mark brings the story of Jesus's crucifixion and death as the climax of his christological narrative. While experiencing the absence of God and crying out, according to Mark, Jesus associates himself with the godforsaken humanity, identifying himself as the most marginalized one on behalf of others. So, the readers can see through how he dies, how Jesus reveals his divine identity to the marginalized, gentile world and is declared by them as God's Son. Also, his victorious resurrection and empty tomb were witnessed by others who were culturally liminal and so unexpected people such as women (see Mark 16:1–6).

2.4. The Death of Jesus, the Son of God (Mark 15:33–41)

When it was noon, darkness came over the whole land until three in the afternoon. At three o'clock Jesus cried out with a loud voice, "Eloi, Eloi, lema sabachthani?" which means, "My God, my God, why have you forsaken me?" When some of the bystanders heard it, they said, "Listen, he is calling for Elijah." And someone ran, filled a sponge with sour wine, put it on a stick, and gave to him to drink, saying, "Wait, let us see whether Elijah will come to take him down." Then Jesus gave a loud cry and breathed his last. And the curtain of the temple was torn in two, from top to bottom. Now when the centurion, who stood facing him, saw that in this way he breathed his last, he said, "Truly this man was God's Son!"

There were also women looking on from a distance; among them were Mary Magdalene, and Mary the mother of James the younger and of Joses, and Salome. These used to follow him and provided for him when he was in Galilee; and there were many other women who had come up with him to Jerusalem.

2.4.1. Introduction

The previous sections of this work have attempted to explain about Jesus's glorious and authoritative coming to earth as the great figure whose aim is proclaiming God's kingly rule through his words and deeds. In so doing, regardless of his universal power and authority over all things, he is seen identifying himself with marginalized and unexpected people. Not only did he go to outcast people but was able to liberate them from their afflictions; and he used them as instruments to proclaim his divine identity which was hidden even to his close followers who were expected to know more.

In this section I extend my analysis to argue that Mark depicts Jesus as himself becoming marginalized to the full for the sake of human beings crying in the absence of God. Here the second evangelist tells his readers that Jesus's identity as the divine Son of God was revealed to and declared unexpectedly by a gentile soldier. Equally unexpectedly, it was culturally marginalized and liminal women who witnessed his death, resurrection and empty tomb instead of the apostles, as might have been expected.

2.4.2. Literary Context

It is obvious that from the very beginning of his gospel, Mark portrays Jesus as the divine Son of God who is able to do many miraculous deeds with his universal authority over all things. Regardless of his unique greatness and supreme authority, according to the second evangelist, Jesus by his own initiative, comes to the marginalized and liminal people to identify himself with them in order to liberate those who have been suffering from physical, social, moral, cultural and spiritual plights. As the protagonist of the proclamation of God's dominion on earth, Jesus's ministry, which covered all the regions of Palestine and Decapolis and their diverse Jewish and gentile peoples, was described by the second evangelist. Does Mark intend his readers to see Jesus himself as a marginalized individual? Yes, as will be discussed, in detail, in the fourth chapter of this work, Mark's readers may understand that Jesus, the divine Son of God, put himself among the marginalized ones, as a marginalized Galilean Jew in all areas of his life by going to every place where they were, in order to set these outcast people free. This included places such as graveyards, roadsides, and low-cast homes during his ministry. It also included being persecuted by religious and political leaders, his family, even by his disciples and finally two bandits who were crucified one on each side of Jesus on the cross. Thus, Mark's readers may understand that Jesus identified himself with marginalized and liminal people, not only by healing or saving them from various plights in the first section of the gospel in which Mark records lots of miraculous deeds of Jesus, but also, as indicated previously, in the second part of his gospel as well (Mark 10:46–52).

Furthermore, in chapter 15, according to Mark, Jesus himself becomes extremely marginalized, at the outer limits of society, due to his horrible death on the cross. He put himself there not for his own sake, but for the sake of many people on earth (Mark 10:45). Mark does not clearly state from what Jesus saves his people, but from the entire gospel narrative the readers understand that Jesus rescues his people from the oppressive power of Satan (3:23–27), as well as from their sins through forgiveness. According to Hooker, forgiveness is part of the salvation that Jesus himself offers to those who respond to his message (1:4; 2:1–12). Additionally, Hooker goes on to explain that those who refuse to repent from their sins are under divine judgement due to their hardened hearts 11:12–20; 12:9; 13:1–36; 8:38; 14:62.[110] Thus, Jesus's death was not to give them temporary relief as a solution to their physical plights, but to save them from their sin which is the ultimate enemy of all human beings. In this whole section about Jesus's death in chapter 15, Mark describes not only Jesus's identification with marginalized and liminal people through his death on the cross but also his experience of abandonment by God which indicates his marginalization in a deeper sense, going to a level beyond anyone else's suffering. Moreover, as the prophecies in the OT about the righteous sufferer indicated in Psalm

---

110. See Hooker, *Not Ashamed*, 56.

22 and many other psalms of lament, Lamentations 5 and Isaianic prophecies about the suffering Servant of the Lord, Jesus may pray and wish to get out of his suffering and death and to be relieved from it. Nevertheless, his marginalization was so extreme that he did not only fear abandonment by God but he experienced it to the full by dying for others; thus identifying himself with outcasts, being crucified between two of them.[111]

In other words, Mark depicts various marginalized people being liberated by Jesus from their troubles. However, Jesus who liberated them after these events from various afflictions, experienced abandonment or forsakenness by God and died as a result of his true obedience to God's will (Mark 14:36).

2.4.3. The Reasons for Jesus's Abandonment and Death

As Mark narrates the story of Jesus's death in this section, it was not only to explain the unique suffering and shameful death of Jesus on the cross, but also to make the significance of his suffering and death clear to his readers and listeners. For instance, Mark wants to show his readers that the suffering and death of Jesus happened as the fulfilment of the prophecies in Scriptures, not as a legend or invention of Mark himself or of the early church.

By recounting Jesus's suffering and death, Mark wanted to show his readers that the people who were around Jesus during his critical moment of abandonment as his witnesses, were the unexpected people, such as Simon of Cyrene (Mark 15:21) and also quite a few women who were among them (15:40–41). Jesus's close friends, the twelve disciples who received lots of instructions from Jesus himself (privately as well as corporately) and so were expected to do better, abandoned Jesus after his arrest (Mark 14:50) and failed to report Jesus's death and resurrection.

Moreover, Mark wants to make clear to the readers the amazing endurance of Jesus during his suffering on the cross by identifying himself with all sinners, paying for their sins and saving them through his death. In other words, in Mark 15, Mark shows his readers and listeners that Jesus, the divine Son of God, who identified himself with miserable people in different regions at various levels, now reaches the climax of marginalization himself, not simply by mixing with outcast people to help them in their physical and social needs but also to become one of them by crying as the

---

111. Bauckham, *God of Israel*, 257.

one who experienced abandonment by God in order to liberate them from their sins. Put differently, readers of the second evangelist understand that Jesus identified himself with the most marginalized sinners not only due to the mockery which is indicated in the first three hours in Mark's account (Mark 15:29–32), but also by going further to death on the cross on behalf of those who felt that they were in the absence of God, darkness (v. 33), in order to save those who repent and trust in the message of the gospel of God (Mark 1:14–15).

2.4.4. Irony in Mark's Narrative

Irony comes where the writing appears to mean one thing but in fact means something different. In the following section, particularly when telling about the death of Jesus, Mark relates several ironies. For example, (1) the title, king of the Jews – the soldiers who crucify Jesus call him king of the Jews but really mean that it is ridiculous to think that anyone should ever have regarded him as king, especially in his shamed and humiliated place on the cross. Here there is not only verbal irony but dramatic irony also, as the readers come to see that despite his crucifixion, he really was the king of the Jews. (2) Jesus was told to prophesy about who struck him, but the readers know he really was a prophet. (3) Jesus is mockingly taunted to tear down the temple, but the readers know that the temple really will be destroyed. (4) Jesus is also told to save himself by coming down from the cross, but the reader discovers that Jesus's life will be saved only as he loses it in death. Much of this irony is part of the larger irony that those who most expected to receive and participate in God's saving reign do not, and in fact, stand behind the death of the one through whom that reign was established. Finally, all throughout, Mark's use of irony portrays God as one who has acted contrary to expectations, away from the centres of power, through a messiah who suffers.[112]

2.4.5. Death of Jesus, the Son of God in Mark's Narrative

The death of Jesus, the Son of God, is very important in Mark's narrative as a result of which Jesus's divine Sonship was revealed. It is recorded not only in the second half of the gospel, particularly in the Passion Narratives

---

112. See Bryan, Class Lecture New Testament One.

but also there are some indications of his coming suffering and death in the early chapters of the gospel.

For instance, Hooker explains that Mark links the suffering and death of Jesus with others before and after Jesus's death, particularly, with the fate of John the Baptist who was presented as the forerunner of Jesus. Although it is not clearly stated as such, if they read the whole story, the readers of the second evangelist can see that the first hint of the coming death of Jesus and its significance is indicated in Mark 1:14. Particularly, the verb in Greek, παραδοθῆναι, that Mark uses when describing the arrest of John, is the same verb he used later to describe Jesus's being handed over into the power of evil (9:31; 10:33; 15:1–15); likewise, is the verb he uses about Judas's betrayal of Jesus (3:19; 14:10, 18, 21, 42, 44). In other words, although in the first round it seems to be unclear, later on, the readers discover that what happens to John and what happens to Jesus in the whole story is similar, although the manner of their death was different.

In addition, even if Mark intervenes something to tell about John's rejection, arrest and death, ultimately, it is all about Jesus's coming rejection, betrayal and death. The reason is that John was the one who prepared the way of the Lord Jesus, not only by preaching about his powerful coming to earth proclaiming God's impending rule through Jesus's words and his divine activities, but also his coming suffering and death which must be fulfilled according to the prophesies of Scriptures. In a nutshell, the readers of Mark's gospel can see how quickly events move to a climax; how inevitably the cross casts its shadow over the whole story.[113] Mark also clearly explains the passion predictions in Mark 8: 27–9:1; 9:31–41; and 10:32–45, as well as the passion narrative of Jesus in Mark 14, particularly, the story of his crucifixion and death in Mark 15.

2.4.5.1. Darkness over the whole land/earth and Jesus's cry of desolation

Since the cry of Jesus's desolation comes after the first three hours of darkness, Mark's readers know that Jesus's cry was caused by his absolute experience of God's absence. It occurred because, as already shown would happen by the prophecies of the OT, Jesus knows that God left him alone on the

---

113. See Hooker, *Not Ashamed*, 47–49.

cross to die. Some attempts to explain the unusual darkness at the time of the crucifixion have been made. For example, some pagan commentators of the Roman era explain it as a solar eclipse rather than a supernatural occurrence during Jesus's death. Similarly, as referred by Brooks, some suggestions are a natural phenomenon such as a dust storm with (sirocco) wind, the presence of heavy rain and dark clouds.[114] However, all this is unlikely since the solar eclipse was impossible at the time of the full moon due to the positions of the sun and moon during the Passover since it occurs when the full moon is behind the earth. In addition, the maximum total duration of a solar eclipse was 7 minutes 31.1 seconds, and the period of totality in Nazareth and Galilee was 1 minute 49 seconds, and [thus] the level of darkness would have been unnoticeable for people outdoors.[115] Therefore, it is possible to argue that the darkness in Mark 15 was a supernatural darkness that happened over the earth, during Jesus's death, as a result of the universe's response to its creator's death.[116] Furthermore, unlike some imaginations of those pagan commentators above who attempted to relate the darkness at the crucifixion to the natural phenomenon, there is no indication of this scientific idea in the text and the whole context of the gospel. Although Luke's statement that "the sun's light failed," Luke 23:45 describes the darkness – he does not indicate anything related to its natural explanation in a technical sense. Rather, Mark's readers are left to understand that these suggestions were very strange explanations to them, since the darkness to them was merely a supernatural manifestation. Moreover, the reference to the darkness in Amos 8:9, "On that day, says the Lord GOD, I will make the sun go down at noon and darken the earth in broad daylight," which expresses the mourning for an only son, the darkness at midday symbolizes the divine judgment that was coming upon the land of Israel due to her rejection of her king.[117] So Mark shows that in the state of absence of God which he entered, Jesus the rejected Messiah, took our judgment on himself. Furthermore, as Bauckham

---

114. Brooks, *Mark*, 260.

115. See Meeus, "The Maximum Possible Duration," 343–348; Kidger, *Star of Bethlehem*, 68–72. For further information, visit "Crucifixion Darkness," http://en.wikipedia.org/wiki/Crucifixion_darkness.

116. See Donahue & Harrington, *Gospel of Mark,* 451–452; see also Brooks, *Mark*, 260; Stein, *Mark*, 715.

117. See Hooker, *According to St. Mark*, 376.

rightly and profoundly explains, in contrast to their experience of God as their light (Ps 27:1; 43:3; 44:3), the OT Psalmists relate the darkness to the state of the dead (Job 10:21–22; Ps 23:4), and describe that God has left his people to die; so it should be understood as though they are in the darkness of death (Pss 88:6, 12, 18; 143:3; Lam 3:2, 6; cf. Ps 44:19; Lam 3:2). Similarly, he goes on to explain that in Mark 15:33–34, it is the three hours darkness which brings Jesus to speak of his experience of abandonment by God. Thus, the readers easily understand that "in both darkness and forsakenness (cf. Ps 88:5), he [Jesus] is already at the gate of death," being extremely marginalized for the sake of others.[118]

The Greek term γῆν (in v. 33) is ambiguous since it can mean both "land" or "earth." However, commentators prefer "the whole land" rather than "the whole earth" because in Mark 15:33–34 it occurs in the genre of historical narrative, and it expresses Jesus's identification with the people of Israel or Palestine and perhaps Judea, since there is no ancient report of such darkness elsewhere at the time.[119] The gospel of Peter 5:15 describes as though the darkness covers only "*all Judea*" due to her sin in rejecting and crucifying Jesus. However, as Bauckham rightly argues "the darkness lay over the whole earth . . . is the universal darkness of death, the abandonment experienced by all who are left by God to suffer and die, that Jesus enters on the cross." Mark's readers discover that the darkness which covers the whole land has universal connotations rather than just the Jews.[120] In other words, the OT image of death which is described as the shroud or sheet that is spread over all nations in Isaiah 25:7 can be considered as the universal problem of death over all peoples.[121]

The Greek translation of the Hebrew phrase Ελωι ελωι λεμα σαβαχθανι ("My God, my God, why have you forsaken me") in 15:34 is the only saying from the cross that Mark records in his gospel. It raises some questions among scholars due to its textual uncertainty. The question is, were these words spoken by Jesus himself in Hebrew or in Aramaic, or invented and added by Mark and his church in Greek? M. Casey thinks that Jesus used

---

118. Bauckham, *God of Israel*, 259.
119. See Brooks, *Mark*, 260.
120. Bauckham, *God of Israel*, 261.
121. See also Bauckham, *God of Israel*, 261, no. 34.

to speak Hebrew in which he used to read the Scripture including Psalm 22, but at the moment of his extreme suffering on the cross he spoke in Aramaic.[122] Further, others correctly suggest that Jesus on the cross used Aramaic but Mark quoted it from Psalm 22 and translated it into Greek to his predominantly Greek speaking readers or audience.[123] This is the third time that Mark mentions Jesus's words in Aramaic. The first was when he exercised his divine power over death in Mark 5:41and then when he prayed to the Father in Mark 14:36. In other words, instead of thinking that Mark and the early church invented this saying and attributed it to Jesus, Mark's readers know that Mark took the words of Jesus in Aramaic and translated them into Greek since the tradition says that his gospel was written to the church in Rome. Finally, whatever language Jesus spoke (whether it was Hebrew or Aramaic), it was a human language in order to communicate to human beings to help and save. Further, as Hooker said, "these words [in Mark 15:34] provide a profound theological comment of the oneness of Jesus with humanity, and on the meaning of his death, in which he shares human despair to the full," Mark's readers understand that Jesus, even during his death on the cross, identified himself with the marginalized humanity crying on their behalf and speaking in the language of common people in first-century Palestine.[124]

Regarding the words, "My God, my God, why have you forsaken me?" borrowed from Psalm 22, Jürgen Moltmann thinks that Jesus is identifying himself with God the Father; so the cry of Jesus in the words of Psalm 22 mean not only "My God, why hast thou forsaken *me*?" but at the same time, "My God, why hast thou forsaken *thyself*?"[125] He goes on to explain that the rejection and agony of Jesus on the cross must be understood as the rejection and agony of God himself; and his rejection in his dying cry must be understood strictly as something which took place between Jesus and his Father, and in the other direction between his Father and Jesus the Son. Furthermore, according to Moltmann, the reason why Jesus cried out

---

122. See Casey, *Aramaic Source*, 88.

123. See Moo, *Old Testament in the Gospel*, 264–268 and Brown, *Death of the Messiah*, 1051–1053.

124. Hooker, *According to St. Mark*, 375.

125. Moltmann, *Crucified God*, 50–51.

on the cross was not to express his personal distress, but it was a call upon God for God's sake, a legal plea, and that he died because of his God and Father.[126] However, although Moltmann correctly points to Jesus's deity and puts emphasis on the unique relationship between God the Father and Jesus his Son, the main reason of Jesus's cry on the cross was different from what Moltmann thought. Likewise, other scholars think differently including that his loud cry emphasizes Jesus's "intense physical suffering . . . the decisive character of this moment in Jesus' struggle against the power of evil"; and "the strength of Jesus, the Son of God"; or "the depth of his emotion."[127] However, the second evangelist says nothing clear to explain this idea. Rather it is appropriate to think that Jesus's loud cry indicates his identification with those who experience God's abandonment and thus crying in his absence, in darkness. Furthermore, the reason why Jesus cries and asks God "Why?" is not for his own sake but was "as the question asked by those with whom his use of the words identifies him. It is their protest that he voices on their behalf."[128]

Further, Jesus's cry on the cross must be understood as his total self-identification with all people in all nations that are marginalized by sin as a result of which they experience God's absence. Thus the readers of the second evangelist understood that Jesus bore the sins of the world while he underwent extreme suffering as "a ransom for many" (Mark 10:45) being abandoned not only by human beings such as his close friends and family but also by his Father. This also indicates his loneliness in Gethsemane (Mark 14:32–41). In addition, Hooker rightly suggests that "at this moment Jesus experiences what Paul elsewhere describes as 'becoming a curse' (Gal 3:13) and 'being made sin' (2 Cor 5:21)," not on his own account but for the sake of others.[129] Jesus, the Son of God, identified himself with all sinners being marginalized himself not only through what he suffered but also by dying

---

126. See Moltmann, 145–153.

127. Donahue and Harrington, *Gospel of Mark*, 447; Evans, *Mark 8*, 507; France, *Gospel of Mark*, 652. For this and other suggestions by scholars, see Stein, *Mark*, 715.

128. Bauckham, *God of Israel*, 262.

129. Hooker, *According to St. Mark*, 375.

on the cross. Thus, Cranfield correctly says, "it is in the cry of dereliction that the full horror of man's sin stands revealed."[130]

Likewise, in regard to the loudness of Jesus's cry (φωνῇ μεγάλῃ in v. 34) and "a loud cry" (φωνὴν μεγάλην in v. 37), scholars have various views. For example, Hugh Anderson thinks that the cry of Jesus in 15:34 is the prayer of the righteous sufferer (quoting the first words of Ps 22), rather than a cry of utter dereliction.[131] So, he thinks that a loud cry of verse 37 is Jesus's call of the judgment of God upon the world. However, as indicated in Psalm 22:2, where the psalmist continuously cries to God without response from God, Hooker argues that the cry of Jesus in Mark 15:37 is a presumptive reference to the cry of Jesus's dereliction in verse 34.[132] Furthermore, Bauckham correctly argues that the loudness of Jesus's cry in both verses (34 and 37) "matches the universality of the darkness: Jesus himself acknowledges his forsakenness for all to hear, while, . . . he prays to God out of it."[133] In other words, Mark's readers recognize that Jesus reached the climax of his mission by declaring his self-identification with the most marginalized sinners of the whole world through his death on the cross and being abandoned by God. His cry was not only due to extreme pain but it was his self-identification with a godforsaken world, for all to hear. Further, Luke's version of Jesus's cry, "Father, into your hands I commend my spirit" (Luke 23:46) which indicates his trust in God, and John's "it is finished" (19:30), which indicates his final victory, seems to be different from Mark's account of Jesus's experience of abandonment. However, since Jesus knows that God's will for him is to die and to bear the sins of the world (8:31; 9:31; 10:34; 10:45; 14:24), and since Mark narrates not only the suffering and death of Jesus but also his triumph of resurrection which marked his vindication by God (ch. 16), his cry must be understood as his victory over sin. The reason is that Jesus cried not on his own account but on behalf of others who are in the shadow of death. In other words, although Mark's concept of Jesus's death seems to be different from that of Luke's and John's accounts, they are not unlike one

---

130. Cranfield, *Gospel According to St Mark*, 458.
131. Anderson, *Gospel of Mark*, 345–347.
132. See Hooker, *According to St. Mark*, 377.
133. Bauckham, *God of Israel*, 266–267; see also Brown, *Death of the Messiah*, 1079.

another; they all are very similar since three of them end with the victorious resurrection of Jesus (see also John 10:17–18).[134]

The idea that Jesus was calling for Elijah to assist him may be based on the traditionally held belief that he would come to help those who were in need and on the belief that Elijah would return (Mal 3:1; 4:5; Sir 48:10; Mark 6:14–15; 8:28; 9:11–13). However, Jesus himself spoke of Elijah as one who had already come and he identified him with John the Baptist who was rejected and put to death (Mark 9:11–13). Thus, here, Mark explains that Jesus links the rejection and death of Elijah (alias John) to his own inevitable rejection and death; therefore, Elijah/John cannot assist Jesus since God his Father left him to die. Also the action of the person who gave Jesus sour wine should be understood as the action of mockery rather than his kindness to Jesus. In the context of Mark's story, there is nothing to indicate anyone's kindness or help to Jesus since his Father left him alone. Likewise, not only Mark but also according to the other evangelists, the offering of wine to Jesus to drink must be seen as a mockery. Therefore, the readers understand that the prophecies of the Scripture must be fulfilled (Ps 69:21). In other words, Mark's readers know that Jesus has come to earth with the purpose of identifying himself with the marginalized and to save them since they are marginalized and liminal in various ways as noted above. It is demonstrated when he was rejected by religious and political leaders, taunted by those who passed by, denied and betrayed by his own disciples and by the two other victims crucified beside him, and even experiencing abandonment by God, in order "to give his life a ransom for many" (10:45).

2.4.5.2. *The splitting of the curtain and the revelation of Jesus's divine identity*

Along with the loud cry of Jesus for all to hear, and his peaceful and voluntary death, there was a second apocalyptic sign.[135] The curtain was torn, opening the way to the presence of God for all. Regarding the torn curtain

---

134. See also Hooker, *According to St. Mark*, 377.

135. The term "apocalyptic" (from the Greek verb ἀποκαλύπτω, to reveal, disclose) refers to revelation or revelatory events, and "apocalyptic sign" in this case indicates Jesus's unique death which was related to the revelation of Jesus's divine identity. In other words, when Jesus died on the cross, the curtain was torn apart and access to the presence of God was made available to all humanity.

of the temple, Mark may intend either the outer curtain separating the sanctuary from the courtyard or the one within the sanctuary in front of the holy of holies. As referred by Stein, it is uncertain because the same Greek term (καταπέτασμα) was used for both.[136] However, since some references in Hebrews (6:19–20; 9:3; 10:19–22) all point it out to be the curtain in the most sacred place in Judaism, Mark's readers understand it as referring to the inner one. Additionally, it is also possible to read a similar story in Josephus about the opening of the gates of the inner court one night as a sign of the temple's future destruction (*War*, VI.5.3).

Therefore, Mark's readers were also told that the veil or curtain of the temple was torn in two, from top to bottom, as an indication of a divine act, symbolizing the future judgment and destruction of the temple against Israel's rejection of her Messiah, Jesus, as well as the opening of the way to God to all humanity. Thus, Mark's readers know that if the death of Jesus opens up access to God in an unprecedented way, it is also the case that it brings judgment on those who thought they knew God best.[137] Moreover, the Greek term ἐσχίσθη regarding the splitting of the curtain of the temple could remind Mark's readers of the rending of heavens in Mark 1:1–10.[138] Finally, it is the second evangelist who tells his readers that Jesus's godforsaken death is the climax of his revelation as the Son of God in his gospel narrative. It is also interesting to understand that Jesus's godforsaken death "transfers the place of God's presence from its hiddenness in the holy of holies to the openly forsaken cross of the dead Jesus."[139]

It is precisely through the godforsaken death of Jesus on the cross, as the outcast, that the barriers were broken down and even Gentiles could recognize the true identity of Jesus as the Son of God (v. 39). Put differently, following Jesus's godforsaken death, when he identified himself with the godforsaken world, the divine identity of Jesus was revealed to, and proclaimed by, humanity.

---

136. Stein, *Mark*, 717; see also Josephus, *Antiq.* VIII.3.3; *War*, 5.5.4–5; LXX Exodus 26:31–33, 36–37.

137. See Bryan, Class Lecture New Testament One.

138. The idea of tearing down the heavens during Jesus's baptism in Mark 1:10, and the torn veil of the curtain during Jesus's death in Mark 15:38 and its significance, will be briefly discussed below in "the revelation of Jesus" "the Son of God" section in chapter 3 of this work.

139. Bauckham, *God of Israel*, 267.

Commentators agree that the "centurion" is the Greek transliteration of the Latin term which refers to someone in charge of a hundred foot soldiers.[140] Since he was standing in front of Jesus, he must be considered to be the executioner of Jesus (vv. 44–45); and "since he is a Roman soldier he can be assumed to have been a Gentile."[141] When this gentile centurion saw how Jesus died, he announced, "Truly this man was God's Son!" (v. 39). Mark does not explain what impressed the centurion and caused him to recognize and proclaim Jesus's divine Sonship. Suggestions have been made which refer to some possibilities in Mark's account, such as the supernatural darkness which came over the land (15:33), the last words of Jesus (v. 34), the loud cry during his death (v. 37), his quick and peaceful death (v. 44), or the unrecorded words of the last cry.[142] In his account, Matthew associates the confession of the centurion with divine manifestations, such as earthquake and "what things had taken place" in Matthew 27:51–54. However, for Mark's readers the reason for the centurion's "exclamation is unmistakably the manner of Jesus death, rather than any accompanying event."[143] Therefore, it is possible to think that the unexpected source, namely a centurion, from whom the declaration of Jesus's divine identity comes makes it so unique because it is an ordinary gentile army officer, a soldier, who recognized and proclaimed Jesus's divine Sonship, rather than anyone from among the Jews, or Jesus's family, or even one of his close disciples.

The title "Son of God" (υἱὸς θεοῦ) lacks the article ("the") in the Greek text. This has led some to interpret the confession for the centurion as "*a* son of God" rather than "*the* Son of God," meaning that according to this Roman/gentile soldier, Jesus is just a good divine man or one of the extraordinary heroes who is worthy of worship. In other words, some commentators think that due to lack of the article ("the"), Jesus must be understood as less than "the Son of God."[144] They also argue that since, so far, Mark has not said anything about a declaration of Jesus as "the Son of

---

140. See Hooker, *According to St. Mark*, 378; Hurtado, *Mark*, 277; Stein, *Mark*, 718.
141. Donahue and Harrington, *Gospel of Mark*, 449.
142. See France, *Gospel of Mark*, 659.
143. Lane, *Gospel of Mark*, 576.
144. See Johnson, "Mark 15:39," 3–22; Harner, "Qualitative Anarthrous Predicate Nouns," 75–87.

God" by any human being, it is unlikely he would mention it here at the end of the gospel (15:39). Additionally, although the centurion's words possibly indicate a religious concept of popular Hellenism, these scholars do not expect such a confession from a gentile, Roman soldier who had no Jewish religious background, to be able, suddenly, to declare Jesus's Sonship of the one true God.

Nevertheless, as pointed out, the readers of the second evangelist need to understand that the phrase "Son of God" should be perceived not by comparing and contrasting grammatical relationships between phrases or words, but by rethinking the entire context of the gospel; particularly, by looking back to the previous references to Jesus as the Son of God.[145] Therefore, I argue that it is not a problem to Mark since throughout the gospel he uses both arthrous and anarthrous nouns[146] to describe Jesus's divine identity or his unique divine Sonship in Mark 1:1, 11; 3:11; 5:7; and 9:7 as will be discussed in the "Son of God" section of the third chapter of this work. In all these references, Mark's readers know that Mark is not saying that Jesus is one of many sons of God, but that he is the only beloved Son, or the Son of the Most-High God/Blessed. In addition, "the connotation of υἱὸς θεοῦ in this context is of divinity rather than merely that of a royal-messianic title."[147] Further, "in the context of Mark's Gospel the absence of the definite article need not blunt the theological significance of the title" but rather the reader must discover that the declaration of a gentile soldier is the confirmation of the climax of Mark's Christology which began in Mark 1:1.[148] Also it is true that for the centurion "the definite article would probably have meant little and mattered less. It is Mark's readers for whom it matters, and for them, . . . Jesus is the Son of God in a unique sense . . . , there can be no question."[149]

Likewise, as briefly noted above, in the Marcan literary ironies, the soldiers (15:18, 26), chief priests and scribes (vv. 31–32), and the high priest and Pilate (14:61; 15:2), have acknowledged Jesus's divine identity although

---

145. See Davis, "Mark's Christological Paradox," 11, 12.

146. "A noun that has an article is called an *arthrous* noun (from arqron, 'article'). A noun that has no article is called an *anarthrous* (i.e. 'not-arthrous') noun." Black, *Learn to Read*, 30.

147. Chronis, "The Torn Veil," 101–106.

148. Donahue and Harrington, *Gospel of Mark*, 449.

149. France, *Gospel of Mark*, 660.

without any understanding as to the true meaning of what they have said. Additionally, Matthew in his account (chs. 14 and 16) mentions this title with and without the definite article, both in anarthrous and arthrous forms (e.g. Matt 26:63 with and 27:40 and 43 without the definite article) to describe the true identity of Jesus as the Son of God.

Therefore, I argue that at Jesus's death on the cross, his divine identity as the suffering Messiah and as God's Son was revealed to the marginalized world. As Hooker argues, "the centurion stands at this point as the representative of those who acknowledge Jesus as God's Son." It is interesting to understand that an unexpected gentile soldier could see, believe and declare Jesus's true identity.[150] Brown also profoundly explains that what Jesus promised to the many from East and West who would sit at table with the Patriarchs while the children of the kingdom (the Jews), who refused it, would be thrown into outer darkness (Matt 8:5–13; Luke 7:1–10), is equivalent to what happened in Mark's account to the gentile centurion at the cross.[151] It is true that the great insight of the centurion is the fulfilment of Psalm 22:28 which says, "All the ends of the earth shall remember and turn to the Lord, and all the families of the nations shall bow down before Him," and of the promise of Jesus that the gospel would be preached to all the nations (Mark 13:10). Therefore, Mark's readers and listeners understand that Jesus is witnessed by a Gentile "human being who is a type of thousands and even millions of Gentiles who later will stand by faith before the cross and confess that the man Jesus of Nazareth is the unique Son of God."[152] Further, it is ironic that while the Jewish religious and political leaders and onlookers were mocking Jesus, and even while his close followers could not grasp who he was, the surprise was that an unexpected gentile army officer makes an amazing confession about the nature of Jesus, and not while Jesus was doing miraculous deeds, but while he was dying on the cross, a very shameful death.

Some understand that Mark wants his readers to know that the reaction of the centurion which followed the loud cry and death of Jesus (v. 37) should be understood as though it accompanied the splitting of the veil of

---

150. Hooker, *According to St. Mark*, 379.
151. Brown, *Death of the Messiah*, 1149.
152. Brooks, *Mark*, 263.

the temple.¹⁵³ Thus, they think that the adverb "thus" in verse 39, refers back to "a loud cry, expired" in verse 37 and the torn veil of the temple in verse 38 indicating that the main reason for the centurion's confession was not only Jesus's death on the cross but also the splitting of the temple curtain. However, I argue that in Mark's account, it was the manner of Jesus's death which brings the declaration of the gentile soldier rather than any accompanying event because this was what he saw (v. 39) rather than how the curtain was torn. Furthermore, Bauckham rightly argues that "the centurion does not, of course, respond to the torn veil, which he could not see, but to what it represents: that the presence of God can now be recognized in how Jesus died (15:39)."¹⁵⁴ The centurion may not have fully understood the meaning or theological significance of his confession because Mark does not explain it. However, from what he declared, the reader discovers that on the openly godforsaken cross of Jesus, his true identity was revealed not only to a centurion but also to all those who experience abandonment or forsakenness in the absence of God. Therefore, I fully agree with Bauckham who says, "the centurion represents all the godforsaken who find the presence of God in Jesus' self-identification with them, the godforsaken."¹⁵⁵ Finally, it is Jesus's godforsaken death on the cross and his self-identification with the marginalized sinners which revealed not only his royal messianic title but also his divine Sonship to God to all humanity.

2.4.6. Jesus and the Women

One of the marginalized and liminal groups of people who are regarded as symbols of weakness in the ancient world are women. At that time, they were not allowed to fully participate in the society in which they were because they were, among others, frequently considered as unclean in various ways. For instance, a man could not touch a menstruating woman, even one from among his/her family members (Mark 5:24–34). However, this was not a problem to Jesus because since Jesus began his Galilean ministry, in the early chapters of his gospel, Mark reports the presence of women with Jesus

---

153. For example, Brown, *Death of the Messiah*, 1144–1145; and Donahue and Harrington, *Gospel of Mark*, 449.
154. Bauckham, *God of Israel*, 267.
155. Bauckham, 267.

(Mark 5:24–34, 7:17; 10:10), even up to the time of his destiny in Jerusalem (15:41). Nevertheless, "prior to 15:40 Mark mentions no women by name except Mary the mother of Jesus (Mark 3:31–35; 6:3) and . . . Herodias . . . due in part to the androcentric bias of his culture which viewed women only in terms of their relation to men."[156]

According to Munro, although Mark understands that there were some women with Jesus, because of Mark's embarrassment at the presence of women, given the ancient context, he refers to them in an obscure manner using common terms such as "they," "many," "people," and "the crowd," because for him, women are not part of Jesus's public ministry, but only present in private places like homes.[157] Similarly, Miller adds that in Mark "the presence of women may be concealed by the masculine plural grammatical terms . . . where there are no men."[158] However, unlike Munro who thinks that women were not part of Jesus's public ministry, Miller rightly argues that women were present around Jesus since the woman with the flow of blood came to Jesus from among the crowd, and he called her forward and praised her for her saving faith publicly.[159] Likewise, Mark records that even though it is rarely seen in the ancient world, in Mark 5:40 the girl's mother is mentioned as being called in along with the father, Jairus, in order to witness the healing of her daughter. Therefore, the readers discover Jesus's concern for women even despite the cultural barriers not only to make them his followers, but also to make them eyewitnesses of three crucial events of the gospel – his death, burial and resurrection and the empty tomb (Mark 15:40–41, 47; 16:1), unlike his close male disciples.

At the conclusion of the crucifixion narrative in his gospel, next to the first gentile witness, the gentile centurion in Mark 15:39, Mark provides the names of several women who were "looking on from a distance" (v. 40). Edwards opines that "even distance is better than absence."[160] Mark's readers know that these women (two of them) were the ones who saw where the body of Jesus was laid (v. 47). They too may have feared persecution since

---

156. Munro, "Women Disciples in Mark," 226; Fiorenza, *In Memory of Her*, 45.
157. Munro, 226–227.
158. Miller, *Women in Mark's Gospel*, 19.
159. See Miller,158; Mark 5:24–34.
160. Edwards, *Gospel According to Mark*, 486.

they had been following and serving the persecuted and crucified Messiah and since families and friends of those who were executed as revolutionaries could also face persecution.[161] Furthermore, Brown points out that although Jesus was not a revolutionary, he was arrested as a revolutionary and accused of claiming to be the king of Jews.[162] He was crucified with revolutionary thieves. France's observation is worth quoting in full:

> The important role played by these women in the closing stages of Mark's narrative . . . is a pointer to something new in the movement Jesus has begun which contrast strongly with the male domination of the society of his [and Mark's] time . . . in a society which gave no legal status to the testimony of women . . . everything will . . . come to depend on their witness to what they have seen and heard.[163]

So, the readers may discover two significant points from this concluding story of Jesus's crucifixion, death and resurrection. First, in contrast to the well-known apostles of Jesus who were expected to do more, but denied and deserted him (Mark 14), these women remained faithful with him to the bitter end to see and to witness his death, burial and resurrection (Mark 16). Although it was expected from Jesus's first followers who benefited a lot from his private teachings and miracles, but who finally denied and ridiculed him, these women demonstrated their undivided devotion to Jesus while following him from Galilee to Jerusalem.

Second, as it was said, "the irony of the absence of the disciples and the presence of the women has been carefully constructed and is heightened by the call to the women to be the first witnesses to the risen Jesus 16:7," not only staying with him to the end devotedly, but also these women were the ones who expected to witness Jesus's crucifixion, burial and empty tomb (15:40, 47; 16:1–8, respectively).[164] Put differently, instead of Jesus's famous male followers, these unexpected women, who were limited by cultural

---

161. See Miller, *Women in Mark's Gospel*, 160.
162. See Brown, *Death of the Messiah*, 1157.
163. France, *Gospel of Mark*, 665.
164. Painter, *Mark's Gospel*, 208.

barriers, became the first instruments to link the news of Jesus's victory to humanity.

Swidler argues that the women cannot be witnesses, according to Jewish law, because their witness is not accepted by the male disciples as their testimony would be considered invalid.[165] Generally, during the first century, according to some apocryphal and pseudepigraphical literature, women are described as evil, unreliable or untrustworthy, irrational, and unclean who cause evil and judgment and were regarded as slaves; furthermore, nobody counts them as persons.[166] In contrast, discussing Josephus's idea that although the law does not accept the witness of women but on some occasions their witness was acceptable, Ilan argues that the witness of women in the gospels is not portrayed in the context of the courtroom.[167] In other words, Ilan proposes that the testimony of the women should not be considered in the context of the civil law; so they can be witnesses in the gospel. Furthermore, I argue that the courtroom or the civil law of the first century, as well as male disciples who were bound by the culture of those days, may not approve the witness of women because they themselves do not understand Jesus's full identity and his main agenda on earth. However, in the reversal value of the kingdom of God in which the first is the last and the last is first, these women who, traditionally, are regarded as weak, and therefore marginalized and liminal, became the main witnesses of Jesus's victorious death and resurrection.[168] Thus, Mark reminds his readers that instead of his close friends (the male disciples) who were expected to stay with him to the end, these women – even those who were not mentioned by name (v. 41) – demonstrated their warm devotion to Jesus by following and serving him and others with him, regardless of such a fearful situation on the way to Jerusalem to be executed.

---

165. Swidler, *Biblical Affirmations*, 201.
166. See Elwell and Yarbrough, *First-Century World*, 74–75.
167. See Ilan, *Jewish Women*, 163–166.
168. See Mark 9:35; 10:43–44.

2.4.7. At the Conclusion of Mark's Crucifixion Narrative, Who Are These Women?

As noted above, Mark, for the first time, mentions three women by their own names in chapter 15. At the burial story, two Mary's are present in 15:47, and in the empty tomb all three of them are present. Mary Magdalene, who is originally from a town called Magdala on the western shore of Lake Galilee, is one of those women whose name is mentioned in all four gospels. She was the one Luke mentions as the woman out of whom Jesus exorcised seven demons (Luke 8:2), although there is no clear biblical evidence of her being the prostitute of Luke 7:36–39 as some scholars suggest.[169] Nothing much is known about the second Mary except the names of her two sons (James and Joses) about whom also nothing much is recorded, although presumably they were well known to Mark's readers (cf. v. 21). James is described as the shorter, which could have referred to his height or his age, among the apostles.[170] He was thought to be the apostle who is "sometimes identified with James the son of Alphaeus."[171] Some attempts to identify this Mary (the mother of James) with Mary the mother of Jesus (cf. John 19:25–27) are unconvincing because as France rightly suggested, it would be strange for Mark to identify her by these younger and lesser-known sons rather than (as in 6:3) as the mother of Jesus, and to place her second to Mary of Magdala.[172] Furthermore, she is not mentioned as the mother of Jesus in Mark 15:47; 16:1 wherein her name appears, and as Bauckham concludes, "no relatives of Jesus appear among the women disciples named by the Synoptic evangelists."[173] Similarly, although Salome is indicated as the mother of sons of Zebedee (James and John) in Matthew 27:56, there is nothing clearly described about her in all four gospels except in Mark 15:41 and 16:1. There are also many others whose names were not mentioned although there are Joanna and Susanna in Luke 8:3 and two sisters (Mary and Martha) in John 11:1–37 and 12:1–8.

---

169. See Brooks, *Mark*, 264.
170. See Hooker, *According to St. Mark*, 379.
171. Brooks, *Mark*, 264.
172. See France, *Gospel of Mark*, 664.
173. Bauckham, "Salome the Sister," 245–275.

In a nutshell, it is true that Mark did not clearly mention specific names of women before chapter 15 due to ancient culture; however, it was not a problem to Mark's Jesus who identified himself with these marginalized and liminal people (women), not only to include them in the company of his followers but also to make them an integral part of his mission. Furthermore, unlike the first male disciples who were expected to do better but deserted him in Mark 14, readers of Mark understand that regardless of the cultural influence in the ancient world, Jesus identified himself unexpectedly with these unsuspecting women to use them as the witnesses of the gospels' decisive events – his death, resurrection and empty tomb.

Finally, the readers or listeners of Mark understand that Jesus identified himself with these neglected women regardless of their marginalized and liminal situation due to their sex and the culture in which they lived and Mark wrote his gospel. As noted above, in addition to her sex, Mary of Magdala was possessed by the oppressive force of demons before Jesus came to her and liberated her. Likewise, although the names of some were mentioned in the gospels, they were not well-known women in society or among the gospel writers because many things were uncertain about them. Still the names of many others were not mentioned in the gospels including Mark 15:41. In other words, in contrast to the well-known chosen apostles of Jesus, these women were from lower strata, so that even their names and families were not clearly described in Mark. However, next to the gentile centurion, the first human being to recognize and declare Jesus's Sonship, although there is no greater indication of their real recognition of Jesus's messianic identity better than any of his male followers, this band of women were described as faithful friends of Jesus, entrusted, as the main people, to follow and serve him and finally to witness the three decisive or significant events of Jesus – his death, resurrection and the empty tomb.

2.4.8. Conclusion

In conclusion, Mark tells his readers and hearers that Jesus's divine identity, as the Son of God, was revealed, declared and finally witnessed by marginalized, liminal, and unexpected people, whereas his close friends, who were purposefully chosen and trained for the expansion of God's kingly rule in Jesus, remained ignorant.

First, Jesus's self-identification with godforsaken humanity in God's absence at the cross was recognized and declared by a gentile army officer, not by anyone else among the Jewish religious group or Jesus's close family or friends. It occurred as a result of Jesus's death on the cross which caused a divine act of God, opening access to his presence to all humanity. Furthermore, this happened by the will of God in fulfilment of the Scriptures.

Mark also makes it clear that the purpose of Jesus's self-identification with godforsaken humanity, entering their marginalized state of God's absence, was not only to suffer on their behalf but also to give himself as a ransom for many in order to liberate them from all sorts of affliction including their sins.

Likewise, the readers get to know that the goal of Jesus's death was not simply to suffer on behalf of others, but according to Mark 16 and other evangelists, it was the victorious resurrection of Jesus and vindication of humankind by God. In other words, Jesus's self-identification with those who were marginalized and liminal people is not simply to suffer and die on behalf of others but to liberate many from their affliction and finally to save/atone humanity through his resurrection.

Second, in spite of the culture of the first century which put women into the social group which could be likened to the outcasts, the unclean or the unimportant, Mark indicates that Jesus had some devoted women who followed and served him from the very beginning of his ministry in Galilee; and Jesus considered by woman as a good model in the expansion of God's kingdom among all nations (Mark 14:6–9). Furthermore, unlike Jesus's male followers, Mark introduces some women by their names and others without their names, not merely as his followers to the end and their service to him and others around him, but also as the witnesses of his ultimate victory through resurrection.

Finally, the readers discover that whereas these women, in the eyes of the Jews around them were neglected ones, in the eyes of God they were channels as well as witnesses of Jesus's victory over death.

2.5. Chapter Conclusion

I have demonstrated from Mark's narrative, particularly in the exegetical study of four episodes above (e.g. Mark 3:7–12; 5:1–20; 10:46–52 and 15:33–41), that the second evangelist has portrayed Jesus as a unique figure, with supernatural authority, progressing forward with the agenda of God's kingly rule on earth through his words and mighty deeds. In addition, despite his universal authority, Jesus by his own initiative comes to the poor and outcasts to identify himself with them even in their marginalized and liminal states as well as to bring a solution to their plights.

First, regardless of opposition from various fronts, Jesus's unique authority is demonstrated over evil or unclean spirits, destroying their kingdom, and liberating those who were possessed by them. Mark also narrates that Jesus's divine identity was revealed to the outcasts not only in Jewish territory but also in the Gentile lands (as discussed in Mark 5), and he was proclaimed by them in all regions.

Second, in spite of discouragements from others around him, Mark's Jesus is portrayed as the one who brings both physical sight and spiritual insight to the blind beggar to see his Royal messianic identity, to declare it and to follow him in his way to the cross in Jerusalem, unlike his first trained apostles. In other words, I argued that Jesus deliberately reveals himself to the marginalized person, rather than to his close friends (his own disciples) who were trained, privately, by Jesus himself and so expected to do more.

Third, as the climax of his christological narrative, Mark brings the story of Jesus's death on behalf of those who are abandoned by God due to their sins and so crying in the absence of God. Thus, the readers of Mark's narrative are to know that, through his unique death, Jesus identified himself with humanity and revealed his divine identity to the marginalized gentile world. Finally, Mark's Jesus, who revealed and identified himself to the marginalized and liminal people to help and heal them, was also declared to be God's Royal Son by them; even some women who witnessed his victorious resurrection and empty tomb also declared as much. As will be discussed in more detail in the fourth chapter of this work, Mark's Jesus is portrayed as though he himself is part of the marginalized humanity.

The next section of this work will carefully examine and evaluate certain titles (e.g. the Messiah, the Son of David, the Son of God, and the Son of Man), from different points of view by scholars with a view to arguing that all these titles ultimately point to the uniquely divine messiahship of Jesus or his divine Sonship to God, yet identifying himself with the marginalized and liminal humanity to save.

CHAPTER 3

The Messianic Identity in Mark's Gospel

3.1. Introduction

Having completed the exegetical part of Mark's narrative in which the second evangelist carefully tells of the story of Jesus's divine identity and his self-identification with the marginalized and liminal individuals and groups, it is appropriate to expound certain christological titles by which Jesus was identified, and which were used as declarations by various people in different ways. Among these titles and/or names of Jesus, only four of them will be investigated in detail here: the Messiah, the Son of David, the Son of God, and the Son of Man.

Some of the titles of Jesus in the Synoptic gospels, particularly in Mark (e.g. teacher and Rabbi, and Lord and Master) are similar and overlap in meaning. It would be outside of the scope of this piece of work to discuss all the titles of Jesus in Mark's gospel in detail, but it would be appropriate to examine these four and their significance because through them, readers can see Jesus's uniquely divine messiahship, yet identifying himself to the unexpectedly poor and outcast people. It is also important to consider that although Jesus was ascribed these four and other equally impressive titles, which did not indicate a marginal identity or position at all, the manner in which Mark's Jesus assume these titles and the way in which he actualized them, reinforces the marginality of Jesus.

First, unlike other messiahs of those days, Mark describes Jesus as the unique Messiah with a unique purpose and goal. His is not of the all-conquering, mighty, victorious king who would deliver God's people (particularly Israel) from the oppression of their human enemies in this world (e.g. Roman Empire), but as the crucified and risen Messiah who would mightily deliver his people from the power of sin and Satan, and give them a different victory, a victory over death. This was a unique understanding of the Old Testament prophecies. This was also the Messiah who identified himself with those who are in need.

Second, he was described as the Son of David with great significance. This was to indicate that Jesus had genealogical evidence to support his claim to be God's Messiah who would come from the Royal line of David as a King. Furthermore, Mark describes him not only as the Son of King David (see Mark 10:46–52) but also as the Lord of David (see Mark 12:35–37; see also Ps 110:1). When Jesus approached the marginalized beggar, Bartimaeus used the royal title, "Jesus, Son of David." He was recognized by the poor and outcast but not at first by his close family members and well-trained disciples.

Third, the title "the Son of God" appears several times at decisive points of Mark's narrative from the very beginning to nearly the end of the gospel. It was declared not only by God, his Father alone, but also by other supernatural beings, demons, and finally by the human being. Furthermore, Mark's readers will learn that Jesus's unique divine Sonship to God was not simply revealed through his miraculous deeds and his divine claim to be able to forgive sin, but further through his shameful death on the cross. By these means he unexpectedly associated himself with marginalized humanity in order to save the world.

Fourth, the title "Son of Man" in Mark's gospel will be examined further because it appears as Jesus's own favourite self-description. It also describes Jesus as the divine Messiah whose person and ministry are understood in terms of vindication through suffering. He is associating himself with oppressed and marginalized people, as well as confirming his glorious return as the judge of the world in fulfilment of the scriptures in Daniel 7:13–14.

As will be discussed next, Mark's Jesus generally is to be understood as the unique Messiah of God with divine authority, yet willing to identify himself with the most marginalized and liminal humanity who experience the absence of God, in order to liberate and save them.

3.2. The Messiah

3.2.1. Definition and Introduction

Before going further, it will be appropriate to define the term "Messiah" in some languages or to clarify its meaning, since it is one of the most used and important titles by which Jesus identified himself and was confessed by others. The term "Messiah" literally means "anointed." It comes from the Hebrew word "*Mashah* or *Mashiach*," or/and from Aramaic "*Meshiha*." The Greek equivalent is Μεσσίας, *messias* or Χριστός, *Kristos*. All these words carry the idea of one who is "anointed" or "the anointed one" of God.

However, there was no commonly held opinion or uniform expectation for the coming of the Davidic king in Judaism. As referred by Bird, some believed that the Messiah would be an earthly warrior (*Pss. Sol.* 17–18), while others conceived him to be a pre-existing and transcendent figure (*1 Enoch*; *4 Ezra*); still others, such as those in Qumran, conceived of two Messiahs, one of Aaron and one of Israel (1QS 9.11; CD 12.22–23; 13.20–22; 14.18–19; 34–20.1; CD-B 1.10–11; 2.1; 1QSa 217–22).[1] All these figures may fit in with different aspects of Israel's sacred tradition of the liberator or saviour, since "A messiah is ordinarily someone raised up, sent, or anointed for a particular task as it relates to the liberation of Israel . . ."[2]

Thus, it can be said that the Messiah, in the Old Testament, originally applied to the kings of Israel who were appointed by God and anointed with holy oil as princes expected to accomplish God's purpose by redeeming or liberating his people Israel from their surrounding enemies.

It is not only some individuals, such as kings, priests and prophets, who were anointed with holy oil[3] for both political and religious purposes, but also some objects and places were anointed and set apart for a special purpose. For instance, the Jewish temple and its objects in Exodus 40:9–11 and unleavened bread in Numbers 6:15 were anointed for a special purpose. Likewise, the concept and function of the term "Messiah" as "anointed one"

---

1. Bird, *Are You the One*, 33–34.
2. Bird, 33–34.
3. For instance, God sets apart some people, such as Cyrus of Persia, for his divine purposes and anointed them without using the oil of consecration (Isa 45:1). The patriarchs in Ps 105 and Israel itself in Hab 3:13 were also said to be God's anointed ones (see Ladd, *Theology of the New Testament*, 132).

is also found in later Judaism (Apocrypha and Pseudepigraphical writings) and in the New Testament's gospels. However, the idea of Messiah and Messianism in the OT, the intertestamental period, Second Temple Judaism and Christianity is too broad to explain in this piece of work.

Thus, here I would like to emphasize in my investigation the concept or the idea of the hoped for or expected Messiah(s) of Israel in the OT and the contemporary Jewish messianic expectations, as well as the messianic questions in the Gospel of Mark.

Does Mark share the traditional understanding of Messiah, or has he reinterpreted it in some way? Here I will particularly discuss the idea of the unique Messiah, Jesus, in the Gospel of Mark, whose real identity is redefined or reinterpreted by himself as the one who revealed himself in unexpected ways to marginalized and liminal people not only to liberate some from their physical plights but also to save many from their sins and death, in my opinion, the most horrible enemies of all human beings.

To do so, some basic questions need to be answered: What did the OT writers or prophets, as well as the contemporary Jewish expectants in Judaism say about the Messiah? Was Jesus recognized as the Messiah during his earthly ministry? Contrary to current Jewish expectations, why did the gospel writers designate Jesus as the Messiah while he did not fulfil/accomplish the expected role of the messiahs of Israel in the first century? What is unique about Jesus's messiahship and its significance in identifying himself with the poor and outcast, the marginalized and liminal ones in the gospels, particularly in Mark's gospel?

3.2.2. The Messiah and the Messianic Hope and Expectations in the Old Testament

It was supposed that the messianic title is found in the Old Testament (e.g. 1 Sam 2:10), however, the simple term "the Messiah" as a title does not occur in the Old Testament.[4] Nevertheless, in later Jewish writings of the period between 200 BC and AD 100 the term is used infrequently in connection with agents of divine deliverance expected in the future.[5] Thus, the OT

---

4. See Ladd, *Theology of the New Testament*, 134–135; Mowinckel, *Cometh: The Messiah*, 4.

5. See de Jonge, "Messiah," 777–778.

readers know that the term "anointed" rather than the "Messiah" is clearly mentioned in association with "three primary offices or ministries in ancient Israel."[6] In addition, from 1 Samuel 2:10, one can learn that even though the term "the Messiah" is not directly stated in the OT, the concept and the meaning of "anointed" or "anointed one" and its significance is familiar enough, particularly with regard to the Davidic descendent.

Further, the OT readers know that David was not the only person who had been anointed as a historical royal figure, since "several historical kings of Israel and Judah, beginning with Saul, are said to have been anointed";[7] nevertheless, Hess and Carroll argue that "Old Testament historians would mention other historical royal figures who were anointed, but none of these was ever recognized as 'the messiah' in a technical sense" other than David. In addition, it was stated that "the conclusion that David was the anointed historical figure par excellence and that the eschatological messiah is to be found in his descendants is reinforced throughout the rest of the Old Testament."[8]

The OT readers also understand that the word [Messiah] always has a qualifying genitive suffix such as "the messiah of Jehovah," and "my messiah," rather than "the messiah."[9] Therefore, as rightly suggested, "functions and roles are often more important than a single title," although the absolute term "the Messiah" does not appear literally in the OT, the concept, the role and its significance is repeatedly used in relation to the Davidic Messiah.[10] Bauckham also suggests that "the Hebrew Bible contains a range of texts that might be understood to refer to the Messiah, and what sort of Messiah one envisaged depended a lot on which texts one emphasized."[11] For this reason, I agree with John Collins when he argues that a messianic figure is

---

6. Bird, *Are You the One*, 34.

7. Collins and Collins, *King and Messiah*, 1. For example Absalom (2 Sam 19:10); Solomon (1 Kgs 1:34, 39, 45; 5:15; 1 Chr 29:22); Jehu (1 Kgs 19:16; 2 Kgs 9:3, 6, 12; 2 Chr 22:7); Jehoash (2 Kings 11:12; 2 Chr 23:11) and Jehoahaz (2 Kgs 23:30).

8. Hess and Carroll, *Israel's Messiah*, 39.

9. See Ladd, *Theology of the New Testament*, 134.

10. De Jonge, "Anointed," 147.

11. Bauckham, *Jesus*, 88.

"an agent of God in the end-time who is said somewhere in the literature to be anointed, but who is not necessarily called 'messiah' in every passage."[12]

Further, some scholars think that the writers of the OT did not indicate that the messiah title applied to an eschatological king.[13] However, since there are some clear prophecies that look forward to the reign of a Davidic king (1 Sam 2:10; Ps 2:2; Dan 9:26 and 2 Sam 7:12–16) and his promised eternal kingdom, I argue that its fulfilment was expected in a greater Son of David in a day of eschatological fulfilment (Ps 89:3; Jer 3:8; Ezek 37:21). In addition, "as the monarchy failed and eventually fell to Nebuchadnezzar in 586 BC, an expectation grew in Israel that God would raise up a new and even greater king like David."[14] Ladd also rightly argues that the most notable prophecies in the OT "were Isa. 9 and 11 in which although he is not called 'messiah,' he is a king of David's line who will be supremely endowed to 'smite the earth with the rod of his mouth, and with the breath of his lips he will slay the wicked' (Isa 11:4) . . . and reign forever from the throne of David."[15] In other words, the idea of the term "Messiah" and its meaning and significance in the Old Testament and other pre-Christian texts (e.g. 1QSa 2:12) point to its relationship to a Davidic king and even beyond its immediate fulfilment in the house of David to its eschatological fulfilment in the messianic king through whom God would establish an everlasting/eternal kingdom over the whole land (Jer 23:5).

In the Old Testament, Zechariah portrays the king as the one who will bring victory and win peace for the people of God in Jerusalem. He will get rid of war, and rule over all the earth (Zech 9:9–10). Even though it is not explicitly stated as such, the colt of Mark 11:2 is to be understood in the Old Testament as the mount of the Messiah in Zechariah 9. However, whereas Matthew 21:5 and John 12:15 clearly mention Jesus's entry into Jerusalem on the donkey, Mark has written it differently. For Mark's readers Jesus's unique messianic role which was predicted in Zechariah 9: 9–10 is fulfilled in Mark 11:1–10 where Jesus was welcomed by the crowds who hailed him as king-Messiah. In addition, in contrast to other victorious warriors of the

---

12. Collins, "He Shall Not Judge," 146.
13. See Dalman, *Words of Jesus*, 289–295.
14. Edwards, *Gospel According to Mark*, 249.
15. Ladd, *Theology of the New Testament*, 135.

OT, Jesus's unique messianic identity is seen by his entry into Jerusalem not as a warrior who comes on a horse or in a chariot but, unexpectedly, as one who rides on a donkey. His victory was to be so different – he wins the peace without the use of the sword. Thus, Mark's readers know that his "Jesus was coming to his people in the paradox of their victorious yet humble king, bringing them dominion and peace."[16] Or to put it differently, I assume that, according to Mark's Gospel, Jesus's messianic identity and his messianic role is revealed in an unexpected fashion that is so different from the popular expectations, as was discussed in chapter 2 of this work.

3.2.3. The Messianic Idea in Judaism

As was indicated in the case of the Old Testament, it was also true that the word "Messiah" is not explicitly stated with great frequency in intertestamental writings either, even though belief in the coming of messiah or the messianic idea is a fundamental part of traditional Judaism.

Nevertheless, throughout first-century Jewish history, there have been many people who appointed themselves, or claimed to be kings or messiahs, or whose followers have declared that they were messiahs.[17]

It is also important to notice that messianic expectation in Israel increased during or after the time that Pompey captured Jerusalem under Rome in 63 BC, and due to the frustration that Israel faced with the Hasmonean dynasty,

---

16. Seccombe, *God's Kingdom*, 503.

17. For instance, as referred by Bird (*Are You the One*, 50–52), first, according to Josephus, Judas, the Galilean led an insurrection in Sepphoris whose bloodshed was motivated by zeal for royal honour. Second, Athronges, who led a revolt in Judea and set himself up in kingship by putting a diadem on his head, was also called a king, imitating the Davidic shepherd-kingship in 2 Sam 2:5; third, Simon a servant of Herod also put a diadem on his head and was declared to be king by a number of people (see *Antiq.* 17.273; *War* 2.57; 17:274). Fourth, as Bird goes on discussing, Josephus also mentions Menahem who led a small group of men who seized the fortress at Masada and then returned to Jerusalem like a king, and fifth, Simon bar Giora who led thousands in the insurrection with some degree of success . . . (see *War* 4.521–34), which has parallels to David's military career in conquering neighbouring tribes. Finally, during the second century, even though he was not designated as "Messiah" or in Hebrew "moshiach" but was called a "Prince" – which had a long history as a messianic title – Simon ben Kosiba was regarded as the Messiah by Rabbi Akiba, one of the greatest scholars in Jewish history. Kosiba fought against Roman Empire and retook Jerusalem. He attempted to accomplish the messianic role by building the temple and resuming its service. Ultimately, however, all of these people were executed without fulfilling the role/mission of the Messiah.

which ruled over Israel in the second century BC after the Maccabean revolt, according to historical sources such as 1 Maccabees and 2 Maccabees.

Thus, the messianic idea and its role in Judaism has always been related to the belief that the Messiah would fight against their gentile enemies and bring military and political liberation, as well as bringing religious redemption to the Jewish people by rebuilding the temple and restoring its service in Jerusalem in order to restore the line of king David.

First, for instance, soon after the death of Pompey (probably around 48 BC), we see that the unknown author of the *Psalms of Solomon* prays for the coming of the kingdom of God through the promised king, the son of David, the anointed of the Lord (*Pss. Sol.* 17:5–23) as the one who destroys the gentile nations and liberates Israel, reigning over them as eternal king (*Pss. Sol.* 17–18). In other words, regarding the messianic expectations in Judaism, the prayer of this devout Jew is "for fulfilment of the Old Testament prophecies of the Davidic king who should rise from among the people to deliver Israel from its enemies, to bring in the kingdom of God, and to rule over it as God's Anointed King."[18] On the contrary, Mark's Jesus, the unique eschatological king-messiah, revealed himself in unexpected ways to unexpected people in order to liberate and save many, not only Israel, from their sins undergoing suffering as a "ransom for many" (Mark 10:45).

Second, "the earliest known instance of the absolute use of the term 'the Messiah' comes from Qumran (1QSa 2:12)."[19] Nevertheless, there are several theories regarding the word "messiah" in the Qumran documents. For instance, some think that the Qumran community looked for two messiahs – one Davidic as military deliverer or king, and one Aaronic as high priest.[20] These scholars think that even though the Qumran community believed that the Davidic Messiah played an important role in their expectation, the priestly Messiah took precedence over the kingly Messiah because he was in charge of the matters of the Law and rituals, while the royal figure would be a Davidic descendant who was to lead God's army into battle.[21]

---

18. Ladd, *Theology of the New Testament*, 135–136.

19. Edwards, *Gospel According to Mark*, 249–250.

20. For further information on this see CD 12.23–13.1; 14.19; 19.10–11; 20.1; 1QS 9.11.

21. See Ladd, *Theology of the New Testament*, 136.

As referred by Charles, another Qumran text, the *Damascus Document*, is thought to have been written by the members of the sect as they looked forward to the coming of not one but two messiahs.[22] The author of this document in 7:18–21 pictures not only two messiahs but also shows that one is a military leader and one is a sage. Likewise, in addition to two messiahs of the *Damascus Document*, as referred by Silberman, another text, the *Manual Discipline* in 9:9b–11 introduces a third idea: the plural, the Messiahs of Aaron and Israel, instead of the singular Messiah of Aaron and Israel.[23] Likewise, even though the specific word "messiah" is not used, the author of the *Testaments of the Twelve Patriarchs* mentions one person from Levi as a priest and one from Judah as a kingly ruler.[24] The Qumranites also expected two messiahs who resemble priestly and kingly descendants of Judah and Levi.

Additionally, others believe that while the Messiah in the *War Scroll* is a prophet rather than a war leader, he would still be known as the prince of the community. In contrast in 4Q Florilegium and 4Q458 he is identified as a war leader.[25] Thus, one can see some contradicting ideas between these texts.

Conversely, others argue that there is only one messianic figure. For instance, it has been argued that "dual messianism is the exception rather than the rule."[26] These scholars make this point by pointing to some "newly available texts (4Q246, [and], 4Q521, which speak of 'the messiah of heaven and earth') and speaks of a single messianic figure, with no implication of a second."[27]

Furthermore, L. D. Hurst states that "A careful examination of the most important literature reveals that the multiple messiahship of Qumran is a creation of modern scholars, not a fact required by the texts themselves."[28]

---

22. Charles, "Damascus Document," 799–834.

23. Silberman, "The Two 'Messiahs,'" 77–82.

24. See Charles, "Testaments of the Twelve." Further, consult "Two Messiahs: The Evidence in the Late 2nd Temple Period." Available: https://jamestabor.com/wp-content/uploads/2012.

25. Consult Jona Lendering, "Messiah," 14. Available: http://www.livius.org/men-mh/messiah_14.html.

26. See Collins, *Sceptres and the Star*, 75; cf. Wise and Tabor, "Messiah at Qumran," 60–65.

27. Collins, *Sceptres and the Star*, 75.

28. Hurst, "Did Qumran Expect Two," 157–158.

Having thoroughly examined the concept of two Messiahs at Qumran, he argues that there is no clear evidence regarding two messiahs in the Qumran writings. Thus, the point here is that the concept of two messiahs at Qumran "may well mean the community from which the Messiah is to spring; or it may be a singular construct ('anointed ones from Aaron [and from] Israel') that points to a traditional pairing of king and priest."[29]

Similarly, I suggest that the idea of two messiahs has no clear supporting evidence. Readers can see that different authors have made multiple suggestions regarding the Messiah in the Qumran documents and sometimes they contradict each other. Thus, one can see that the idea of a dual messiahship may not appear in the Scriptures.

However, in the scriptures, rather than the Qumran texts usually called the Dead Sea Scrolls, there was no clear distinction between priests, kings and prophets because ancients regarded kingship as something religious. For instance, it is not surprising to see that King David sometimes acted as priest (2 Sam 6:12–19) and sometimes as a prophet predicting the future (2 Sam 23:1–7). Therefore, it is possible to think that the royal messiah who is the eschatological king of Israel is to be understood as the priestly messiah who is the eschatological high priest. He is the Davidic King Messiah.[30] Finally, whether it is one or two messiahs at Qumran, I argue that there are profound differences with the Messiah of the gospels.

In contrast to the role of messiah of Qumran, which basically has a militaristic connotation most obviously against Rome, Jesus, the King-Messiah of Mark's gospel, identified himself with the poor and outcast in order to liberate and save them.

Third, according to two apocalypses (*4 Ezra* 7:28–29 and *4 Ezra* 12:32–34) from the first century AD, the messiah ("my messiah") was mentioned as the one who is revealed with others and reigns over the messianic kingdom for four hundred years and then dies with them. He is also mentioned as the one who comes from the offspring of David and brings all to his judgment seat, finally destroying the wicked for their ungodliness and delivering God's people. Similarly, as discussed by Bird in the *Apocalypse*

---

29. Hurst, 179–180.
30. See Collins, *Sceptres and the Star*, 75.

of Baruch (*2 Baruch*), the Messiah is revealed by God and reigns in the temporary messianic kingdom (*2 Bar.* 29:3; 30:1) and defends and restores God's people (Israel) defeating their gentile enemies.[31] Finally, it is obvious that the messianic expectation in Judaism and/or in the intertestamental writings tells us that the messiah is expected to fight against gentile nations and their kings and to conquer them, and then to bring political and/or national liberation to Israel, as well as religious restoration by rebuilding the temple for the nation. In short, whereas their messiah would free Israel from her oppression by gentile enemies, Mark's Jesus is the unique Messiah with unique purpose of saving many through a unique and unexpected way, his own shameful death on the Romans' cross.

The next section will seek to examine the messianic expectation in the Gospels, particularly in Mark's gospel, which shows his readers what the Jewish messianic hope was and Jesus's unique messianic identity and role which was totally different from all other sources mentioned above.

3.2.4. The Messianic Hope and Expectation in the Gospels

All in all, in the Old Testament in Judaism and in first-century Christianity, or in the Gospels in the New Testament, the task of the Messiah has never been limited to one single role, and the ways in which interpreters have explained his role have been diverse. However, as repeatedly noted above regarding this idea in the OT and Intertestamental literature, N. T. Wright stated the major and common expectations that the Messiah must have accomplished saying that:

> The main task of the Messiah, over and over again, is the liberation of Israel, and her reinstatement as the true people of the creator god [sic]. This will often involve military action, which can be seen in terms of judgment as in a law court. It will also involve action in relation to the Jerusalem Temple, which must be cleansed and/or restored and/or rebuilt.[32]

Therefore, when one comes to the messianic hope entertained by the Jewish people, and the messianic expectation and role of the Messiah in the Gospels,

---

31. Bird, *Are You the One*, 57–59.
32. Wright, *New Testament*, 320.

one finds a hope similar to that reflected in the *Psalms of Solomon* in which the people expected a messiah to appear as a son of David, a warrior and conquering king-messiah or Lord-messiah (*Pss. Sol.* 17:23–33; 18:7). Similarly, students of the Gospels will find a messianic hope that the Messiah would appear (John 1:20, 41; 4:29; 7:31; Luke 3:15) as a kingly son of David (Matt 21:9; 22:42) to fulfil the expected messianic mission, and would be born in Bethlehem (John 7:40–42; Matt 2:5) and remain forever (John 12:34).[33] Ladd continues to say that "the most important element in this expectation is that the messiah would be the Davidic king."[34] In other words, even in our canonical Gospels, the messiah of Jesus's day was expected to deliver Israel from the yoke of their heathen (Roman) enemies, to establish the earthly kingdom, and to secure the temple for purity of worship, because the hopes for deliverance in those days were always related to the themes of national or/and political liberation of the Jewish nation and restoration of their religious matters.

It is not only in the Gospel of John 6:5–15[35] and Luke 19:38 that Jesus was seen as the Davidic king who provides people's physical needs, but also in the Gospel of Mark. Here he was apparently considered as a great provider of people's physical needs due to the crowd's great enthusiasm and high aspirations to Jesus at the feeding of the five thousand in Mark 6:31–44, and Jesus's reference as the "son of David" during his triumphal entry into Jerusalem (Mark 11:8–10). Eventually, the Romans' action in executing Jesus as "king of the Jews" in Mark 15:26 indicates that Jesus was regarded as the one who would overthrow Roman Empire/rule in order to offer the Jewish people an earthly political Davidic kingdom; because "A mighty leader who would overthrow Rome is precisely what the people desired of their messiah."[36]

Mark's readers know that in ancient Judaism the concept of the messiah who would suffer such a horrible fate that Jesus described in Mark 8:31

---

33. See Ladd, *Theology of the New Testament*, 137; Bird, *Are You the One*, 92.

34. Ladd, 137.

35. It is also important to notice that Jesus explicitly rejected the militaristic association of his messiahship, by the crowd when they attempted to make him king by force due to his reputation as a great miracle worker and national deliverer.

36. Ladd, *Theology of the New Testament*, 137.

was totally unexpected even though there were many references to his true nature in the Jewish Scriptures. Jesus, in the canonical Gospels (particularly Mark), totally rejected the ideas that the term "king" or "messiah" suggested to the popular mind, but affirmed that his messianic identity and mission meant something altogether different – something which no one expected.

For instance, as already indicated earlier regarding Peter's confession of Jesus as the Messiah or Christ, some scholars think that Jesus rejected Peter's confession of his messiahship "as a merely human and even diabolical temptation."[37] Oscar Cullmann also argues that Jesus rejected the idea of his messiahship confessed by Peter precisely because Jesus considered it a satanic temptation in order to persuade him to play the role of a Jewish political messiah by destroying the Roman's contemporary political structure and restoring Israel's earthly Davidic kingdom as God's people.[38] Further, according to Weeden, since Jesus rebuked Peter as Satan for confessing him the "Messiah," Mark has put Peter alongside Satan as the opponent of Jesus.[39]

Conversely, however, one can see that the whole tendency of Mark up to chapter 8 is to lead the twelve (and the readers) to affirm that Jesus is the Messiah. Thus, even though it is insufficient, Peter's confession of Jesus as Messiah is not totally wrong because Mark presents Peter as one who was chosen by Jesus for a great purpose (Mark 3:13–19) and has become a significant part of the proclamation of God's kingdom, and he benefited from Jesus's private teaching and mighty deeds. Therefore, I argue that according to Mark, Peter's confession should not be seen as false but insufficient, needing correction because it does not include Jesus's suffering messiahship; or at least, "whatever Peter's concept of messiahship is, it is not the same as Jesus's concept."[40]

Thus Peter was not totally rejected because of his rebuke of Jesus, but was depicted as someone who could not understand the necessity of the cross for which Jesus came to earth (Mark 8:31) despite the fact he considered Jesus to be the Christ, because his thoughts did not comply with the will

---

37. Fuller, *Foundation of New Testament*, 109.
38. Cullmann, *Christology of the New Testament*, 122. See also Dinkler, "Peter's Confession," 169–202.
39. See Weeden, *Tradition in Conflict*, 66.
40. Sweetland, *Journey with Jesus*, 56; see also Kingsbury, *Christology*, 94–97.

of God, but with human aspirations dominated by satanic values.[41] In short, Mark portrayed Jesus as the unique King-Messiah who was not fully understood even by his close friends, the disciples, but revealed himself to the unexpected poor and marginalized ones.

3.2.5. Conclusion

In conclusion, even though the term "Messiah" is not explicitly stated in the Old Testament and intertestamental writings, the concept and its meaning as the "anointed one," and its function and significance, is found in Davidic descendant or the Davidic Messiah, according to the OT prophesies which would be fulfilled in a greater Son of David in whom God would establish the eternal kingdom.

However, unlike the messianic concept of the contemporaries in the OT and the first century Judaism, as well as of the kingly conqueror of the *Psalms of Solomon*, the second evangelist believes that Jesus is the unique Messiah whose messiahship was redefined or reinterpreted by himself in a unique and unexpected sense. In other words, contrary to the OT and his contemporaries, "Jesus was defining his own role in the saving reign of God that was already bursting in among the political and religious realities of Galilee and Judea."[42] For instance, Mark redefines Jesus's messiahship in terms of the suffering, death and resurrection of Jesus as the royal Davidic Messiah who defeats Israel's enemies in this age with a Messiah who must fulfil his destiny through his suffering and victorious death. Further, in Mark's gospel, Jesus's messiahship is closely related to his divine Sonship (Mark 1:1), rather than just a traditional messiah concept.

To put it differently, the Markan Jesus did not explicitly claim to be the Messiah, because he did not fit the popular expectation of such a figure; yet he did not deny it, but rather gave his own definition to it. Furthermore, concerning the term Messiah, "Jesus seems to have preferred his activities to speak for him, rather than claim a specific title for himself."[43]

---

41. See Painter, *Mark's Gospel*, 126; see also Edwards, *Gospel According to Mark*, 251–252.

42. Bird, *Are You the One*, 115.

43. Bauckham, *Jesus*, 88; see also Bird, *Are You the One*, 36; Collins, "He Shall Not Judge," 146.

Finally, the messiahship of Mark's Jesus is so different and totally unexpected since his kingdom is not political, nor even religious, but so unique whose main purpose is to save people giving his life as a ransom on their behalf (Mark 10:45). The next section will explore the concept of the title, the "Son of David" in which Jesus was recognized as the royal messianic figure, yet associating himself to the marginalized and liminal people.

3.3. The Son of David

3.3.1. Introduction

Another christological title by which Jesus was understood and proclaimed was "Son of David."[44] The Old Testament looked forward to the ideal king who would come from the Davidic line (Jer 23:5; 33:15). Therefore, Jesus's contemporaries wanted him to fit into the mould of the royal Davidic Messiah precisely because he came from the line of David (Rom 1:3), and conceived him as a messiah-king hoping that he would liberate Israel from the Roman yoke by armed force, probably with divine assistance. Similarly, the title "Son of David" also is mentioned as the Lord's anointed in the *Psalms of Solomon* as the warrior and conquering king who would liberate Israel, destroying their gentile enemies (17:23).[45] Likewise, Jesus was recognized and declared as the Son of David in the Synoptic Gospels.[46] However, obviously Jesus accomplished none of these (Jewish expectations).

---

44. It is true that the two titles "Messiah" and "Son of David" were closely associated by some first-century Jews (and so would have been an obvious way for Bartimaeus to address Jesus). Mark's Jesus seems to resist at least some of the Zionist implications of both "Messiah" and "Son of David" titles (see Mark 12:35–37, where Jesus distances himself from Davidic ties) by indicating that he is also the Lord of David (Ps 110:1). This seems to fit Mark's own theological and socio-political concerns: he is separating the apocalyptic nature of Jesus's messiahship – which he affirms – from specific hopes for the re-establishment of the "Davidic kingdom of Israel." Thus, though these two titles are similar and interpret one another, the "Son of David" appears in Mark 10 as the one whose role is reinterpreted or redefined what this meant. He emphasized his unique concern and ability to have compassion and mercy on the poor and unwanted people. In other words, by the term "Son of David" in Mark 10, Mark wants his readers to grasp the possibility of God's reign on earth through the merciful King-Messiah who is also the Son of God who identified himself with the weak.

45. See Miura, "Son of David," 882.

46. For example, Matt 9:27; 12:23; 15:22; 20:30; Luke 1:27, 32, 69; 2:4, 11; Mark 10:47–48; 11:1–10; 12:35–37.

So, what does Mark mean by "Son of David?" How does he picture Jesus, as the "Son of David" in relation to the marginalized and liminal individuals and groups of people in his Gospel? Contrary to the contemporary Jewish expectations for militaristic and political Messiahs, and unlike Jesus's first followers and friends who could not recognize his full identity, and unlike the scribes and teachers of the law, how does Mark's Jesus reveal himself to the marginalized people, and how is he declared by them with this title, and why?

In the next two episodes (Mark 10:47–48 and 12:35–37), Mark tells his readers that Jesus is the "Son of David," but this title is insufficient to describe Jesus's unique and full identity. Even though it is correct, Mark's Jesus is not only the Messiah of Israel to help or liberate them from their surrounding enemies and do miracles as many messiahs of those days did, but as the Lord of David and the powerful Son of God, to save many from their sins paradoxically through his unique death on the cross (10:45, 52; 15:33–39).

3.3.2. Jesus the Son of David (Mark 10:47–48)

The first time in Mark's Gospel that Jesus is addressed with the title "son of David," is by the marginalized beggar, Bartimaeus. According to Ladd this title appears only once in Mark (10:47), for it would have less meaning to a gentile audience than to Jewish readers.[47] Unlike Matthew (1:2–25) and Luke (3:23), it is true that Mark has no genealogy that connects Jesus with King David; nevertheless, Mark tells the story of Bartimaeus addressing Jesus as son of David, the man from the village called Nazareth (10:47). Some scholars, according to Jewish tradition, suggest that the title, "Son of David" points to Solomon because he is David's son with his great ability of healing and exorcism;[48] however, this is unlikely because there is no clear evidence to connect this title to Solomon;[49] plus, Bartimaeus's healing is not exorcism. Rather, it is important to think that this title indicates Jesus's royal messiahship with his unique ability to heal and save (Mark 10:52).

Thus, the readers of the gospel discover that Mark clearly indicates that "in attributing 'Son of David' to Jesus, that the eschatological expectations

---

47. Ladd, *Theology of the New Testament*, 142.
48. See Chilton, "Jesus ben David," 92–97; Duling, "Solomon," 235–252.
49. However, one can think that if it was not a title, it could apply to Solomon.

associated with David are being fulfilled in Jesus."[50] However, as it was discussed above regarding the insufficiency of Peter's confession of Jesus as the "Messiah" in Mark 8:29–30, Bartimaeus's confession of Jesus as the "Son of David" too is correct because it characterizes Jesus as the descendant of David (Mark 10:47–48; 11:9–10; see also Ps 110:1), but insufficient because it does not include Jesus's passion, even though he was on the way to Jerusalem to die a shameful death. Additionally, Mark's characterization of the Son of David is totally different from the first-century Jewish expectations for the title, and of *Psalms of Solomon* 17 which describes him as a warrior king who fights for Israel against their gentile enemies. Rather, Mark's Jesus is uniquely recognized and declared as the one who uses his unique supernatural authority to heal and save others.[51]

In the next section, the readers recognize that even though traditional Jews believed that the Messiah had to be a son of David as someone from the line of David's family, Jesus appears to be arguing that this makes no sense because the Scriptures describe David himself pointing to the Messiah as his "Lord" rather than his "son." Therefore, it is appropriate to discuss the concept of the title and its uniqueness related to Jesus as well as its unique significance in Mark 12:35–37.

3.3.3. Is Jesus Son of David or Lord of David? (Mark 12:35–37)

Having challenged the opposing authorities from various groups of religious parties (e.g. Pharisees 12:13–17; Sadducees 12:18–27; and scribes 12:28–34), Mark's Jesus takes the initiative and begins teaching people (the large crowd) on his messianic nature and identity since Mark's audience (Jews and early Christians)[52] as well as the scribes (the teachers of the law)

---

50. Kingsbury, *Christology*, 106.

51. It is also true that Mark utilized the OT sources to describe the title, Son of David, and reinterpreted it in the Son of David tradition unlike the militaristic and political aspect of the term. Moreover, it would be appropriate to consider an OT Davidic tradition being linked to God's mercy to his oppressed people which reminds the readers of something in the Davidic tradition that is more geared toward God's compassion (e.g. Isa 40:11; 61:1–3), especially if one takes into consideration the prophetic judgment on the kings not fulfilling their obligations as kings by taking care of and showing mercy to their subordinates (e.g. Ezek 34). See Mark 10:47–48, 52; see also Hahn, *Titles of Jesus*, 262–263.

52. The early church understands that Jesus who was the seed of David according to the flesh (Rom 1:3–4) is the lord of David in the Spirit (Mark 12:36) because he is ultimately

understood that the Messiah would come from David's family. Unlike some questions by religious leaders in the previous sections, in this episode Jesus asks them a question based on the Scriptures (Ps 110:1) in order to correct the view of the scribes about the Messiah. It reads:

> While Jesus was teaching in the temple, he said, "How can the scribes say that the Messiah is the son of David? David himself, by the Holy Spirit, declared, 'The Lord said to my Lord, "Sit at my right hand, until I put your enemies under your feet."' David himself calls him Lord; so how can he be his son?" And the large crowd was listening to him with delight. (Mark 12:35–37)

Regarding Jesus's identity related to Davidic Sonship in this episode, scholars understand and interpret it in various ways. For instance, some understand that Jesus completely refuted or denied the idea of his Davidic Sonship.[53] Others think that Jesus's Davidic Sonship was not totally rejected but of little or no value to Jesus's messianic identity, as well as to Mark's Christology.[54] The reason is that the same person in Psalms 110:1 who is quoted in Mark 12:36, cannot at the same time "be both David's lord and David's son, and, since the Psalm speaks so clearly of the Messiah as David's lord, David's Sonship must be excluded."[55] However, this is unlikely, because there was no ambiguity in the early Christian writings which clearly indicated the Davidic descent of the Messiah (Rom 1:3; additionally, see 2 Tim 2:8; Acts 2:24–36 and 13:22–37) as the fulfilment of the promise that God made to David in 2 Samuel 7:12–14. Furthermore, a careful reader understands that the same Jesus of Mark said nothing against this title (Son of David) when he was confessed by the blind Bartimaues in Mark 10:47 and acclaimed by the crowd as such (Mark 11:10). Rather, Jesus's temple-action in Mark 11 and following riddles in 12:35–37 clearly show Jesus's

---

the Son of God (Mark 1:1, 9–11; 3:11; 5:7; 9:7 and 15:39).

53. See Burger, *Jesus als Davidssohn*, 152–159, 64–70; Cullmann, *Christology of the New Testament*, 131–133; Nineham, *Gospel of St. Mark*, 330–331; Kelber, *Kingdom in Mark*, 95–96; Wrede, *Messianic Secret*, 168, 175.

54. Best, *Following Jesus*, 140; Meier, *Marginal Jew*, vol. 1, 240, fn. 55; Achtemeier, "And He Followed," 115, 130–131.

55. Wright, *Jesus and the Victory*, 509.

deep roots in the Davidic tradition. Moreover, the point of the question "so how can he be his son?" in verse 37 is not to reject the idea of Davidic Sonship or descent of Jesus Messiah but to emphasize "that a much higher view of his origin is necessary since David calls him 'lord.'"[56]

Therefore, it is possible to conclude that Jesus's question in Mark 12:35–37 quoted from Psalm 110:1,

> is closest to ancient catechetical riddles that can be traced back to medieval and even patristic times . . . This kind of riddle is based not on comparison, but on paradox. . . . Jesus's question does not imply that David's son *cannot be* David's lord, but it challenges the reader to resolve the paradox: David's son *can* be his master if he is the Messiah, who exceeds even his renowned ancestor in the destiny of Israel.[57]

In other words, I argue that Jesus did not reject his Davidic descent, by asking "how?" in verse 37, but he points to the Scriptures that spoke of his incomparable and supernatural origin, long ago, rather than a human descent. In addition, as noted above, since he did not repudiate his Davidic Sonship when he was declared as such, it is unlikely to think that he rejected it in Mark 12. Rather, Mark's readers know that Jesus himself declared that he is the one who was to fulfil the messianic promises of the OT (see Luke 4:21), and thus expanding it, because Jesus is not only the descendant of David, but also he is more than the "son of David" – as will be discussed below, he is the Son of God.

Bultmann and others also think that Jesus's Davidic Sonship is not genuine, but is a product of the early church's interpretation or invention.[58] Nevertheless, as indicated above, since in the early Christian writings, including Mark 10:47–48 and 11:9–10, Jesus is clearly acclaimed in this title as "son of David," Kingsbury is right in saying that "Mark is not at pains to discount or indeed to reject a Son-of-David Christology."[59] In addition, Cranfield correctly argues that "the unanimity of the early Christian

---

56. Taylor, *Person of Christ*, 492.

57. Beavis, "From the Margin," 32.

58. Bultmann, *Theology of the New Testament*, 28; Vermes, *Complete Dead Sea Scrolls*, 62–63, 189–190; Funk, *Gospel of Mark*, 187–188.

59. Kingsbury, *Christology*, 103; Bock, *Blasphemy and Exaltation*, 220–222.

tradition about Jesus' Davidic descent makes it most unlikely that this saying is the creation of the early Church."[60] In other words, it is impossible to think that the contradiction in this saying implies that the early church invented the idea of Jesus's Davidic lineage, since the early tradition clearly and widely supported this idea (Rom 1:3–4; 2 Tim 2:8; Acts 2:24–36; Matt 1:1). Furthermore, the Davidic Sonship of Jesus was mentioned by David himself in Psalm 110:1 and is used by Jesus himself in Mark 12:35–36. Thus, I conclude that the Davidic Sonship of Jesus was not the invention of the early church but rather Mark points to the Scripture which speaks of David himself who declared it by the Holy Spirit, since "Ps 110:1 was already part of a messianic narrative and was read messianically."[61] Therefore, the readers of Mark 12:35–37 are to discover "Jesus's use of Ps 110 and the title 'son of David' in the context of Jewish interpretation of eschatological deliverers and without having to resort to the *Sitz im Leben* of the early church, with its apologetics and Christological readings of Scripture."[62]

Ladd also argues that "a better interpretation is that Jesus is accusing the scribal experts of an inadequate understanding of the Messiah. He is indeed David's son; but this is not enough."[63] First, it is inadequate because in both cases, here and with Peter in Mark 8:29 declaring that Jesus is the Christ but not being able to understand his passion as the suffering Son of Man, according to Jewish messianic expectations it is difficult to believe that the Messiah must suffer. In addition, when Peter (and the disciples) declared that Jesus is the Christ or Messiah, Jesus did not reject it as though he was not the Messiah, but he implicitly accepted it and added that he must suffer many things (Mark 8:30–33). In other words, "to speak of Jesus' messiahship apart from his destiny as the Son of Man, therefore, is inadequate."[64] Likewise Bartimaeus in 10:47-47 correctly appealed to Jesus, the healer, as the Son of David in his royal messianic title, but the concept of the cross was not clearly there; and so "apart from the event(s) of the cross (and resurrection), however, one cannot 'think' about Jesus as God 'thinks' about him

---

60. Cranfield, *Gospel According to St Mark*, 381.
61. Horbury, *Jewish Messianism*, 34, 58, 96–97, 113.
62. Bird, *Are You the One*, 131.
63. Ladd, *Theology of the New Testament*, 142.
64. Matera, *New Testament Christology*, 17.

(1:11; 9:7; 8:31d), which is to say that one cannot penetrate the secret of his identity (15:39)."[65] Thus, it is possible to say that both the confessions of Peter in Mark 8 and of Bartimaeus in Mark 10 are correct but insufficient, for they do not clearly picture the full truth of Jesus's identity. In addition, the term "Son of David" is insufficient "not simply because it accorded too low a status to the exalted Jesus, but because its background made it misleading in a Jewish context and meaningless in a Gentile one."[66] Finally, the scribes (the teachers of the law) could not understand Jesus's real identity, for which reason Jesus raised a correcting question based on Psalm 110:1.

Second, it is true that in both stories Jesus is understood as, and acted as, the Messiah or Christ (Mark 8:20–30),[67] as someone from the royal family of David, the promised descendant of Israel's greatest king who was expected to fulfil contemporary Jewish hopes. However, Bartimaeus's appeal to Jesus to "have mercy on me" in Mark 10:47–48 must not be interpreted or understood in the political or militaristic terms of *Psalms of Solomon* 17–18, because he was not engaged in any militaristic or political affair for Israel against their gentile enemies, but rather he does something totally unexpected by healing others and dying for others as a ransom (Mark 10:45). Thus, "for Mark, there is something more mysterious about Jesus as son of David than was commonly thought (see 12:35–37)" because he is the lord of David according to the Scriptures in Psalm 110:1.[68] As the Son of David, Jewish people expected Jesus to fulfil his messianic role by demonstrating his power to his own benefit by destroying his enemies in order to save himself from his death, but unexpectedly, as the Son of God, he demonstrated his unique divine messianic authority by healing people from their afflictions; in doing so, saved others through his death on the cross (Mark 10:45; 15:31–39).

Moreover, third, it is important to see how Jesus himself redefines his messianic identity and role in terms of the divine Son of God and suffering

---

65. Kingsbury, *Christology*, 113.

66. Hooker, *According to St. Mark*, 292.

67. The reason for this is that the messianic role was, generally, linked to liberation and giving peace to Israel; however, Jesus avoided doing so, for he had a different agenda as the unique Messiah with a totally different mission: to suffer, die, raise again and, in doing so, to save many (Mark 8:30–31; 10:45).

68. Painter, *Mark's Gospel*, 151.

and vindicated Son of Man in both halves of Mark's gospel. Unlike the contemporary expectations of a warlike conquering king who was expected to defeat his enemies in a bloody battle, unexpectedly, Jesus was engaged in a battle different from the current military and political battle. In other words, a redefinition or reinterpretation of what Davidic Sonship means to be engaged in the real and redefined battle against the enemies of God and his people rather than gentile armies and their kings.[69]

In a nutshell, it is clear that Mark wanted his readers to know that Jesus is a descendant of David, and yet in doing so to discourage the popular messianic expectations of the day. Likewise, as the son of David, Mark's Jesus was not engaged in a physical battle to fight against human enemies of Israel but, as the Lord of David and Son of God, he fought and won the battle against the sins of many through his shameful death on the cross. Unexpected but far more glorious.

3.3.4. Conclusion

As discussed above, it is true that the traditional Jews and the early Christians (e.g. in Rom 1:3–4; 15:12; 2 Tim 2:8) including Mark's readers accept the Davidic descent of the Messiah (Mark 10:47–48; 11:10) because the OT clearly points to it. Nevertheless, even though they are experts of the law, the scribes[70] could not fully understand the message of Jesus's question in Mark 12:35–37 – "How can Jesus be both the son of David and the lord of David?" Or "how can David's Lord, at the same time, be his son?" However, the readers of Mark know that in this episode, Jesus's question, "so how?" in Mark 12:37, is not an indication of his rejection of his Davidic descent, because Mark clearly indicated that Jesus is the Son of David (e.g. Mark 10:47–48; 11:10), but it is to affirm that he must be much more.

The answer to this question, according to Kingsbury's careful investigation of Jesus's exegesis of Psalm 110:1, is that "the Messiah is the 'son' of David because he is descended from David; by the same token, the Messiah is also the 'lord' of David because, as the Son of God, he is of higher station

---

69. See Wright, *Jesus and the Victory*, 509.
70. The scribes, generally, know that the Messiah comes as the "Son of David" according to the prophecies of the OT as the "branch" of David (Jer 23:5–6; 33:15–16; Zech 3:8 and 6:12) or a "branch" from Jesse's stamp (Isa 11:1).

and authority than David."⁷¹ In other words, Mark's readers know that Jesus who identified himself with the marginalized and liminal people at different levels in various ways as the suffering Son of Man, is much more than the Son of David; he is the Lord of David, so the Son of God (1:1, 11; 9:7; 3:11; 5:7; 15:39). As indicated above in the exegetical section (ch. 2) of this work and will be elaborated in the next section, he is the unique Son of God who won the ultimate victory of God on the cross identifying himself with the poor and outcast, not only by visiting and healing them in public places and giving them temporal relief physically, emotionally and socially, but also by identifying himself with them on the cross while he was suffering and dying in the absence of God. He did so in order to liberate or save many, not only Israel, from their ultimate and true enemies namely, in my opinion, Satan and death.

Thus, the next section will seek to examine the idea of the title "the Son of God" in Mark's gospel because, as discussed above, "the titles 'messiah' and 'son of David' are inadequate to describe fully the significance of Jesus, who is also the powerful Son of God⁷² . . . who will be exalted in the resurrection."⁷³

3.4. The Son of God

3.4.1. Introduction

The phrase "the Son of God" is the most important title to understand the revelation of Jesus's divine identity in the Gospel of Mark. According to Mark, this title is the highest title which can be given to Jesus.⁷⁴ Nevertheless, Mark describes him not only as the divine Son of God due to his divine

---

71. Kingsbury, *Christology*, 112–113.

72. In other words, as will be discussed below, for the second evangelist, the "Son of God" is more important than the term "Messiah" because his divine Sonship is a ground for his election to his messianic office. It is true that Jesus's divine Sonship identifies him as a royal messianic figure. Furthermore, the divine affirmation of Jesus's divine Sonship in Mark 1:11 and 9:7 alludes to the Israelite king in Psalm 2:7 which is evidenced by Jesus' triumphal entry in Mark 11:1–11 and his anointing at Bethany in Mark 14:1–9. Thus, his divine Sonship is to be understood as God's messiah and king in a unique sense because "as God's Son, Jesus . . . will rule over not only the people of Israel but also the entire world" (Winn, "Son of God," 890; consult also Rogers "Unveiling Mark's High Christology," at http://www.answering-islam.org).

73. Beavis, *Mark*, 182.

74. See Feneberg, *Der Markusprolog*, 156; also Achtemeier, *Mark*, 44.

activities by liberating those who were marginalized and liminal, but also he presents him as the one who was revealed and declared as the suffering and vindicated messianic Son of God whose main purpose is to atone or to save the marginalized humanity through his unique death and glorious resurrection. To put it differently, from the very beginning to the end of his gospel, particularly at decisive points of his story, the second evangelist tells his readers that Jesus's real identity as the Son of God is revealed, understood and declared from various sources, expected and unexpected. For instance, first, Mark himself in 1:1; second, supernatural beings (e.g. God in Mark 1:9–11; 9:7, and demons in 1:24, 34, 3:11–12; 5:7); third, Jesus himself indirectly hinted it in 12:6 and at his trial 14:61; and finally, a human being (the gentile soldier) during Jesus's crucifixion in 15:39, acknowledged that Jesus is the Son of God.

Furthermore, as Bauckham states, "A purely functional account of Jesus' divinity in this Gospel [Mark] is not adequate; rather Mark shares with early Christian writers in general . . . a Christology of divine identity." Mark tells his readers about Jesus's divine identity as demonstrated not only through miraculous deeds and divine functions in his narrative (i.e. he forgives sin, thus judging on God's behalf), but he also points to the OT texts (e.g. Isa 40:3 and Mal 3:1–3) which are mentioned in Mark 1:2–3, to describe Jesus's divine messianic identity in scriptural terms.[75] In saying this, Bauckham means that to focus on a purely functional account is inadequate because it does not sufficiently focus on the question of what it means for God to be God. For him, the crucial question is one of identity which is revealed through Jesus's miracles and his suffering. This is his way of moving the discussion beyond the question of whether a given NT writer attributes to Jesus the function of deity. In other words, because they shared fully the monotheism of their Jewish contemporaries, the NT writers were not simply trying to show that Jesus was divine due to his divine activities or works of power, but rather to show that Jesus must be included within the divine identity of one God, since this identity was uniquely revealed and understood, ultimately, through his suffering and crucifixion.[76]

---

75. Bauckham, *God of Israel*, 264–265.
76. See Bauckham, x–xi.

Thus, it can be said, Mark wanted to define Jesus's divine identity as described in the Scriptures long ago, and "to show that Jesus fulfils the expectations of the prophets that God would one day come to his people for deliverance and judgment."[77] As noted earlier in the introduction of this work, in Mark 1:2–3, Mark shares with early Christian writers in those scriptural terms (e.g. Isa 40 and Mal 3) which would be fulfilled in John's ministry regarding Jesus's unique identity and in his uniquely divine name (YHWH), the name which refers "not to divine function, but to the unique identity. Jesus, according to Mark, participates in this unique identity of the God of Israel," and the title "Son of God" according to Mark, "indicates Jesus' unique relationship to God as one who participates in the divine identity."[78]

However, clearly the phrase the "Son of God" has a variety of meanings in the OT, in the religious writings of Judaism, as well as in the Roman traditions. It is true that it caused ambiguity in the minds of some people as they encountered this gospel, but this was not a problem for Mark since he wanted his readers to know Jesus as the divine "Son of God" in a unique sense.[79] For Mark, Jesus is the one who revealed himself and was declared to be the Son of God, from various sources, particularly by unexpected ones such as the poor and outcasts rather than the expected ones, even his first followers or disciples. The uniqueness of his divine identity was ultimately demonstrated on the cross where he died a shameful death for others, rather than that he did something miraculous for himself or for his family and friends.

Therefore, the next section will examine the idea of the phrase "Son of God" with several meanings in the OT, in the writings of first-century Judaism and the Gospels, in order to interpret it and determine the core concept of the phrase. In particular, some passages in which Mark mentioned the revelation of Jesus's unique divine Sonship to God (Mark 1:11; 9:7; 15:38–39) or Father-Son relationship (Mark 14:61–62) will be given special, though brief, attention. Finally, Jesus's divine Sonship in Mark and his unique self-identification with the marginalized and liminal people, to help and to save them, will be noted.

---

77. Thielman, *Theology of the New Testament*, 59.
78. Bauckham, *God of Israel*, 265.
79. See Gundry, *Mark*, 1.

3.4.2. Meaning of the Title "Son of God"

As indicated above, it is not only Jesus who is called the Son of God in the Gospels. This term has come to have several meanings as Bible students carry on studying the history and the significance of this expression in the OT and in the religious literature of Judaism and the Roman tradition. For instance, Adam was called the son of God in a similar sense that Seth was the son of Adam (Luke 3:38). Likewise, the Scriptures describe all Israel as God's son, his firstborn (Exod 4:22–23; Hos 11:1; Deut 14:1; Jer 3:19, 20; additionally, see *Psalms of Solomon* 18:4 in the first century BC and *4 Ezra* 6:58 in the first century AD). Angelic beings are also called "sons of God" in Genesis 6:2, 4; Job 1:6; 38:7; and Daniel 3:25.

The emperor or the king in the Roman tradition was described as the "son of a god."[80] Similarly, "[i]n the Egyptian royal ideology, the pharaoh was actually a god or divine. Furthermore, in Assyrian ideology, the king was adopted as the son of God."[81]

In summary, it is true that according to a couple of texts in the OT the king could be called God's son (e.g. 2 Sam 7:14; Ps 2:7), and it is also true that in an equally small number of texts from Jewish literature of the New Testament period, the royal Messiah, the expected son of David, is called Son of God, even though such texts are remarkably rare. They do not explain why Mark and other writers of the Synoptic Gospels give such prominence to the term "Son of God" applied to Jesus.

Therefore, as will be discussed later, due to these and other confusing reasons in Mark's day, the second evangelist was motivated to alert his readers to clearly know that in Jesus, God's Sonship is unique and exclusive beyond all other expressions of the term. Thus, it can be said that for Mark it is the most meaningful description of Jesus. It refers to no mere status or office, but as will be demonstrated below regarding the revelation of Jesus in Mark 1:10–11, it is a profound relationship with his divine Father.

3.4.3. Divine Man – θεῖοV ἀνήr – *Theos Aner*

Scholars of the Christology of the NT in the Gospel narratives, think that one of the major possible backgrounds for the "Son of God" Christology

---

80. See Hengel, *Son of God*, 21–24, 30.
81. Fuller, *Foundation of New Testament*, 31.

is the Greek concept of "divine man" (*Theios Aner*), because some of the divine functions of Jesus in the Gospels are similar, though not identical, to the activities of the divine men in Hellenism. So, Walter Liefeld discusses the awareness of students of the history of religion regarding "the similarity between certain aspects of the figure of Christ in the Gospel narratives and the Hellenistic portrayal of an apotheosized figure."[82] "These include extraordinarily gifted men, perhaps miracle workers and healers, who are grouped under the general designation of *Theios Aner*, or "divine man."[83] Kingsbury also explains the idea of the divine man as "a heroic figure of the past [who] could be regarded as a supernatural being endowed with divine wisdom and the divine power to perform miracles."[84]

Thus, on the one hand, some scholars think that there is no difference between the Jesus of the Synoptic Gospels and other miracle workers of Hellenism, precisely because both possess divine power and the ability to perform various sorts of miracles. In other words, it is a mark of some older scholarship on Mark to see the Gospels' portrait of Jesus as fitting into a common type known as a "divine man" (*Theios Aner*), a semi-divine figure such as an apotheosized hero or leader. For instance, having pointed out several examples of OT figures who were considered divine men, in ancient writings (e.g. Moses and others), Bieler describes the nature of the ancient Greco-Roman idea of "divine man" – *Theios Aner*.[85] For him, too, the divine man is the one who is considered to be superhuman in his person, with unique gifts, divine wisdom and the divine power to do miracles.[86] Similarly, while discussing his detailed study on the figure of the divine man, Hans D. Betz describes those who exalt themselves as though they had been showing the characteristics of *Theios Aner* in their practical lives as well as their activities.[87]

Bultmann also emphasizes the Hellenistic concept of the divine-man Christology as though it has a direct relationship to the idea of the "Son of God" in the Gospels; and so believes that the term "divine man" is central

---

82. Liefeld, "Hellenistic 'Divine Man,'" 195.
83. Liefeld, 195.
84. Kingsbury, "The 'Divine Man,'" 243.
85. Bieler, *Theios Aner*, 4–5, 113; see also, Kingsbury, *Christology*, 26–27.
86. See Bieler, *Theios Aner*, 73–97, 129, 141.
87. Betz, *Lukian von Samosata*, 100–143.

for Mark's Christology.[88] He also explains that during the Hellenistic period, there were a whole series of "divine men" who claimed to be such and were regarded as "sons of (a) god" and were also worshiped in the cult. Thus, he classifies the gospel materials in terms of Hellenistic literature. Hence, he says, "the Synoptic Gospels . . . picture Jesus as the Son of God who reveals his divine power and authority through his miracles."

Willi Marxsen is in total agreement with Bultmann's view of the Son of God in Mark with its relationship to divine-man Christology in Hellenism. However, Marxsen does not believe that the Gospel of Mark is to be read and understood in the Hellenistic churches of Paul, but it was written to help Galilean Christians to await the *parousia* of the risen Jesus.[89]

Moreover, according to Bultmann, it can be said that the Gospel of Mark was at home in the Hellenistic churches of Pauline persuasion; hence for him, there is no difference between the concepts of the Son of God (for the figure of Jesus) in Mark's gospel and in Pauline theology, except the idea of preexistence in Paul. In other words, it is appropriate to understand that he believes that Mark's Jesus is a divine man similar to the idea of Pauline theology in the sense of Hellenistic divine-man Christology.[90]

Finally, as discussed previously, for these scholars, the title "Son of God" in the Gospels has a Hellenistic origin in nature. Thus, the students of this subject can easily recognize that the idea of *Theios Aner* or divine man in Hellenism is all about exalted figures (such as wonder workers and heroes), including Mark's Jesus, due to their extraordinary gifts of power and ability to perform miracles. Put differently, according to these scholars, the concept of the figure of divine man in Hellenism and Jesus of the Gospels is reminiscent of the most exalted figures among others with especial gifts and ability of doing miracles. In contrast, Mark's readers clearly see that none of the *Theios Aner* figures of Hellenism were interested in helping the poor and marginalized as Mark's Jesus did.

One example of this is Apollonius of Tyana, of the first century AD, about whom Philostratus wrote. As referred by Talbert, in his *Life of Apollonius*

---

88. Bultmann, *Theology of the New Testament*, 130.

89. See Marxsen, *Mark the Evangelist*, 92–94.

90. See Bultmann, *Synoptic Tradition*, 347–348; see also Betz, "Jesus as Divine Man," 117–120.

of Tyana, Philostratus described Apollonius as a sage and miracle worker as well as a recognized divine man. Apollonius was considered a son or child of Zeus, or even godlike by the people, due to his miraculous deeds including raising a girl who seemed to be already dead.[91] But, Philosratus had never described Apollonius as either a son of Zeus or a son of God, other than pointing out that some people thought him to be a son of Zeus and so divine in the Greek sense, due to his goodness which showed him to be a "divine man with greater access to God than other men have."[92]

There are some points of similarity between the Jesus of the Gospels and Apollonius of Tyana. For example, both were known as miracle workers, exorcists, and healers, including raising the dead (e.g. while Apollonius was said to raise a young girl, Jesus raised a daughter of Jairus in Mark 5). They both were described as itinerary teachers or preachers who traveled from their original places to several countries with their own agendas. For example, whereas, according to Philostratus, Apollonius traveled from his home in Cappadocia to several places (e.g. Italy, Spain, Egypt, India and up the Nile River to Ethiopia),[93] Mark's Jesus of the Gospels traveled from Nazareth, his hometown to various regions in and around Palestine. They both attracted followers/disciples and communities to admire their deeds and ethical teachings that continued even after their deaths.

Nevertheless, unlike Jesus's community, the community of Apollonius was mainly based in Cappadocia and focused on the wealthy and well-educated (see Philostratus 8.31). Also, as noted earlier in the introductory section of this work, contrary to Apollonius's teaching, the main focus of Jesus's teaching and miracles were on a greater portion of the Roman population, many of whom were ordinary, uneducated, poor and destitute, including outcasts. In other words, while the movement of Apollonius targeted a small segment of the elite and wealthy of society, including those who had the ability to study philosophy, Jesus's focus was on the ordinary people who lived in the lower strata of society, many of whom had to work hard to support their families.

---

91. Talbert, "Concept of Immortals," 419–436. See Philostratus, 1.2, 21; 3.28, 39; 4.45; 5.24, 36; 8.15; also Bieler, *Theios Aner,* 7, 28.

92. Edwards, *Gospel According to Mark,* 69.

93. For further understanding, see Philostratus, 5.24, 37, 62; 6.11, 15

Unlike Apollonius's movement which lasted only until the late fourth century and remained stagnant in and around his home area, Cappadocia, the Jesus movement which began with himself continued to spread throughout many regions through his twelve disciples and the subsequent followers today.

Therefore, I argue that it is unlikely that Mark attempted to associate the Jesus of the Gospels with the divine man (men) of Hellenism because the title "Son of God" was not synonymous with "divine man," and was not common even in Hellenism. This interpretation is to be rejected largely due to its inadequacy to describe the unique divine nature of Jesus's Sonship to God, which ultimately involves his suffering and death as well as the performing of works of power.[94] Howard Marshall is correct in saying that "the use of *theios* with reference to men endowed with superhuman qualities appears to have no essential relationship to the concept of Son of God."[95] Likewise, having surveyed the use of the concept of "divine man" in Hellenistic literature, in connection with the "Son of God," some scholars rightly conclude that even though the adjective θεῖος is used frequently but the term θεῖοV ἀnhr was rare in occurrence (and is by no means a fixed concept but a fluid expression at least in the pre-Christian era). It is also true that there are no clear texts in the Gospels indicating that such divine people or individuals were usually considered to be "sons of gods."[96]

Furthermore, even though there are some points of similarity between the figure of Jesus in the Gospels and other revered figures, such as Hellenistic divine men, the most obvious point may now be made: nowhere do the Gospels, either in suggested sources or in the extant texts, contain the term, divine man "*Theios Aner*."[97] In addition, even though a concept of the divine man is all about the exceptionally gifted person having a higher, revelational wisdom and a divine power to perform miracles, he was not to be considered a deity but a mixture of the human and the divine, or a superhuman.[98] Thus the term, "divine man" is never applied to Jesus in the New Testament.

---

94. See Bauer, "Son of God," 770.
95. Marshall, "Son of Man," 3.636.
96. See Kingsbury, *Christology*, 33–35.
97. See Liefeld, "Hellenistic 'Divine Man,'" 204–205.
98. See Betz, "Jesus as Divine Man," 122–123.

Fuller is also right in arguing that the term "Son of God" is never used for the "divine man" concept in Hellenistic Judaism.[99] It is also concluded that neither emperor worship, the mystery religions, the Hellenistic "divine man" concept, nor Gnosticism can provide a basis for understanding the New Testament Son of God title.[100] Put differently, there is no evidence that relates the Jesus of the Gospels in a straightforward way to the divine man of Hellenism because Jesus is presented as the unique Son of God throughout the Gospels with a unique identity and purpose. His purpose is not to save himself from his death on the cross, but to save many others (Mark 10:45), particularly those who are marginalized and liminal rather than those who were considered exalted such as so-called divine men. Additionally, contrary to the idea of Hellenistic divine-man Christology, in Mark, Jesus's unique, divine Sonship is also recognized and declared by marginalized humanity while he was dying a shameful death on the cross Mark 15:39. Thus, one could argue that the uniqueness of Jesus according to Mark is highlighted by the (deliberate) use of a term ("Son of God") that had a general ring of familiarity, in conjunction with actions which completely subvert more general notion.

Further, pointing to the idea of Psalm 2:7 which reads, "You are my son; today I have begotten you," and to the western text of Acts 2:22 which reads, "Jesus of Nazareth, a man attested to you by God with deeds of power, wonders, and signs that God did through him among you," Bultmann argues that, according to Mark's story, "Jesus becomes the Son of God (that is, divine man) by the Spirit conferred upon him at the baptism."[101] Branscomb, also thinks that Jesus was appointed to be the Messiah, the Son of God at his baptism, and thus was installed in that messianic office.[102] In other words, these scholars interpret the terms "Son of God" during Jesus's baptism in terms of adoption Christology, as though Jesus became the Messiah or Son of God at his baptism.[103]

---

99. See Fuller, *Foundation of New Testament*, 69.

100. See Taylor, *Person of Christ*, 59–60.

101. Bultmann, *Theology of the New Testament*, 131; see also Wrede, *Messianic Secret*, 73–75; Hahn, *Titles of Jesus*, 342–345.

102. See Branscomb, *Gospel of Mark*, 16.

103. See also Bultmann, *Synoptic Tradition*, 247–248; Dibelius, *From Tradition to Gospel*, 271–272.

However, this is unlikely because instead of quoting Psalm 2:7 as the only text from the OT to describe Jesus's divine Sonship in Mark, a careful reader combines it with the prophetic words from Isaiah "Behold my servant, whom I uphold, my chosen, in whom my soul delights" (42:1) which identifies Jesus as the long awaited, promised messianic king and servant of Yahweh. In other words, Jesus's divine Sonship to God was a result of the scriptural prophecies being fulfilled in the Synoptic Gospels, not the occurrence of Jesus's adoption during Jesus's baptism. Moreover, even though the pericope (Mark 1:9–11) is entitled "the Baptism of Jesus," the baptism is mentioned simply in verse 9 while the rest of the story focused on what Jesus saw and heard immediately afterwards, which is the most important point of the pericope describing the revelation of Jesus's real identity as the divine Son of God.[104]

It is not just "You are my son" which is how God addresses the Messiah in Psalm 2, but the terms "You are my Son, the beloved" or "You are my beloved Son," in Mark 1:11 speak about the permanent messianic status of Jesus because it affirms what Jesus is, not what he has now become.[105] Similarly, as Mark's focus in introducing John the Baptist was about being, not becoming, Jesus's forerunner, so the focus of his attention in Mark 1:11 is to introduce who Jesus already is, not his becoming what he was not before.[106] Put simply, in Mark 1:1–13 both John the Baptist and Jesus receive a divine affirmation; the former was affirmed as the forerunner and the latter was affirmed as the Son of God. Thus, the readers recognize that Jesus's divine

---

104. See France, *Gospel of Mark*, 73.

105. See Ladd, *Theology of the New Testament*, 165; France, *Gospel of Mark*, 82.

106. See Kingsbury, *Christology*, 67. However, even though Jesus is described as the Son of God throughout the Gospel's narrative rather than as adopted during his baptism, the words "You are my son . . .," spoken at Jesus's baptism may be taken as evoking the wider context of those words in Psalm 2:7, especially the following clause "Today, I have begotten you." Psalm 2 describes the words of God to his anointed/appointed King, and these words in particular suggest that at the point of anointing/appointing (Today) the king is adopted as God's Son (since "begetting," with reference to God, is clearly metaphorical). The wording of the psalm suggests that at a specific point in time the person designated as king "became" God's Son. John's emphasis in his Christology of Christ's pre-existence highlights the character of the Synoptics' Christology in its description of Jesus being the Son of God, typically seen as a high Christology.

identity was affirmed, rather than God's supposed adoption of Jesus as the Son of God or of his being enthroned as the Son of God (Ps 2:7).[107]

The voice continues saying, "with you I am well pleased" in Mark 1:11. It fits the idea "on whom my good pleasure has settled." Thus, it is a clear allusion to another part of the prophesies of Isaiah which reads,

> Here is my servant, whom I uphold, my chosen, in whom my soul delights; I have put my spirit upon him; he will bring forth justice to the nations. (Isa 42:1)

This is all about the servant of the Lord, the Messiah, anointed with God's Spirit for a unique mission in his world history. Thus, the readers of Mark's narrative know that God's Spirit is continuously at work in all the activities of Jesus, on earth, because he is continuously in touch with his heavenly Father who uniquely loved him.

Further, as discussed below, similar to the only beloved son of Abraham in Genesis 22:1 and 16, it is rightly argued that there must be something in Mark's mind since his term "ἀγαπητός" in Mark 1:11 signifies "only" or "unique."[108] It also "can mean 'only,' as in 12:6, where the 'beloved' son must be an only son since he is the heir."[109] Mark's repetition of the words of the heavenly voice in Mark 1:11 and 9:7 obviously shows Mark's declaration of Jesus's unique Sonship already, rather than his adoption.[110]

Thus, instead of putting the words "the servant" in Isaiah 42 and "the Messiah" of Psalm 2, separately, as though opposing each other, combining both together "offers a suggestive basis for Mark's presentation of the paradox of a suffering, unrecognized Messiah."[111] It is worth noting that Jesus was affirmed or declared by the heavenly voice as the only uniquely beloved Son of God already. Likewise, he was dedicated to his messianic mission by identifying himself with the purpose of helping and saving those who are poor and outcast, and thus marginalized in the lowest scale of society. Bauckham also rightly argues that "Jesus cannot be said to be the Son

---

107. See also France, *Gospel of Mark*, 82; Stein, *Mark*, 58.
108. See Turner, "OUIOSMOUOAGAPHTOS," 113–129, 362.
109. Stein, *Mark*, 59.
110. See Hooker, *According to St. Mark*, 48.
111. France, *Gospel of Mark*, 81.

independently of his mission: the two are inseparable" for Jesus's being and his mission go together.[112]

As pointed out earlier, Weeden does not believe that Mark's Jesus is the divine Son of God, but rather he is the suffering Son of Man who dies and rises again. Contrary to Bultmann's view which sees *Theios Aner* as contributing positively to Mark's portrayal of Jesus, Weeden argues that Mark attempted to improve inaccurate views of Jesus among his readers who associated Jesus with a theology of glory, and to correct this with the "theology of the cross," emphasizing Jesus's suffering in the passion predictions in the second half of the gospel, particularly in Mark 8–10.[113] In other words, he thinks that, "the disciples, with their *Theios-Aner* Christology and *Theios Aner* lifestyle, reject Jesus's suffering, Son-of man Christology."[114] Mark therefore corrected a "divine man" (*Theios Aner*) Christology, with an emphasis on the Passion story (or the suffering of Jesus) in the second half of his gospel, and a Christology of power in weakness. According to Weeden, Mark vehemently rejects the *Theios Aner* tradition except for the purpose of utilizing these elements to correct the wrong understanding of the disciples regarding Jesus's real identity. Thus, he asserts that this "*Theios-Aner* position" was considered by Mark to be "an aberrant and insidious bastardization of the faith."[115] In other words, he opposes the Son of God Christology in the first half of Mark's gospel precisely because, for him, as briefly mentioned in the introductory section of this work, Mark's Jesus is the suffering Son of Man as described in the second part of the gospel.

So Weeden thinks that Mark emphasizes that "Jesus' role as a suffering servant was not only the central and most important element in his messiahship but was the role specifically ordained by God and the role by which he was finally accurately identified by man."[116] To put it differently, Weeden believes that the title "Son of God" in Mark's first section is a false Christology which was wrongly or erroneously understood by his disciples; so it must be understood in the light of another title, namely, "Son of Man."

---

112. Bacukham, "Sonship," 113.
113. Weeden, *Mark*, 147–149.
114. Weeden, 68.
115. Weeden, 147.
116. Weeden, 52–53.

Furthermore, for Weeden and his supporters, Jesus is not a Messiah of earthly glory, but of self-emptying, suffering love of God and humankind.

Similarly, Perrin argues that Mark's concern was to correct a false Christology under the title "Son of God," which was already established in his community but was insufficient to express his Christology, due to its divine-man associations, and instead to teach a true Christology under the title "Son of Man."[117] He agrees with Weeden that the second evangelist set out to "correct" an improper view of Jesus that existed among Mark's community. But to Perrin, "Mark's correction lay not in correcting inaccurate views of *theologiae gloriae* among Mark's readers, but how, in the narrative, Son of Man seemed to correct a less than satisfactory Son of God description."[118] As an example of this, Perrin also observes that "Peter confesses Jesus as the Christ but then exhibits a false understanding of the meaning of that confession, in all of which he is representing Mark's church"; and he also makes clear that "Mark uses Son of Man to correct and give content to a christological confession of Jesus as the Christ."[119] For him, Peter's confession of Jesus as the Christ was not only incorrect or inadequate, but demonic; thus a wrong understanding of the disciple which needed correction and so was replaced by Jesus himself by the true title, "Son of Man." Finally, Morrison correctly argues that both Weeden and Perrin "are less positive about the divine man concept as an acceptable category for Mark's presentation of Jesus. In fact their view has been reduced to the phrase 'Corrective Christology,' though the content of the correction is different for each."[120]

Kelber also agrees in principle with Perrin[121] and Weeden, but he believes that the false Christology that Mark emphasized and opposed as a Hellenistic "divine man" Christology, which regarded Jesus as a superhuman figure endowed with miraculous powers and supernatural knowledge,

---

117. See Perrin, "Christology of Mark," 108–121; also Telford, *Interpretation of Mark*, 129, see also Weeden, *Tradition in Conflict*, 68.

118. See Morrison, *Turning Point*, 242.

119. See Telford, *Interpretation of Mark*, 130.

120. Morrison, *Turning Point*, 242.

121. While Perrin thinks that Mark's purpose, in doing so, was to "teach the Christians of his day a true Christology in place of the false Christology that he felt they were in danger of accepting" (Perrin, *Modern Pilgrimage*), Kelber feels that the false Christology was already established in Mark's community (Kelber, *Mark's Story*; see also Amoss, *Introduction to the Christology*). For further information, consult http://www.qis.net/~daruma.mark-c.html

was already established among Mark's audience.¹²² For him, it had been the Christology of the prestigious church of Jerusalem which was destroyed by the Romans during the Jewish War in 70 CE, due to their failure to grasp the true nature of God's kingdom, thereby causing tragedy for the people of Jerusalem "whose Kingdom hopes had gone up in the flames of the temple conflagration." In addition, Mark's opponents may have represented an elitist type of Christianity, proud of its esoteric knowledge and miraculous powers and filled with the conceit of knowledge itself to constitute the elect.¹²³

So, the scholars mentioned above tend to think that this is the reason why Mark's Jesus wanted to use the title "Son of Man," as a corrective to the erroneous understanding of "Son of God." In other words, for them the title "Son of God" in Mark is not a proper title to describe Jesus's real identity precisely because it was an erroneous understanding of Jesus's disciples who believed that Jesus was a divine man. Plus, they think that Jesus did not employ it in a reference to himself, but rather he used the suffering "Son of Man" as the only adequate christological title (which was not suppressed as other titles) as his real and ultimate self-designation¹²⁴

For instance, they argue that when Peter confessed, "You are the Messiah" in Mark 8:29, Jesus's reaction was extremely powerful against Peter's idea, saying that the Son of Man must undergo suffering, and be rejected by the elders, chief priests, and scribes, be killed, and after three days rise again (v. 31). In saying this, they thought that Jesus rejected his divine messiahship which was confessed by Peter. However, as noted above, Jesus's response to Peter's confession "you are the Messiah" was not total rejection, but challenged the insufficiency of Peter's confession precisely because it did not include Jesus's destiny of suffering, death and resurrection; the very reasons for which he came to earth in order to save or atone for many who are marginalized in the absence of God.

Likewise, these scholars believe that when Jesus was addressed as the Messiah, the Son of the Blessed One [God] in 14:61, Jesus accepted it, interpreting it however, by means of a use of Son of Man. In other words,

---

122. Kelber, *Kingdom in Mark*, 138.

123. See also Kelber, 22, 135–137.

124. See Perrin, "Christology of Mark," 92–93, 112–113, Weeden, *Tradition in Conflict*, 65–67, see also Kingsbury, *Christology*, 31–32.

when he was asked "Are you the Messiah, the Son of the Blessed One?" Jesus's reaction to the question of the high priest was positive saying, "I am [God's Son]; and you will see the Son of Man sitting at the right hand of Power, and coming with the clouds of heaven" (v. 62),[125] but in doing so, they think that Jesus identified himself as the Son of Man rather than the Son of God. To put it simply, these scholars believe that Mark's Jesus spoke about both titles (the Christ and Son of God) for himself, and corrected them by using the Son of Man.

Nonetheless, similar to less explicit but still affirmative wordings in Matthew, Σὺ εἶπας ("You have said so") in 26:64, and Luke, Ὑμεῖς λέγετε ὅτι ἐγώ εἰμι ("You say that I am") in 22:70, Jesus's reply, Ἐγώ εἰμι ("I am") in Mark 14:62 is in the affirmative to the question of the high priest. For instance, when Judas asked Jesus "Surely not I, Rabbi?" concerning his plan to betray him, Jesus's answer was, "You have said so" in Matthew 26:64, which is similarly affirmative though seems more ambiguous than "Yes." Therefore, Jesus's answer to the high priest in Mark 14:62 must be taken as affirmative. The next statements, "you will see the Son of Man seated at the right hand of the Power," and "coming with the clouds of heaven" in 14:62, also indicate Jesus's unique Sonship as the fully divine and exalted one to whom victory and dominion belong (see also Dan 7:13; Ps 110:1). Thus, Ladd rightly argues that Jesus's view or claim on this issue is "far more than messiahship; it involved messiahship of an exalted Son of Mankind." In other words, Ladd goes on to explain that Jesus, who was standing before their court to be judged by the Sanhedrin or high priest, will one day, as the vindicated Son of Man, come and judge the world (Mark 14:62), because he is the one who "claimed the prerogative of final judgment, a function that belongs to God alone."[126] Thus, Jesus is to be understood as the unique Messiah who is sitting at the right hand of God, who is equal to God, and who holds the final destiny of the whole universe as the deliverer and Judge of all human beings (see also Mark 8:38).

In conclusion, however, as noted above, even though the concept of the divine man of Hellenism and the Jesus of the Gospels has similarities in some

---

125. See Telford, *Interpretation of Mark*, 128–129.
126. Ladd, *Theology of the New Testament*, 168.

superficial ways, the second evangelist does not indicate any clear evidence to his readers to understand the title "the Son of Man" in the passion story (in the second half of Mark's gospel) as correcting the title "Son of God" in the first half.[127] In short, it is rightly argued that there is no evidence which tells us that Mark's Jesus was ever proclaimed clearly as a miracle worker or "divine man."[128]

Instead, readers are to "read Mark's gospel as a unified message that makes sense of both miracle and passion as interwoven strands of Jesus' mission."[129] Put simply, it is unlikely that Mark attempted to split his gospel into two sections, with the first half of the gospel all about Jesus the divine man and a wonder worker, and the second half about Jesus the suffering Son of Man (a human being). It is true, rather, that the Gospel of Mark is a unified work of an evangelist telling his readers that Jesus is the Royal Messiah and divine Son of God as recognized and declared to be so by God, by demons and even by unexpected individuals in the narrative. Either title ("Son of God" or "Son of Man") is not superior to the other but both work together for the purpose of making clear the real and full identity of Jesus as the glorious Son of God, and the suffering and vindicated Son of Man, whose unique and true identity was ultimately revealed, recognized and proclaimed in an unexpected manner, (particularly Jesus's death on the cross), and by unexpected people who were marginalized and liminal. Thus, it is important to briefly note what the Gospels, rather than any other sources, say about Jesus the Son of God.

3.4.4. "Son of God" in the Gospels

Several scholars have claimed that Jesus never claimed the title "Son of God" for himself. For example, Wolfhart Pannenberg believes that "the Pre-Easter Jesus neither designated himself as Messiah (or Son of God) nor accepted such confession of him from others."[130] He also goes on explaining that Jesus's claim to act with the authority of God does not mean that he

---

127. See Kingsbury, *Christology*, 44.
128. See Moule, *Origin of Christology*, 147.
129. Henderson, *Christology and Discipleship*, 10–11.
130. Pannenberg, *Jesus – God and Man*, 327.

understood himself either as Messiah or Son of God; instead his consciousness of unity with God expressed itself indirectly – in his activity.[131]

Nevertheless, those who received Mark's gospel knew that Jesus was acknowledged as the Son of God on various occasions. For instance, as mentioned above and will be discussed briefly below, Mark, from the very beginning makes it clear that Jesus is the Son of God (Mark 1:1). Jesus was also understood and proclaimed as the Son of God by God himself from heaven at his baptism (Mark 1:11) and at the transfiguration (Mark 9:7). Demons, the supernatural beings, too, recognized and hailed him to be the Son of God due to his supernatural power over them (Mark 3:11; 5:7). Matthew 16:16 understands Peter's confession of Jesus to be the Messiah not simply in the common sense of the first-century messiahship but in a unique sense, by divine revelation as the Messiah, Son of God. In addition, Matthew mentions the term "Son of God" on various occasions (e.g. Matt 14:33; 27:40; 27:43). Also, "places where Matthew adds the phrase do not change but only accentuate this tradition."[132] Therefore, Fuller is correct in arguing that "Jesus did not 'claim' to be the Son of God, or directly call himself such, but he did know that he stood in a unique relationship of Sonship to God."[133]

In other words, as noted above, it is true that in the Synoptic Gospels the title "Son of God" was not directly used by Jesus as the title by which he designated himself but rather he refers to himself, obliquely, as the "Son" which relates Jesus closely to God the Father in a unique sense (e.g. Mark 12:6; 13:32; Matt 11:27; 28:19; Luke 10:22). In these episodes, Jesus more significantly called God "my Father" not only in speaking like "the Son" but also in acting as the "Son" through his divine knowledge, supernatural revelation and forgiveness of sins (Mark 2), as well as in acting with total obedience as the agent of God's kingdom. Jesus also addresses God as "Abba" to indicate his unique relationship to him as his Father. Therefore, it will be appropriate to briefly discuss below the unique relationship between Jesus as "the Son" and God as "the Father or Abba" in the Gospels, particularly in Mark.

---

131. See Pannenberg, 327–328.
132. Ladd, *Theology of the New Testament*, 162.
133. Fuller, *Mission and Achievement*, 84.

3.4.5. Jesus as the Son

One of the two titles in the Synoptic Gospels that Jesus explicitly used of himself is "the Son" (the other is "the Son of Man"). Jesus's designation of himself as the "Son" is very important in understanding Jesus's divine identity as the Son of God, because he identified himself as Son, and he identified God as his Father, and God addressed him as "my beloved Son" (Mark 1:11; 9:7).

Regarding this title (Son), some people have different views. For instance, Pannenberg thinks that Jesus may not have spoken of himself as Son, but the Palestinian community created this idea precisely because Jesus had spoken of God as his Father. Furthermore, Pannenberg interprets the relationship of Jesus as Son to the Father in terms of obedience.[134] In a similar vein, Gunther Bornkamm believes that the title or name "Son" came to us as a result of the creative Christology of the primitive church.[135] Jeremias also thinks that the term "the son" in Mark 13:32 was not a designation for the Messiah in Palestine, hence it could have arisen only in Hellenistic society; thus, he thinks that the phrase "nor the son" in Mark 13:32 is an addition and not authentic. Nonetheless, since he believes that "the Father" is equivalent to Aramaic "Abba," it must be original.[136]

However, the readers of Mark's gospel are to understand Jesus's unique Sonship in his unique relationship to God, his Father (Mark 12:1–12; 13:32). So, Moule rightly argues that the idea of Jesus's unique divine Sonship goes back to Jesus himself.[137]

For instance, Jesus publicly and openly accepted the full title "Son of God" for himself at his trial, while claiming special association with God, highlighted by a resulting charge of blasphemy (see Mark 14:61–64). As Anthony Rogers said, "'Son' is not a messianic title, but is to be understood in the highest sense, transcending messiahship,"[138] Jesus is not simply the Messiah but the Son (of God). As the Son he has a unique relationship to the Father. Therefore, it can be said that the three Synoptic evangelists

---

134. See Pannenberg *Jesus: God and Man*, 158–159.
135. See Bornkamm, *Jesus von Nazareth*, 226.
136. See Jeremias, *Prayers of Jesus*, 37.
137. See Moule, *Origin of Christology*, 30–31; see also Mark 14:61–62.
138. See Rogers, *Unveiling Mark's High Christology*.

(Matthew, Mark and Luke) each affirm that Jesus is the divine Son (of God) rather than merely the Messiah; in other words, his divine Sonship is a basis for all his divine functions.[139]

Nevertheless, Hahn thinks that the absolute title "the Son," which is mentioned in the Synoptics, derives from Jesus's use of "Abba," for God, which is rooted in the OT messianic tradition in 2 Sam 7:14. In other words, Hahn tries to distinguish between the titles "the Son" and "the Son of God" because, for him, there is "no clear reference to the designation of God as Father in any place where the title 'Son of God' is used."[140] Van Iersel criticizes Hahn, suggesting that the title Son of God itself is probably derived from "the Son."[141] For Walter Grundmann, "the Son" is the oldest Christological or theological title which is developed separately into the designations Son of Man and Son of God.[142]

However, there is no evidence that the Synoptic evangelists held these titles in tension (giving prominence to the one title over the other). In other words, trying to distinguish between these titles or giving priority to one title against another is an unnecessary matter since the NT writers use both titles interchangeably and thus both should be taken as equivalent. For example, Mark mentions "the Son" in Mark 13:32. Also he does it in the same sense and with the same significance or purpose elsewhere with "the Son of God."[143] James Edwards also rightly concludes that both "the Son" and "the Son of God" relate the same idea: the unique filial relationship of Jesus to God.[144] Finally, it is appropriate to argue that Jesus's divine Sonship to God "has deliberately been based on the evidence of his use of Abba and not on an explicit saying about his Sonship."[145]

3.4.6. God as Abba as Father

The term "Abba" in the Gospels, is used by Jesus as his typical address to God as his Father in a unique sense (e.g. Mark 14:36). He never referred to God

---

139. See Schreiner, *New Testament Theology*, 239–240.
140. Hahn, *Titles of Jesus*, 279–280, 313.
141. See Van Iersel, *Reading Mark*, 180–181, 185–191.
142. See Grundmann, "Χριστός," 46.
143. See also Marshall, *The Origins of New Testament*, 88.
144. See Edwards, "Son of God," 109.
145. Bauckham, "Sonship," 107–108.

as the Father, of either Israel as a nation or Israelites as many individuals, but as his Father ("my Father"). This clearly indicates that the Father-Son relationship between God and Jesus is unique and unparalleled with anyone else precisely because the term Αββα ὁ πατήρ is found only on Jesus's lips during his prayers (e.g. Mark 14:36; Luke 23:34, 46; John 11:41; 12:27–28). Therefore, Jesus's use of Abba in addressing God as his Father clearly "reveals the heart of his relationship with God."[146] Further, Jesus does not include anyone else with himself in calling God "our Father." He mentions the term "your Father" in Matt 6:9 to indicate God's Fatherhood to his first followers through him (Jesus himself); so it is true that Jesus "was the unique Son through whom the eschatological gift of Sonship was bestowed on others." As Bauckham goes on to affirm "it was Jesus' own relationship to God as Abba which he shared with his disciples: their Sonship derived from his own."[147]

Moreover, according to Jeremias, the term "Abba" in reference to God does not appear in ancient Judaism, nor in "rabbinic literature which corresponds to this use of 'my Father' by Jesus."[148] Thus, the readers are to learn that Jesus's Sonship to God is unique and exclusive to Jesus alone. Further, Jesus's claim to "unique Sonship cannot be separated from his path to the cross, nor from his resurrection as the Father's seal of approval on the accomplishment of the filial mission."[149] Therefore, it is important to note, briefly, that according to Mark Jesus's Sonship to God was a divine revelation.

3.4.7. The Revelation of Jesus in Mark's Gospel

Mark in particular narrates three key revelatory moments in which Jesus's divine Sonship to God was clearly declared by God the Father and by a human being. The first of these events comes in the vision that Jesus received during his baptism near the beginning of Mark's Gospel (Mark 1:11). Then again at the mid-point of the story (9:7) at the transfiguration of Jesus on the mountain top, the Father repeats his declaration about his Son. The last of these revelatory events, the tearing of the veil of the temple and the

---

146. See Jeremias, *Prayers of Jesus*, 62.
147. Bauckham, "Sonship," 107.
148. Jeremias, *Prayers of Jesus*, 53, 57; see also Michael, "The Son of Man," 639.
149. Evans, *Historical Jesus*, 113.

confession of the gentile centurion occurred at the time of Jesus's death in the near end of the Gospel (Mark 15:38–39).

These events are revelations about Jesus's unique Sonship of God. In two of these events the readers understand that the voice is that of God the Father, saying that Jesus is indeed his uniquely beloved Son. In the final passage (15:38–39) it is a gentile centurion who declared Jesus to be God's Son at the cross. Thus, it is appropriate to briefly discuss three of these revelatory events in Mark's story.

Mark's readers knew that God the Father declared that Jesus was his uniquely beloved Son during his baptism. It reads,

> In those days Jesus came from Nazareth of Galilee and was baptized by John in the Jordan. ¹⁰And just as he was coming up out of the water, he saw the heavens torn apart and the Spirit descending like a dove on him. ¹¹And a voice came from heaven, "You are my beloved Son; with you I am well pleased." (Mark 1:9–11)

Meier pointed out that "Behind agapētos ["ἀγαπητός"] in this text may lie the Hebrew 'yahid'."[150] The Hebrew word strictly means "only," "only one." But in a context of family relationships, when applied, e.g. to a son, it may mean "only beloved" or "uniquely beloved."[151] In other words, the word beloved or ἀγαπητός, when used of a son (or a daughter) often had the sense of "the only child," the child who is especially loved precisely because he or she is the only son or daughter. For instance, when Abraham was requested to sacrifice his son Isaac, the Hebrew calls Isaac Abraham's only son, but this is translated, in the Greek version of the Old Testament by "ἀγαπητός," beloved. Further, Meier goes on to say, "in the LXX, in every instance where yahid in the Hebrew text is translated by agapētos, it is used of an 'only' or 'only beloved' son or daughter who has died or who is destined for death such as Isaac in Genesis 22:2. 12. 16 and Jephthah's daughter in Judges 11:34."[152] Put another way, in the Hebrew God says to Abraham, "Take your son, your only son, whom you love." In the Greek

---

150. Meier, *Marginal Jew*, vol. 2, 188–189.
151. See Rogers, *Unveiling Mark's High Christology*.
152. Meier, *Marginal Jew*, vol. 2, 188–189.

this becomes "Take your beloved son, whom you love." Something similar happens in the story of Jephthah's daughter, which is also a case of a father being obliged to sacrifice a beloved daughter. The Hebrew simply says that she was Jephthah's only child, but the Greek version says she was his "only child, very dear (ἀγαπητός) to him." The Greek translator wanted to express the two aspects of the Hebrew word – indicating both an only as well as a beloved child. In this sense, Jesus's God's Sonship does not indicate merely his messianic status or his messianic office but his profoundly unique relationship to his divine Father.

Thus, it is possible to argue that the heavenly voice in Mark's story declares Jesus to be God's only and beloved son. If other humans or angels might be called sons of God for various reasons, Jesus is singled out as son in a unique sense, his father's only son, and moreover dear to his father. Further, one can understand that God did not say "my beloved son" to any of the others either in the OT or in Judaism except Jesus, because in Mark's Greek, the adjective "ἀγαπητός" reveals that God has identified Jesus as his "only" or "unique" beloved Son.[153]

Second, contrary to other "son (sons) of God or gods" in the midpoint of Mark's story, at Jesus's transfiguration God self-announced that Jesus is his uniquely beloved Son, who must be listened to or obeyed. The passage reads,

> Six days later, Jesus took with him Peter and James and John, and led them up a high mountain apart, by themselves. And he was transfigured before them, ³and his clothes became dazzling white,⁴And there appeared to them Elijah with Moses, who were talking with Jesus.⁷Then a cloud overshadowed them, and from the cloud there came a voice, "This is my beloved Son; listen to him!" (Mark 9:4–8)

Before this happened, in the previous chapters of Mark, the readers hear that Jesus has healed the sick and cast out demons, he has forgiven sins, and stilled a storm, he walked on the water and has miraculously fed crowds of people. And on the basis of all this evidence, when Jesus asked his disciples who they think he is, Peter, speaking for all the disciples, said: you are the Messiah, understanding that Jesus is the expected king of Israel (Mark 8:27–30).

---

153. See Turner, "OUIOSMOUOAGAPHTOS," 113–129, 362.

Immediately Jesus begins to explain to the disciples that he is going to suffer and be rejected by the Jewish authorities and put to death before rising from the dead. With this new teaching of Jesus, Peter was confused because this was not what he thought should happen to the expected Messiah of Israel.

When one comes to the story of transfiguration, Jesus took three of his first followers (Peter, John and James) with him up a high mountain, where they were given an extraordinary experience. Then Jesus appeared with two great prophets (Moses and Elijah), of Israel's history in the OT. In this story, Peter suggested making three temporary dwellings, one for each of them. In doing so, he categorized three of them (Moses, Elijah and Jesus) on a great and equally glorious level, thinking that these three were the three great figures of the messianic age. Mark's readers know that Peter had already recognized Jesus to be the anointed king, the Messiah (Mark 8:29) and Elijah as the high priest of the renewed Israel. Moses, then, the greatest of the prophets, would be the prophet in this ideally reconstituted Israel. So, Peter makes his poor suggestion of honouring each of them with some sort of tent.

Nevertheless, the point here is that God corrected Peter not to level Jesus, his Son in the same category as Moses and Elijah, but decisively distinguished him from them. Put differently, Peter's thoughts are sharply contradicted by the divine voice. Ignoring Moses and Elijah, God specifies Jesus as his beloved son: "*This* is my beloved son" confirming what he had already said to Jesus at his baptism but now reveals to the three disciples. Thus, this singles out Jesus as unique, unlike the equally great heroes in Israel's history like Moses and Elijah since "Moses and Elijah are God's servants; Jesus is God's beloved Son (Mark 12:6)" . . . [and] "the good news centers on Jesus Christ, the Son of God, not Moses or Elijah."[154]

Moreover, for Mark "Son of God" means much more than the Messiah since many people (e.g. Peter and the twelve disciples) recognized and confessed, as well as the crowd considered him to be the Messiah, hailing his entry into Jerusalem precisely because Mark's Jesus is God's unique and uniquely beloved Son. When the three disciples look around, they see that

---

154. Stein, *Mark*, 418–419.

Moses and Elijah had disappeared, or were taken up in the overshadowing cloud, but Jesus is still there with them. He is the one to whom they should listen.

Third, as indicated above, the last event of revelation is the moment of Jesus's death on the cross. This time Jesus is declared God's Son, but not by God, but by a human being (a gentile centurion) who saw Jesus die. The centurion did not speak his remarkable insight for anyone at that time and place to hear, but it was a revelation to all the readers of Mark's narrative. The readers are meant to see that Jesus is truly the Son of God in his death, in the extreme point of his following of his Father's will for the salvation of the world through him.

Thus, it is appropriate to argue that the declaration, "Truly this man was God's Son," is made by a Gentile, the Roman centurion (not necessarily Roman by nationality, but certainly Gentile). It happened at the cross because he was in charge of the group of soldiers who had crucified Jesus and stayed there to see the job properly finished. Even though it was not possible to know precisely what led him to this conclusion, Mark recorded that Jesus's way of dying led the gentile centurion to this understanding. It is significant that this declaration was made by a Gentile. His words are ambiguous in the Greek – which literally says "Truly this man was son of God." He could be saying "this man was a son of God" or "this man was the Son of God." The former would be more plausible in the mouth of a pagan Gentile though clearly the latter is what the Gospel has taught readers to think Jesus is, the absolutely unique son of his divine Father. Perhaps Mark intended the ambiguity. The centurion meant as much as he could have understood within his non-monotheistic worldview, but the readers can see that he says more than he meant, the appropriate final revelation of Jesus's unique divine Sonship in Mark's story.[155]

In addition, demons, who are supernatural beings also, unexpectedly, declared that Jesus was the Son of God (Mark 1:24; 3:11–12, 5:7). Therefore, it can be said that Jesus's unique relationship to God, as his unique Son, is clear throughout Mark's narrative. Furthermore, a careful reader of this Gospel knows that while Jesus is the uniquely beloved Son of God with unique

---

155. See Edwards, *Gospel According to Mark*, 479–480; see also France, *Gospel of Mark*, 659–660.

power and supreme authority, recognized as such by supernatural beings (e.g. God his divine Father and demons), he identified himself with those who are marginalized at the lowest social level, to help and liberate them.

Further, Jesus's divine Sonship or God-like divine actions were demonstrated, in Mark's Gospel, when he forgave the sin of the paralytic in Mark 2:5, and when he calmed the raging storm in (Mark 4:41) and controlled nature (Mark 6:45–52), which is the business of Yahweh alone (see Ps 65:7; 89:9; 107:28–30). Mark tells his readers that Jesus is not simply the Son of God in the religious sense of the day but he is the unique messianic Son of God who is able to share the very nature of God, yet at the same time, identify himself with the poor and outcast. As rightly said, "he is not the Son of God because he does certain things; he does certain things because he is the Son of God."[156]

Finally, the readers of the second evangelist know that, in Mark, if part of what it means for God to be God is that he identifies with the outcast, the poor, and the lonely, then Jesus's crucifixion shows us a surprising truth about the Messiah; crucifixion shows us what it means for God to be God. In addition, it is important because it helps explain why for the NT writers crucifixion is not held in tension with Jesus's deity ("Jesus was crucified even though he was God"), but is the demonstration of his deity ("Jesus was crucified and this shows that he was God"). In other words, Mark's Jesus suffers precisely as the Son of God and, in doing so, reveals something about what it means to be God; the cross shows us that suffering is not simply something that God requires of others – it is something he does for others.

As mentioned above, it is also true that in Mark's Gospel, episodes of Jesus's divine functions such as forgiving the sin of the paralytic in ch.2, his calming the storm in ch.6, and judging on God's behalf in Mark 13; Mark 14:62, all point to Jesus's divine identity, but the question is not fully answered in the Centurion's mind until he "saw how Jesus died" (Mark 15:39). Thus, the readers can conclude that the divine identity of Jesus as the divine Son of God is ultimately "revealed not only in his deeds of divine

---

156. Stein, *Mark*, 58.

authority, nor merely in his coming participation in God's cosmic rule, but also in his godforsaken death."[157]

3.4.8. Conclusion

As discussed above, some scholars have attempted to view Jesus as a typical Hellenistic divine man or wonder-worker, and others as a merely suffering Son of Man who revealed his power in weakness. However, since Jesus did not fulfil the contemporary expectations of the people in miraculous ways, I argue that it is impossible to think that Jesus accepted this "divine man" type role of the Son of God.[158]

Rather, the readers of the second evangelist know that Jesus is the Son of God in a unique and exclusive sense in which no other human being can be identified, precisely because, for instance, God does not say "my beloved Son" to anyone in the gospels (including so-called Hellenistic divine men) except Jesus, (see Mark 1:11), who is worthy of obedience (Mark 9:7). Likewise, nobody either in the OT or in contemporary Judaism addressed God as "Abba" or "my Father" except Jesus (e.g. Mark 14:36).

Furthermore, it is not simply due to his works of power or miracles, or even his divine functions as noted above, but Mark's main concern was to make clear the relationship between Jesus's divine Sonship and his unique death.[159] In other words, the secret of Jesus's unique identity which began to be disclosed at his trial in 14:61–62 (even though the Sanhedrin thought that it was blasphemy in Mark 14:64), was fully revealed and declared at his death. Therefore, the readers understand that Mark's Jesus was acclaimed as the divine messianic Son of God in unexpected ways and the vindicated Son of Man, yet associating himself with those who are sick, poor and lowly in Mark's first half. He also ultimately identified himself with marginalized humanity in the absence of God in Mark's second half; not so much in political or religious arenas doing miracles but in particular through his shameful death on the cross (Mark 15:33–39).

---

157. Bauckham, *God of Israel*, 266.
158. See Ladd, *Theology of the New Testament*, 162–163.
159. See Dunn, *Christology in the Making*; see also Mark 15:39.

3.5. The Son of Man

3.5.1. Introduction

The title "Son of Man" is the favorite self-designation of Jesus among all the titles in the Gospels and is one of the most important titles of Jesus in the Synoptic Gospels. The Synoptic Evangelists placed this title exclusively and solely on the lips of Jesus sixty-nine times, of which fourteen are found in Mark's gospel and thirteen times in John. Nobody in the Gospels addressed Jesus with this title except when the crowd echoed Jesus's own words in John 12:34. Jesus had just used this title when referring to himself in verse 23. In a similar way the angel repeated Jesus's own word in Luke 24:7. Apart from the Gospels, the term appears four times, in the vision of Stephen in Acts 7:56;[160] Hebrews 2:6 cf. Psalm 8:5; Revelation 1:13 and 14:14; Daniel 7:13, but only Acts 7:56 is used as a title for Jesus.[161]

The origin and meaning of this expression is controversial; and its interpretation in New Testament scholarship has been debated by New Testament scholars over many years, and a satisfactory agreement has yet to emerge.

Therefore, it would be appropriate first to investigate and discuss the background of this title, "Son of Man" in the OT, in Jewish Apocalyptic literature and in the Synoptic Gospels. In Mark's gospel we see Jesus who is the glorious Son of God identifying himself with humanity from the very beginning, particularly with those who are in a great need in various ways.

The subsequent section attempts to answer some specific questions. Which sources lie behind this enigmatic phrase, "Son of Man"? How and why did Jesus use this title? What concept and significance did this title have for the people during Jesus's life time? Finally, in the Son of Man sayings in the Gospels, particularly in Mark, what did Mark intend to say to his hearers and readers?

---

160. It is believed that the writer of Acts is also the writer of Luke, hence refers to "the Son of Man" as reference to Jesus's glory in heaven due to his previous ascension to sit at God's Right hand (see Luke 24:51).

161. See Stein, *Mark*, 135–136.

3.5.2. The Background of "Son of Man"

The term "Son of Man" is found in both the canon of the Hebrew Bible (Old Testament) and the New Testament as the translation of Hebrew phrase; nevertheless, biblical scholars find it difficult to determine the exact source, meaning and the proper usage of the phrase. In its most fundamental sense, it simply refers to human beings or humankind in Judaism. Its Hebrew expression *ben-'adam* refers to a particular person or simply human being (e.g. Ezek 2:1) or to humankind in general (e.g. Ps 8:4). Similarly, in the Greek New Testament, ὁ υἱὸς ἀνθρώπου or "the Son of Man" is a literal Greek translation of the Aramaic *bar nasha*, or more likely *bar enasha* that "could be used to mean 'the man,' 'a man,' 'somebody' or 'humankind in general . . . [which] simply means an individual member of the group, . . . and we should understand that the figure seen in Daniel 7:13 was 'one like a man' or 'a human figure.'"[162]

3.5.2.1. The Son of Man in the Old Testament

The most clear source or origin for "the Son of Man" expression is the Old Testament. As we have seen it is a common idiom in the Hebrew Bible (OT) pointing to the idea of humanity. In this regard, for instance, the book of Ezekiel comes to the minds of Bible readers. In Ezekiel, the phrase "son of man" occurs 93 times addressed by God to the prophet, not by his own name but as *ben adam*, "as an individual creature drawn from the genus man and contrasted with God";[163] hence some interpreters believe that the background for Jesus's usage in the Gospels is in Ezekiel.[164] However, Ladd rightly argues that this is unlikely for it does not "explain the eschatological use of 'Son of Man' in the Gospels" because for some scholars its usage in Ezekiel (cf. Dan 8:17) indicates only Ezekiel's (man's) weakness apart from God's help to accomplish the prophetic task."[165] Nevertheless, it is possible to argue that regardless of this expression in Ezekiel, it is appropriate to make

---

162. Marshall, *Origins of New Testament*, 64.
163. Michael, "The Son of Man," 613.
164. See Richardson, *Theology of the NT*, 20; Sidebottom, *Christ of the Fourth*, 71–78.
165. Ladd, *Theology of the New Testament*, 146. See also Stalker, "Son of Man," 2829.

the general conclusion that it expressed a real identification of the term "son of man" with humankind.[166]

Likewise, Psalm 8:4 reads:

> What are human beings that you are mindful of them, mortals that you care for them?

Does the Psalmist use the phrase "son of man'" as a Hebrew parallelism to just mean the same as "man" (i.e. humankind)? Referring to Christ's humiliation as an essential counterpart to his exaltation in Hebrews 2:9, the writer of Hebrews quotes Psalms 8:4–6 in Hebrews 2:6–8 which reads:

> What are human beings that you are mindful of them, or mortals, that you care for them? You have made them for a little while lower than angels; you have crowned them with glory and honour, subjecting all things under their feet.

In other words, it is possible to suggest that in quoting Psalm 8:4–6, the author of Hebrews has an ample ground to interpret this term (son of man) within the messianic motif. Furthermore, the "man" in Psalm 80:17 could be interpreted as the king.[167] Similarly, regarding this, Stalker suggests that "this is an appeal in an age of national decline, for the rising of a hero to redeem Israel; and it might well have kindled the spark of messianic consciousness in the heart of Jesus."[168] Nevertheless, Stein argues that "there is general agreement, however, that the use of the title in the Gospels is not derived from its usage in Psalms or Ezekiel."[169] In addition, C. H. Dodd argues that although there is something in the minds of early Christians that reminds them of the concept of this phrase in the book Ezekiel, there is no clear evidence in the New Testament; thus, Ezekiel cannot be a primary source of testimonies.[170]

Rather, the most probable occurrence of the term "Son of Man" in the Old Testament is found in Daniel 7:13–14 which is the Aramaic section of the book of Daniel. In its original use an expression, "one like a son of man,"

---

166. See Carter, "Son of Man," 485.
167. See Rowe, "Daniel's Son," 81.
168. Stalker, "Son of Man," 2829.
169. Stein, *Method and Message*, 136.
170. See Dodd, *According to the Scriptures*, 117.

or its Aramaic equivalent "*bar enasha*" is not a title but it is only a description of a distinct figure. Further, as Marshall says, "the force of *like* is that the figure is not a man but is like a man, just as the beasts are 'like' different animals."[171] Thus, according to Jesus's usage in the Synoptic Gospels this expression refers to someone "like" a human with certain rights and authority.[172] In other words, even though it is not a title in Daniel 7, the phrase "Son of Man" is by far the most important scriptural source in the Old Testament for Jesus's usage of this expression, as a title, in the apocalyptic sense.

Daniel 7:13–14 reads:

> As I watched in the night vision, I saw one like a human being coming with the clouds of heaven. And he came to the Ancient One and was presented before him. To him was given dominion and glory and kingship that all peoples, nations, and languages should serve him. His dominion is an everlasting dominion that shall not pass away, and his kingdom is one that shall never be destroyed.

Here in Daniel's vision, in contrast to the four beasts/animals which represent four great pagan empires of antiquity, a figure "one like a human being" or "one like a son of man" appears as humankind or "a human who rides the clouds to the Ancient of Days to receive ruling authority."[173] Furthermore, the authority of the one like a son of man in Daniel 7:13 and the identification of the Saints of the Most-High in Daniel 7:27 are clearly tied.

With regard to the identity of the holy ones or the Saints of the Most-High in Daniel 7:18, 27 scholars hold various views. While Martin Noth holds that they are celestial or heavenly beings since the term "the holy ones" in the OT is used to indicate heavenly beings, it refers to the ones on high rather than on earth; thus the term "the saints of the Most High" in Daniel 7 should be given the same meaning (angelic).[174] J. Collins also argues that they are angelic beings because "the expression 'holy ones,' used substantively, in the Hebrew Bible refer to angels or supernatural beings

---

171. Marshall, "Son of Man." 778.
172. See Bock, "Son of Man," 894–895.
173. See Bock, 895
174. See Noth, "Holy Ones," 215–228.

in the great majority of cases"[175] but, Collins points out that Noth himself "freely admits that the adjective 'holy' is often applied to human beings, and that Israel can be called a 'holy people'."[176] Likewise, J. Goldingay sees that they are celestial beings in some ways – angels or glorified Israelites.[177]

However, "the angelic argument becomes almost irrelevant for the OG [Old Greek] because the holy ones are called the 'holy people of the Most High' (λαῷ ἁγίῳ ὑψίστου) rather than the 'people of the holy ones of the Most High' . . . 7:27)"; further, even though there is no word "people" in Daniel 7:27, the concept that the eleventh horn makes war against the holy ones and wears them out in 7:21, 25 suggests that the holy ones are not angels but people.[178]

Thus, others argue that they are the people of God in Israel. Identifying the "Son of Man" in Daniel 7:13 with the "Saints of the Most High" in 7:27, Straton suggests that the figure (Son of Man) is symbolic of Israel as a whole or collective entity, and a personification of the holy people (of Israel) rather than a personalized Messiah.[179]

Still others have tried to identify the "one like son of man" with either an individual angelic figure, Archangel Michael as the heavenly representative of Israel or Gabriel,[180] or "involving an eschatological figure (either a messiah or another eschatological deliverer)."[181] Burkett also observes that "first-century interpreters of Daniel 7:13, in the extant sources at least, assumed that the one like a son of man was an individual, the Messiah."[182]

Nevertheless, Cullmann argues pointing out to the representative character of the Son of Man in contrast to the beasts,

> as *representatives* of the world empires, but the "man" is the nation of the saints itself. The incongruity suggests that the

---

175. Collins, *Apocalyptic Imagination*, 104–107; see also 1 Enoch 14:22–23 which is closely related to Daniel 7, thus they are clearly angelic.
176. Collins, *Apocalyptic Vision*, 125.
177. See Goldingay, "Holy Ones on High," 195–197.
178. See Reynolds, *Apocalyptic Son*, 38–39.
179. See Straton, "Son of Man," 36, see particularly, Mowinckel, *He That Cometh*, 350; also, *Cometh: The Messiah*, 350–352.
180. See Schmidt, "Son of Man," 22–28.
181. Bock, "Son of Man," 895.
182. Burkett, *Son of Man Debate*, 113.

"man" may also originally have been representative of the nation of saints. Representation easily becomes identity in Judaism. According to the Jewish concept of representation, the representative can be identified with the group he represents; . . . [thus it] includes the idea that the figure of *the* Man represents all men.[183]

Therefore, in contrast to the four beasts which represent the worldly empires that are alien to God and oppressed his people arising out of the earth and their temporary kingdoms, "the one like a son of man is essentially the *representative of Israel*, who comes before the Ancient of Days and receives authority, power, and a kingdom . . . ; the human figure has the same role as Israel's king, who was the representative ruler of the people before God."[184] Thus, the readers understand that unlike the temporary kingdoms of this world, the one like son of man of Daniel 7 is the one who descended from heaven to help the faithful or restored people of God who suffered for a while but receive sovereignty to share God's rule over the nations forever and ever. Put simply, the term "son of man" in Daniel 7:13–14 is very important to understand that after the sovereignty of pagan empires (four kings) came to an end, the sovereignty of the saints of the Most-High (v. 27) would be established. So, Daniel sees one like a son of man coming to the sovereignty which the beast had lost, and it is given to the Son of Man to rule the whole universe forever, as the eternal king sitting on the throne.[185]

Thus, what is unique about the idea of the Son of Man in Daniel 7 similar to this expression in the Synoptic gospels? So, next, it will be noticed whether there is the idea of suffering of the Danielic son of man before he comes to glory and dominion, indicating to the Markan suffering and dying Son of Man who ended up with vindication and glorious resurrection.

3.5.2.1.1. Suffering of the Son of Man

Does "one like a son of man" of Daniel 7:13 who identified himself with the saints of the Most-High (i.e. humanity) in verse 27, suffer? As referred

---

183. Cullmann, *Christology of the New Testament*, 40–41.

184. Bird, *Are You The One*, 86, 97–98; see also Marshall, *Origins of New Testament*, 66–67.

185. See France, *Divine Government*, 75.

by Longenecker, relating the idea of the Son of Man or Messiah of the Similitudes in *1 Enoch* 37–71 to explain the "one like a son of man" in Daniel 7:13, some scholars think that Danielic Son of Man is only a transcendent and exalted figure rather than humiliated or suffered one.[186] For example, William Manson thinks that even though the powers of evil in the symbolic beast figures are present in the context of Daniel's vision (Dan 7:2–12), contrary to the transcendent heavenly son of man, nothing in Daniel 7:13–14 suggests that this transcendent figure entered in his glory through suffering; thus, "no ideas of this kind are hinted at in Daniel or in those sections of the Jewish books of I Enoch and IV Ezra which continue and develop the Daniel tradition."[187]

However, Moule argues that,

> the fact remains that in Daniel 7:21, 25, the specially aggressive "horn" on the beast's head "made war with the saints of the Most High;" and it is precisely with those saints of the Most High that the Son of Man is identified . . . if so, the Son of Man, . . . stands for a loyal, martyr-group who are brought to glory and vindicated through suffering.[188]

Thus, in other words, son of man in Daniel 7 is a suffering figure. Nevertheless, David Seccombe, thinks that it is true that the saints of Daniel 7 had been persecuted suffering by the pagan empires and their rulers, "however, there is nothing in Daniel's description which connects this suffering with the Son of Man."[189] In other words, Seccombe goes on to argue that even though the son of man of Daniel 7 identified himself with afflicted humanity to help and to share his kingdom authority with them, he remained the glorious figure whose destiny is universal and has everlasting dominion.

In other words, even in the pre-Christian thought, the Son of Man of Daniel 7:13 – who received eternal sovereignty, and yet identified himself with the saints of the Most-High (i.e. faithful people of God) who first was persecuted by the worldly empires (v. 21, 25), and later was vindicated – has

---

186. Longenecker, "'Son of Man'," 153–154.
187. Manson, *Jesus the Messiah*, 7–8.
188. Moule, *Birth of the New Testament*, 174; see also Best, *Temptation and the Passion*, 164; Dodd, *According to the Scriptures*, 117; Dalman, *Words of Jesus*, 264–266.
189. Seccombe, *King of God's Kingdom*, 442.

shared his eternal glory and honor with them forever and ever. In addition, Hooker argues that "the saints who are now crushed on earth are recognized in heaven as those to whom the dominion belongs, and stand even now before the throne of the Most High . . . , and that he will end their suffering and give them the kingdom."[190] Therefore, from Daniel's vision in chapter 7, one can learn that there are two elements of humility and suffering as well as majesty and sovereignty of the saints through the Son of Man who identified himself with them as their representative. In short, Collins is correct in suggesting that the theme of suffering followed by exaltation is a core point of Daniel.[191]

Moreover, Hooker goes further back and argues that Jesus's saying about the Son of Man is rooted not only in the vision of "one like a son of man" in Daniel 7, but in the creation stories themselves. Indeed, in other words, she sees the language of Daniel's vision as itself rooted in the creation stories. It is precisely a son of *man*, a human being, who is to be given dominion over an earth that is at present ruled by *beasts* (Dan 7:1–14). Daniel, like various intertestamental authors, sees Israel as the true descendent of Adam, and the victory of the son of man as the God-given victory of Israel over her oppressors[192]

Casey has also argued that the Aramaic idiom behind the Greek ὁ υἱὸς τοῦ ἀνθρώπου simply means something like "a man such as me."[193] Thus, it is possible to see that Hooker's and Casey's approach point in a similar direction of interpretation: that when Jesus used the term "Son of Man," he was referring to himself, but precisely as a human being, one whose activity could in principle be imitated.[194]

Henderson has related this term "the Son of Man," in Daniel 7:13, to the phrase "the saints of the Most High" in verse 27. These she takes to be the faithful messianic community established by Jesus (i.e. faithful followers of Jesus), to proclaim God's act of forgiveness with the authority of Jesus, which is "implicitly conferred upon those who 'trust' in God's kingdom." She goes

---

190. Hooker, *Son of Man*, 29.
191. See Collins and Harlow, *Eerdmans Dictionary*, 177.
192. Dan 7:27, see also Hooker, *Son of Man*, 71–72.
193. See Casey, *"Son of Man" Problem*, 61–68.
194. See also Casey, 272.

on to say "in this respect, those who lift up the pallet must be seen as Jesus' followers at least in the broadest sense."[195] Furthermore this section appears to refer to Jesus as a mere man associating himself with those who were oppressed or who suffered in the eyes of people but on the day appointed he appears vindicated by God as the judge of the world.

In other words, not only Israel in general or the faithful remnant in particular but also Jesus's present and future followers with whom he identified himself must be understood as the ones who received power and authority, regardless of their suffering and death, to continue doing his agenda on earth.

3.5.2.2. *The Son of Man in Jewish Apocalyptic Literature*

3.5.2.2.1. In *1 Enoch* or the Similitudes

As discussed by Bird, another important possible source to discuss the phrase "son of man" and the development of its tradition is the book of Enoch in the Jewish Apocalyptic literature, particularly the second book of *1 Enoch* in chapters 37–71, which is known as the Similitudes or Parables of Enoch.[196] The Similitudes of Enoch also featured the term "Son of Man" and described this figure as a pre-existent, heavenly creature whose main function was to act as judge at the apocalyptic event. Since the writing was generally thought to pre-date Christianity, some scholars believed that the phrase, "the Son of Man" was recognized in the Judaism of Jesus's time and, thus, Jesus adopted this idea and applied it to himself. Furthermore, on the one hand, Rudolf Otto holds that the book of Enoch is the key to understanding the thoughts and works of Jesus.[197] This is an extreme view. Similarly, for some, as in the book of Daniel, the Son-of-Man concept was built primarily on or influenced by the Similitudes of Enoch,[198] but once established, it was read into other works as well, such as *4 Ezra* 13.[199]

On the other extreme, J. Y. Campbell argues that it is "a conglomeration of fragments of different kinds and diverse origins"; and totally corrupted

---

195. Henderson, *Christology and Discipleship*, 73–74; see also Hooker, *Son of Man*, 182.
196. Bird, *Are You The One*, 93–94.
197. See Otto, *Kingdom of God*, 385.
198. See Kummel, *Theology of the New Testament*, 77–78; Witherington, *Christology of Jesus*, 244–245.
199. See also Beyschlag, *Die Christologie*, 9–34; cf. Casey, *"Son of Man" Problem*, 17–18.

and thus unlikely to be of much use in determining the origin of the phrase. He also points out that "most of the extant manuscripts of the Ethiopic Enoch belong to the eighteenth century; none can be confidently dated earlier than the sixteenth."[200] Likewise, a few British scholars who were influenced by Campbell, including C. H. Dodd were reluctant to build their arguments on evidence drawn from the Similitudes though they show some positive attitudes towards those chapters as early Jewish origin. Therefore, because of this uncertainty, they have no confidence to accept that the Similitudes are reliable pre-Christian documents at all, and therefore they cannot be used with any confidence to elucidate the concept of the Son of Man in the New Testament.[201]

Bowker admits that "the problems of dating of these documents are difficult, and refers to the Similitudes which are entirely absent from the text in the caves of Qumran"; thus, he observes a difference between the Similitudes and other parts of Ethiopic Enoch which are found in the Qumran text.[202] According to Milik, "The Similitudes are probably to be considered the work of a Jew or a Jewish Christian of the first or second Century AD, who reutilized the various early Enoch writings to gain acceptance for his own work."[203]

Stalker has also suggested that the whole structure of the Book of Enoch is confused. Thus he says, "it must always have invited interpolation, and interpolations in it are recognized as numerous. The probability, therefore, is that the passages referring to the son of man are of a later date and of Christian origin."[204]

Still others believe that even though Jesus's use of the phrase "Son of Man" has a sense of his familiarity with the Enochic idea of the "apocalyptic son of man," it is still uncertain.[205] Therefore, it can be concluded that there is not any clear evidence to show that Jesus used the Similitudes for the concept of the term "Son of Man." Hence, "we can use it only to

---

200. Campbell, "Origin and the Meaning," 145–155.

201. See Dodd, *Interpretation of the Fourth*, 116–117; see also Milik, *Ten Years of Discovery*, 33.

202. See Bowker, "Son of Man", 25–26.

203. Milik, *Ten Years of Discovery*, 33; Hindley, "Towards a Date," 553–554.

204. Stalker, "Son of Man," 2830.

205. See Carter, "Son of Man," 485.

understand contemporary Jewish thinking in which the Son of Man has become a messianic title for a pre-existent heavenly being who comes to earth with the glorious kingdom of God."[206] Finally, whereas there is no idea of the suffering Son of Man in the Similitudes, there is this concept of suffering of "one like a son of man" who identified himself with the saints of the Most-High [i.e. faithful people of God] in Daniel 7. The suffering Son of Man, in the Synoptic Gospels particularly in the second half of the Gospel of Mark, is the one who identified himself with the marginalized humanity and liminal individuals and group of people. This idea will be discussed shortly in the next section about the Son of Man in the Synoptic Gospels, particularly in Mark.

3.5.2.2.2. *4 Ezra*

The opening line of the vision in the book indicates that *4 Ezra* was written in the end of the first century AD as a clear reference to the events of 70 CE. It reads:

> In the thirtieth year after the destruction of our city, I, Salathiel, who am also called Ezra, was in Babylon. I was troubled as I lay on my bed, and my thoughts welled up in my heart, because I saw the desolation of Zion and the wealth of those who lived in Babylon. (3:1–2)

According to Metzger, although the author of *4 Ezra* writes about the destruction of Jerusalem by the Babylonians, the desolation of Jerusalem by the Romans in AD 70 is the main focus of the story or event.[207] Thus, the readers learn that chapters 3–14 of *4 Ezra* contain seven visions, their introduction and explanation. Furthermore, the sixth vision in chapter 13 tells us of the vision of the man from the sea, calling him "man" and its

---

206. Ladd, *Theology of the New Testament*, 147; cf. Charlesworth, *Old Testament Pseudepigrapha*, 1985.

207. Metzger, "Fourth Book of Ezra," 520.

interpretation, calling him (my) son or servant.[208] Several scholars also point out that *4 Ezra* has been greatly influenced by the book of Daniel.[209]

For example, as in Daniel 7:3, *4 Ezra* 11:1 mentions the eagle (i.e. Roman Empire) that rises from the sea and is destroyed in both Daniel 7:11 and *4 Ezra* 12:3.[210] Then, in both Daniel 7:13 and *4 Ezra* 13:1–12 a human-like figure appears. Likewise, a dream or vision of Ezra and a description of the human-like figure is mentioned in both Daniel 7:2, 7, 13 and *4 Ezra* 13:1, 3. Furthermore, the "clouds of heaven" in Daniel 7:13 and in *4 Ezra* 13:3, the "powerful wind" in Daniel 7:2 and *4 Ezra* 13:1, and the term for God as the "Most High" in Daniel 7:22, 25, 27 and in *4 Ezra* 12:32; 13:29 all indicate a clear influence of *4 Ezra* by the book of Daniel 7.[211] In addition, a human-like figure of *4 Ezra* 13 is also called God's son in verses 32, 37 and 52 in the interpretation of the vision. Thus, Bird states "that is achieved by identifying the 'figure of a man' with God's 'Son,' and earlier in *4 Ezra* 7:28–29 the Messiah is designated precisely as 'my Son'."[212] Straton also believes that at that time the Son of man was understood as the Messiah and further identified as the Son of God in *4 Ezra* 13:23.[213] In other words, even though the human-like figure of *4 Ezra* was never called "Messiah," his characteristics and activities indicate his messianic nature in *4 Ezra* chapters 7, 11–12. Thus, the readers may conclude that both Daniel 7 and *4 Ezra* 13 can be interpreted messianically together with other OT passages such as Psalm 2:7 and 2 Samuel 7:13–14.[214]

---

208. Even though some texts such as Latin and Syriac refers to the human-like figure of 4 Ezra as son/my son in 13:32, Stone prefers the word "servant" since both son and servant come from the Greek παῖς (see Stone, *Features of the Eschatology*, 71–75). However, Collins rightly argues that 'the Greek παῖς could still reflect Hebrew "son" rather than "servant" cf. 2:16; it recalls Psalm 2 where God calls the Anointed king "You are my son, this day I have begotten you." In other words, although in the Greek translation of 4 Ezra the word παῖς is used, it does not mean "servant," but it can just easily mean "child" or "son" (see Collins, *Apocalyptic Imagination*, 2nd ed., 207; cf. Nickelsburg, "Son of Man," 141).

209. See Hooker, *Son of Man*, 49–50; Lacocque, "Vision of Eagle," 237–258; Casey, *Son of Man*, 122.

210. See Collins, *Apocalyptic Imagination* 2nd ed., 196.

211. See Lacocque, "Vision of Eagle," 241.

212. Bird, *Are You The One*, 95.

213. See Straton, "Son of Man," 37.

214. See also Bird, *Are You The One*, 95.

Moreover, some scholars notice the messianic nature of the human-like figure in the vision of *4 Ezra* 13; thus he is presented as the Messiah in the interpretation.[215] For instance, as the expected Messiah of the first century, he is considered the one who destroys ungodly nations (13:37–8), and carries out judgment from his mouth similar to the messianic branch of Isaiah 11:1–4 (cf. *4 Ezra* 13:10–11, 37–9). J. Moo also argues that the Messiah of *4 Ezra* in 13:5–6 is the one who reigns in a way that no one who dwells on earth expects.[216] In addition, as referred by Reynolds, it indicates that similar to the Similitudes of Enoch in 48:2–6 and 62:7, the human-like figure of *4 Ezra* is presented as pre-existent (*4 Ezra* 13:26), defender of the righteous remnant (*1 En.* 48:4–7; 62:11–16; 71:16–17; and *4 Ezra* 13:23–29), and a warrior-judge (*1 En.* 46:5; 62:3; 69:27; also 52:6; cf. 53:7; and *4 Ezra* 13:9–11, 37–39, 49).[217]

Thus, finally, some scholars think that, similar to Daniel 7 and the 1 Enochic Similitudes, the book of *4 Ezra* is another Jewish composition which represents pre-Christian expectations with regard to the idea of the "Son of Man" as the eschatological agent of redemption.[218]

However, as noticed above, in the case of *1 Enoch*, particularly the Similitudes, it is impossible to put up any argument about Jesus's use of the title "Son of Man" on evidence drawn from *4 Ezra* – as well as other Apocryphal works – since *4 Ezra* was probably written by a quietist Pharisee in the latter part of the first Christian century.[219]

In addition, there is no clear emphasis on the concept of the suffering Son of Man in any non-canonical sources including both *1 Enoch* and *4 Ezra* describing Jesus's real and full identity as both the divine Son of God and, the suffering and vindicated Son of Man as we see it in the Synoptic Gospels. This is particularly seen in Mark, though there is something related to the death of a human-like figure and those who were with him in *4 Ezra* 7:28–29. These two first century apocalyptic writings (the Similitudes and

---

215. See Charlesworth, "Concept of the Messiah," 205; Caragounis, *Son of Man*, 130; see also Burkett, *Son of Man Debate*, 105–106.

216. See Moo, "Messiah," 525–536.

217. Reynolds, *Apocalyptic Son*, 41–53.

218. See Cullmann, *Christology of the New Testament*, 139–144; Fuller, *Foundation of New Testament*, 34–43; E. Schweitzer, "Son of Man," 119–129.

219. See Dodd, *According to the Scriptures*, 116–117.

4 Ezra) used Daniel by indicating the greatly exalted figure of a divine status rather than the one who identified himself with the suffering humanity.[220] In other words, unlike the second evangelist, none of these apocryphal texts describe their "son of man" figure as the suffering and crucified one as well as his resurrection on the third day to redeem others.

Therefore, among three proposed sources above (Dan 7, the Similitudes or Parables of *1 En.* and *4 Ezra* 13), only Daniel 7 is a pre-Christian source to clearly express the idea of the title, Son of Man, in the Synoptic Gospels, particularly in the second part of Mark's Gospel as we will discuss it later. Furthermore, even if there may be some possible elements one can interpret in some ways, there are no compelling thoughts on the idea of the suffering son of man in *1 Enoch* as well as in *4 Ezra*, particularly, as compared to that of both implicit and explicit expressions in Daniel and in the Synoptic Gospels. In other words, unlike the book of Daniel 7 and the Synoptic gospels, none of these apocryphal texts (such as *1 Enoch* or Similitudes which depicts "son of man" as only pre-existent, heavenly judge and exalted one and *4 Ezra* 13 describing him as the messianic figure who comes out of the Sea as the one whose earthly role is to restore Israel) describe the crucifixion and resurrection of their redeeming figure three days later.[221] In contrast *4 Ezra* 13 describes him as the messianic figure who comes out of the Sea and whose earthly role is to restore Israel. Additionally, both the Similitudes of *1 Enoch* and *4 Ezra* are the books from the fourth – first century BC. They are also Jewish and not Christian literature. The teachings about the Messiah in both *1 Enoch* and *4 Ezra* are only predictive about the Messiah and not directly about the life and works of Jesus.

The next section will seek to discuss the use and the significance of the term "Son of Man" in the Gospels in general and in the Synoptic Gospels in particular as the most important potential sources for Jesus's divine identity. Furthermore, particular attention will be given to Jesus's unique identity as the authoritative and/or glorious Son of God and the Suffering Son of Man in Mark's gospel, and his unexpected self-identification with humanity,

---

220. See Collins, "He Shall Not Judge," 118, 211.
221. See Collins and Harlow, *Eerdmans Dictionary*, 213.

especially with those who are marginalized and liminal people to save them in various ways, as noted above.

3.5.2.3. The Son of Man in the Synoptic Gospels

The term "the Son of Man" occurs throughout the New Testament, and eighty-one times in the Gospels. Sixty-nine of these are found in the Synoptic Gospels thirty times in Matthew, fourteen times in Mark, twenty-five times in Luke, thirteen times in John, once in Acts and Hebrews and twice in Revelation. As it has already been mentioned, the expression, "the Son of Man" appears almost exclusively on the lips of Jesus in the Gospels, with fourteen of them rooted in Mark, where it is presented as Jesus's favorite expression of his own self-identification. In other words, apart from four Gospels where the expression "Son of Man" appears on the lips of Jesus as typical of the way in which he spoke, the only exceptions are found in John 12:34; Revelation 1:13; 14:14, and particularly in Acts 7:56 where Stephen declared, while he was dying, "Look," he said, "I see the heavens opened and the Son of Man standing at the right hand of God!"

Even though it is not totally satisfactory, scholars classify the Son of Man sayings in the Synoptic Gospels in three distinctive categories. Group A groups the expression "Son of Man" to his present activity during his earthly ministry (eg. Mark 2:10, 28; Luke 7:34; 9:58; 19:10); group B referring it to his future suffering, death and resurrection (e.g. Mark 8:31; 10:45; 14:21, 41); and group C connecting it to his apocalyptic (final) coming as the exalted one and final judge of the world (e.g. Mark 8:38; 13:26; 14:62; Luke 12:8, 40; 17:22–30; 18:8; Matt 10:23; 19:28). In these three groups or categories, sayings of Jesus reveal him as the One who is destined for sovereignty and victory through humiliation, rejection and suffering.

Moreover, many scholars agree that Jesus spoke primarily in Aramaic although it was not the only language he used to speak because he read the Hebrew scriptures in the synagogues (e.g. Luke 4:18–19),[222] and possibly Greek as he was able to converse with the Roman prefect Pontius Pilate with no need of interpretation.[223] Aramaic, according to Dalman, was the

---

222. See Williams, "Expressing Definiteness," 66.
223. See Witherington, *Christology of Jesus*, 236; Lukaszewski, "Issues Concerning the Aramaic," 14.

first language of Galileans including not only Jesus but also his first twelve followers. This was their native language.[224] Further, Dalman goes on to explain that Jesus's primary focus was on preaching the good news to the poor, ordinary, and the marginalized ones; thus it is appropriate to think that Jesus had paid great attention to help these people in need mainly in the language they understood best.[225] Also, instead of Hebrew, a more literary language, Greek was a less known language to the unprivileged or marginalized people at that time; in other words, it "would have been used only by the aristocracy."[226] Still, it is possible to suggest that Jesus spoke in Aramaic when he uttered his Son of Man sayings.[227]

However, some scholars question the authenticity of the expression, the "Son of Man" in the Gospels. Therefore, even though a comprehensive analysis and critique of this idea is not the main focus of this piece of work, it is important to raise briefly the issue of authenticity of the Son of Man sayings in the Gospels. In this regard, first, some believe that the Son of Man sayings are inauthentic; they are attributed to Jesus not by himself as his self-designation but by the early (Hellenistic) church community as its creations or products, hence they do not reveal Jesus's self-consciousness.[228]

Second, others think that only some, but not all, of the Son of Man sayings, are authentic. For example, it was thought that the Son of Man sayings which speak of his future coming (apocalyptic sayings) are alone authentic, referring to someone else other than Jesus.[229] In other words, these authors say that any of these sayings which apply this expression to the earthly Jesus are a latter addition by the Hellenistic church;[230] thus, with the term "Son of Man," these scholars believed that Jesus was not referring to himself as

---

224. See Dalman, *Words of Jesus*, 10; also Acts 2:7; see also Evans, "Messianic Hopes," 39.

225. See also Dalman, *Words of Jesus*, 11.

226. Lukaszewski, "Issues Concerning the Aramaic," 14.

227. See Tejada-Lalinde, "Jesus as the Son," 12. For further information of this whole idea, consult http://digitalcommons.fui.edu

228. For example, see Vielhauer, "Erwagungen zur Christologie," 55–91, 92–140; Conzelmann, "Gegenwart und Zukunft," 277–296; Perrin, *Rediscovering the Teaching*, 173–199; 1974, 57–83.

229. See Bultmann, *Synoptic Tradition*, 2nd rev. ed., 152; *Theology of the New Testament*, 28–32, Bornkamm, *Jesus von Nazareth*, 228–231; Fuller, *Foundation of New Testament*, 119–125; and Higgins, *Jesus*, 185–195.

230. See Bultmann, *Synoptic Tradition*, 2nd rev. ed., 155.

the coming Son of Man but to another apocalyptic figure who comes to judge the world in the end. Put simply, adherents to this view thought that it was not Jesus himself but the early church that attributed this expression to him in apocalyptic sense so identifying him as the future coming Son of Man. In contrast, Cranfield rejects this idea arguing that "there is no scrap of evidence that Jesus expected one greater than himself to come, and there is much evidence to the contrary."[231]

Hurtado goes further arguing that the primary linguistic function of the expression, "son of man," in the gospels is to refer to Jesus rather than to make a claim about him; thus he concludes that "the son of man" can be used in sayings that stake various claims about Jesus, but it is the sentence that conveys the intended claim or statement, not the son of man expression itself. Instead, we are to attribute to the referent, Jesus, the import of these sentences.[232] In other words, according to these scholars, the expression, "son of man" in the gospels is to be translated as an exclusive self-reference of and by Jesus, and so to refer to Jesus himself rather than a claim about him by anyone else.[233]

Eduard Schweizer believes that the Son of Man sayings that speak of the earthly life of Jesus are authentic but he is skeptical about the suffering Son of Man and some of the apocalyptic Son of Man sayings, unless he interprets them in terms of Jesus's exaltation by God after his rejection, suffering and humiliation.[234] Further, Schweitzer thought that Jesus's primary focus was on Ezekiel's son of man (*ben adam*) to understand and explain the concept of the son of man as lowly and humiliated but latter vindicated by God to be the final judge[235] Nevertheless, he believes that "son of man" sayings about parousia were created by a group in the early church.[236]

However, third, still others argue that the expression the "Son of Man" in the Gospels are highly likely to be authentic and show Jesus's

---

231. Cranfiled, *Gospel According to St Mark*, 274; Moule, *Phenomenon of the New Testament*, 68; see also, Marshall, *New Testament Christology*, 51, 73.

232. See Hurtado, "Summary," 159–177.

233. See also Bock, "Use of Daniel," 90–92; Hurtado, "Summary," 160–161.

234. See E. Schweizer, "Son of Man," 119–129; "Son of Man Again," 256–261; *Jesus*, 166–171; cf. Marshall, *New Testament Christology*, 71–72; Black, "Son of Man," 305–318.

235. E. Schweizer, "Son of Man," 121–122.

236. See also Schweizer, "Son of Man Again," 259–260.

own self-understanding. For example, some strongly argued that in the original Aramaic, the term "Son of Man," usually referred to an individual; thus Jesus used it as a self-designation in specific reference to Daniel 7:13.[237] Furthermore, Bock argues that "the consistency of the term's use by Jesus and the lack of its use as a confessional term of the early church elsewhere in the NT makes it extremely unlikely to have been the creation of the church."[238] In other words, the limitation of the term, Son of Man, to the lips of Jesus in the canonical Gospels rather than its confessional or creedal usage by the early church makes its authenticity stronger and clearer. Bock also goes on to argue that "the textual memory of the exclusiveness of its use by Jesus tells us that the expression held a special place for Jesus that the church both recalled and honored."[239] Put simply, the early church is not the origin or producer of this expression but one that faithfully echoes or repeats what Jesus himself said according to the Gospels' tradition,[240] because her mission is to build on a known Jesus's tradition rather than creating a new one. However, it is possible to suggest that presumably, on the same basis, the early church might – even inadvertently – have attributed some Son of Man sayings to Jesus which did not originate with him, precisely because they knew that this was one of his favourite expressions.

Finally, having determined that the Son of Man sayings in the Gospels are highly likely to be authentic, it is now important to briefly survey the main focus of each evangelist in his own way of expressing the significance or usage of the title "the Son of Man" because each evangelist describes the term "Son of Man" with varying emphases.[241] It is also important to pay particular attention to the idea and/or usage of this expression in the Gospel of Mark where he describes Jesus as the glorious or divine figure and yet the suffering and vindicated Son of Man who identified himself with the marginalized and liminal humanity.

---

237. See Bruce, *This Is That*, 26–30; see also Muller, *Expression 'Son of Man'*, 1; Owen, "The Son of Man Debate," vii; Bock, "Use of Daniel," 90–92; Hurtado, "Summary," 169–171.
238. Bock, "Son of Man," 897.
239. Bock, 897.
240. See Moule, *Origin of Christology*, 22.
241. See Bock, "Son of Man," 896.

3.5.2.3.1. The Gospel of Matthew

In the Gospel of Matthew, Jesus uses the title, "Son of Man" when describing his own mission. As indicated above, more than any other canonical gospel, the phrase "Son of Man" appears thirty times in this gospel even though this term is absent in its first seven chapters. As in two other Synoptic Gospels (Mark 8:27 and Luke 9:18), Matthew's Son of Man sayings come after Jesus's question to his first followers, "Who do people say that the Son of Man is?" (Matt 16: 13). Peter's answer to the question in the Synoptic Gospels is similar which says "you are the Messiah" in Mark 8:29, "the Messiah of God" in Luke 9:20, and "You are the Messiah, the Son of the living God" in Matthew 16:16. Jesus's next step was telling his followers that he (the Son of Man) must undergo great suffering, and be rejected by the Jewish authority, and be killed, and on the third day be raised (Mark 8:31; Luke 9:22; Matt 16:21). In other words, whereas the disciples of Jesus understood him as the Messiah, or a Davidic king who destroys his enemies, Jesus unexpectedly spoke of his suffering, death and raising in terms of the Son of Man, rather than the Messiah.

Also, as in Mark 2:10, the Matthean Son of Man is described as the one who has authority on earth to forgive sins (Matt 9:6). Hence, the reader infers that the implication of the authority of the Son of Man to forgive sins and his lordship over the Sabbath in (12:8) as well as his claim to universal authority in 28:18–20 shows that the Matthean Son of Man is a heavenly figure who has authority on earth. In this regard, Muller affirms that, according to the first evangelist, the authority of Jesus is different from the authority of the human beings.[242] It is also possible to see that the authority of the Matthean Son of Man in 9:6 has clearly been influenced by Daniel 7:14 in which the authority or dominion given to the "one like a son of man." It is true that there is no clear evidence that the expression "Son of Man" was used as a title in any Jewish literature including Daniel 7, unless only to describe a human figure who appeared in a vision opposite to animals. However, as in other canonical Gospels, Matthew's Jesus's usage of the definite article "the Son of Man" or "that Son of Man" was a demonstrative because it refers to the Danielic son of man (7:13–14) in which Jesus sees his

---

242. See Muller, *Der Ausdruck*, 175–6; see also Matt 7:28–29; 11:27; 21:21–27.

own unique mission of vindication and glorification following his rejection, suffering and death.[243] In other words, even though it has not appeared as a title in Daniel or other Jewish literature before the time of Jesus, according to Matthew, it is a title in Jesus's understanding of his own unique mission.

As mentioned above, unlike the Son of Man figure who appears as a heavenly and glorified redeemer, as well as pre-existent being in the Similitudes (*1 Enoch*) in which nothing appeared about his suffering and death, the Matthean Son of Man is described as the one who will fulfil the destiny of suffering, death and resurrection after three days (Matt 17:9, 12; 20:18; 26:24, 45). As will be seen shortly, it is also obvious that other Synoptic Gospels describe Jesus as the suffering, dying and rising Son of Man which is reminiscent of "one like son of man," in Daniel 7, who identified himself with the saints of the Most-High, the faithful people of God who were afflicted and then vindicated (see Dan 7:21–22, 27). In short, Matthean scholars understand that "the expression would simply mean that this human is called to and destined for rejection followed by vindication."[244]

Also, "some seven or eight sayings are found only in Matthew, the bulk of which point to Jesus' coming as judge (Matt 13:41; 16:28; 24:30a; 25:31; 19:28)."[245] Matthew describes the identity of Jesus as the Apocalyptic Son of Man who will come to judge the world. In other words, it is Matthew's peculiar teaching to emphasize Jesus's glorification and his judgmental activity as the coming Son of Man (see also Matt 24:30a, 39). In short, unlike Mark's emphasis on the suffering and vindicated Son of Man, the first evangelist puts great emphasis on the judgment role of Jesus as the Son of Man. For example, the readers of Matthew understand that the Matthean Son of Man is to receive authority 9:6; 12:8 which reflects the authority of the Danielic son of man in 7:14 and the thrones of Daniel 7:9. However, comparing the Enochaic son of man in *1 Enoch* 45:3; 55:4; 61:8; 62:2–5; 69:27, 29, to the Matthean Son of Man who sits on a throne of glory in Matthew 19:28; 25:31, some scholars think that the judgment role of the Matthean Son of Man is based on the Enochaic son of Man rather than

---

243. See Moule, *Origin of Christology*, 11–22.
244. Bock, "Son of Man," 898.
245. Bock, 899.

the Danielic figure.²⁴⁶ Caragounis also says that Matthew 19:28 and 25:31 "are quite likely direct quotations from the Parables."²⁴⁷ Nevertheless, even though there are some strong similarities between the Son of Man sayings in Matthew's account and the Similitudes, for the reasons mentioned above, including the dating of the Similitudes of *1 Enoch* which is uncertain, it is unlikely to prove that those sayings in Matthew are dependent on the Similitudes.²⁴⁸ A. I. Wilson also notes a difference in that *1 Enoch* 61:8 talks of a judgment that happened on the "holy ones in heaven above" – surely a reference to angelic beings – while the account of judgment in 62:2–3 has quite a different tone to that in Matthew."²⁴⁹

Therefore, it is possible to argue that the Matthean Son of Man who has universal authority in the present (9:6; 12:8; 28:18) and the Son of Man who will return in the future on the clouds of heaven (in glory) is much more like the Danielic son of man (Dan 7:13; see also Matt 24:30; 26:64) rather than the Enochic son of man although there are some similarities between Matthew and the Similitudes of *1 Enoch*. Finally, it is the Danielic son of man, a mere human being, who identified himself, first with the afflicted people of God but later is given authority and vindicated, similar to the Matthean Son of Man who identified himself with the suffering humanity, as in other Synoptic writers.

3.5.2.3.2. The Gospel of Luke

Along with Matthew and Mark, the Son of Man sayings appear on the lips of Jesus himself twenty-five times in the Gospel of Luke. Nine of these sayings are shared with Mark and ten of them with Q. Again, there are six Son of Man sayings peculiar to Luke (Luke 17:22; 18:8; 19:10; 21:36; 22:48; 24:7).

As other Synoptic writers, Luke also mentions the Son of Man sayings in three distinct categories: first, he introduces Jesus as the Son of Man with the authority to forgive sins (Luke 5:24) and refers to the Son of Man's present activities (7:34; 9:58).

---

246. See Reddish, *Apocalyptic Literature*, 165.
247. Caragounis, *Son of Man*, 171; see also Theisohn, *Der auserwahlte Richter*, 153–154.
248. See also Hare, *Son of Man Tradition*, 177–178.
249. Wilson, *Will These Things Happen?*, 243.

Second, he describes Jesus as the suffering, dying and raising Son of Man (9:22, 44; 18:31; 22:22, 48; 24:7) however, the Lucan Son of Man is described as the one whose suffering and rejection led him to his exaltation and future coming.[250] In other words, Lucan readers clearly discover that Jesus's exaltation would happen through suffering and rejection (22:69) before his glorious return.

Higgins suggests that due to the absence of the terms "coming with the clouds of heaven" in Luke's version about the Son of Man before the Sanhedrin, but its appearance in Matthew 26:64 and Mark 14:62, particularly the terms "from now on" in Luke 22:69 denotes the Son of Man's exaltation to the right hand of God rather than to his future coming.[251] However, since there are a number of references to the future coming of the Son of Man (e.g. 9:26; 12:40; 18:8; 21:27), it is possible to suggest that the lack of the terms "coming with the clouds" in Luke 22:69 is just to indicate Luke's emphasis on the immediacy of the exaltation of the Son of Man soon after his suffering, death and resurrection.

Likewise, in contrast to Matthew and Mark, Luke emphasizes the Son of Man's role in salvation.[252] Thus, Luke's Jesus is to be understood as the one whose mission as the Son of Man is clearly related to the salvation of the lost (Luke 19:10); he also reminds his readers and hearers to stand firm and be ready for the Son of Man's exaltation and glorious return (Luke 12:35–40; 18:8; 21:34, 36).

Third, Luke, as the other Synoptic evangelists, describes Jesus's role of judgment when he returns in glory; in other words, Jesus's forensic or judgmental role as the Son of Man is clearly reported in Luke's narrative (see Luke 12:8, 40; 17:22–30; 18:8; also, Matt 10:23; 19:28; Mark 8:38; 13:26; 14:62).

As with the other Gospels, there are also similarities between the Son of Man concepts in some Apocryphal books or Jewish apocalypses, such as the Similitudes of *1 Enoch* and *4 Ezra*, and the Gospel of Luke. For instance, Marshall discusses that the day of Yahweh (the Lord) in *1 Enoch*

---

250. Luke 17:24–25; 22:69; see Marshall, *Gospel of Luke*, 660–61; Tödt, *Son of Man*, 110–111.

251. See Higgins, *Jesus and the Son*, 96.

252. Luke 21:27–28; see also Schneider, "Der Menschensohn," 282.

45:3; 61:5; *4 Ezra* 13:52 is called the day of the Son of Man in Luke 17:24, 30.[253] While speaking about the coming of the Son of Man, Luke's Jesus speaks about his coming to cast fire on the earth (Luke 12:40–59) which reminds of *4 Ezra* 13:10–11. In addition, the activity of the Son of Man when seated at the right hand of God in Luke 22:69 is similar to the idea of people standing before the Son of Man in *1 Enoch* 62:5–9; so, both indicate his act of judgment.

Similarly, the readers of the third Gospel can clearly see the Danielic influence in the gospel. Some scholars see Daniel 7:13–14 as the background of the Greek term ὁ υἱὸς τοῦ ἀνθρώπου,[254] and others such as Casey notice the Danielic influence in 9:26; 12:40; 18:8; 21:27; 22:69.[255] In short, the readers of Luke's gospel can sense that there are two elements of clouds and/or glory in Luke's mind as he refers to the dominion and glorious coming of Danielic son of man.

Finally, it is true that there are striking similarities between those apocryphal books of the Similitudes and *4 Ezra*, and the Gospel of Luke as they speak of the figure of the Son of Man. However, there are also some significant differences since the Similitudes and *4 Ezra* describe the preexistent, exalted and glorious Son of Man, free from suffering, who destroys sinners and defends righteous people, whereas the Lukan Son of Man, as other Synoptics, is described as the one who has unique divine authority to forgive sins identifying himself with the marginalized and the lost to save them. It is in this gospel that salvation is sovereignly granted to those outside the bounds of normal expectation, for example, to the poor (Luke 1:50–53; 4:18; 6:20), sinners (5:27–32; 7:28, 30, 34, 36–50) and the marginalized ones (15:1) including Gentiles (4:24–27). Similar to other Synoptic Gospels, rather than the Jewish apocalypses, Luke's Jesus is also the one who is exalted after suffering and death, and would come again as the final judge of the world pointing out to the prophesy in Daniel 7:13–14 as its OT background as discussed thus far.

---

253. See Marshall, *Gospel of Luke*, 661.
254. See Lindars, *Jesus Son of Man*, 139; Tuckett, "Lcuan Son of Man," 213; and Catchpole, "Angelic Son of Man," 261–262.
255. See Casey, *Son of Man*, 161–196.

3.5.2.3.3. The Gospel of Mark

It is, now, time to turn to Mark's Gospel to investigate how the second evangelist used the phrase ὁ υἱὸς τοῦ ἀνθρώπου in his Gospel. He does this in a way similar to the rest of the New Testament using the definitive form. As briefly discussed above in case of Matthew and Luke, Mark, also reports the Son of Man's sayings, exclusively from the mouth of Jesus, in three categories: first, the authority of the Son of Man on earth to forgive sins and his lordship over the Sabbath, second, his suffering, death and resurrection and third, his exaltation and future coming as the final judge. In Mark's Gospel the term or the title (Son of Man) occurs fourteen times,[256] the bulk of which speaks of the prediction of the suffering and rejected Son of Man.[257]

3.5.2.3.3.1. The authority of the Son of Man on earth

Mark begins to use this title, "the Son of Man," by reminding his readers and hearers of Jesus's shocking claim to have authority on earth to forgive sins (Mark 2:10) and furthermore his authority or lordship over the Sabbath (2:28). In both these verses (2:10 and 2:28), the underlying authority of the Son of Man's (Jesus's) actions are called into question by the Jewish leadership or authorities. However, since the scribes asked: Who can forgive sins but God alone (2:7), it is possible to know that Mark in his first Son of Man saying reports that his Son of Man is identical to God, to whom alone the prerogative of forgiving sins against God belongs. Thus, from this context the readers understand that Jesus as the Son of Man claims the divine authority to forgive sins.[258] Edwards also says, in Mark "2:10 'Son of Man' depicts Jesus' authority to forgive sins, thereby alluding to the 'son of man' figure in Daniel 7:13–14, who likewise is empowered with God's authority."[259] Put simply, regarding the concept of granting forgiveness to others, the Markan Son of Man seems to be, implicitly, related to the Danielic son of man figure.

Nevertheless, H. L. Chronis, thinks that there is no a clear evidence of a specific Old Testament background to the Markan Son of Man sayings.[260]

---

256. Mark 2:10, 28; 8:31, 38; 9:9, 12, 31; 10:33, 45; 13:26; 14:21, 41, 62.
257. Mark 8:31; 9:9, 12, 31; 10:33, 45; 14: 21 [2x], 41.
258. See Ladd, *Theology of the New Testament*, 152.
259. Edwards, *Gospel According to Mark*, 80.
260. See Chronis, "To Reveal," 459–481.

Furthermore, Casey argues that one cannot see the specific concept of the authority to forgive sins in the Danielic son of man.[261] In contrast, other scholars argue that the Danielic son of man is to be understood as the background of the Markan Son of Man sayings in some ways.[262] I would like to suggest that as in other Gospels, the readers and hearers of the second evangelist would probably recognize the Danielic influence, in this matter, in the Markan Son of Man sayings at least in a broader sense. For instance, since the Danielic son of man has eternal dominion or authority from God over all things, though not explicitly, it may or is even likely to include authority to forgive sins.[263] As indicated above, since the Danielic son of man serves as the kingly representative ruler rather than a symbol of the holy ones, his role of judgment also might include granting forgiveness to others. Thus, Hooker goes on to say that the forgiveness of sins is "an activity which we might well have expected from the Son of Man . . . because forgiveness is at once the destruction of evil and the expression of a relationship existing between the Son of Man and other men."[264] In other words, as G. H. P. Thompson suggests, "one aspect of God's judgment is forgiveness of men's [and women's] sins and this activity is now operative in the mission of Jesus";[265] in the judgmental role of the Son of Man, one may understand the two elements of destroying evil and saving the lost through forgiveness.

Further, following their condemnation because of their iniquity, the kings and rulers of the earth petition the Enochic Son of Man for mercy (*1 En.* 62:9, 11; see also 63:1, 5, 8–9). In short, in addition to the Danielic and Markan Son of Man sayings, one understands that the petitions or prayers of the kings and rulers of earth for mercy clearly shows the Enochic Son of Man's ability or authority to forgive sins. Regarding the Son of Man's authority to forgive sins, the consistency between the Markan Son of Man

---

261. See Casey, *Son of Man*, 160.

262. See also Kirchhevel, "'Son of Man'," 181–187; Marcus, "Son of Man," 38–61, 37–86.

263. However, whether or not people thought about this authority as including forgiveness of sins, Jesus could have given new meaning to a familiar idea such as the "'Son of Man'" and his authority. In other words, one does not necessarily have to find all the potential NT significance of an expression in an OT occurrence to say that this occurrence serves a background for the NT saying.

264. Hooker, *Son of Man*, 93.

265. Thompson, "The Son of Man," 205–206.

and "one like a son of man" in Daniel 7 seems to be related to each other, especially since the Danielic son of man is said to receive kingly authority from the Ancient of Days (God) for ever and ever.[266]

Another example of the authority of the Son of Man on earth appears in the context of Mark 2:1—3:6 in which opposition and conflict occurred between the Jesus and the Jewish religious authorities; this conflict was obviously caused by the nearness of the kingdom of God that Mark's Jesus preached. Among the Sabbath controversies, Mark 2:28 records Jesus as saying "so the Son of Man is lord even of the Sabbath." This had to do with eating in a way that apparently violated the law.

According to some scholars, such as Vermes, this idea is interpreted generically as though the Sabbath was given to humankind because "God made man [humankind] lord of all creation, including the Sabbath."[267] In other words, Vermes argues that since the Sabbath was created by God for the benefit of man, humankind is the master of the Sabbath. However, this view is unlikely because even though the first term used is generic ("humankind" in v. 27), Jesus did not continue to use this term in the next verse (v. 28) but he changed it into the definitive statement, "the Son of Man." Even though it is true that the Sabbath was, generally, a gift to humankind, "the available evidence does not speak of humans ruling the Sabbath or overruling some Sabbath regulations."[268] Put another way, God created the Sabbath (Gen 2:3) and gave it to humankind as a responsibility to take care of and enjoy it but God alone is the Lord of all creation, including the earth.

Thus, similar to Mark 2:10, where Jesus claims the authority of granting forgiveness to the paralytic, or the sinner, he also claims to possess authority over the Sabbath in Mark 2:28 alluding both accounts to Daniel 7:14 and the authority or dominion given to that son of man. Furthermore, "this is because, as Daniel 7 makes it evident, only the Son of Man was given authority over all humankind and human kingdoms and human institutions."[269]

Therefore, since almost all the Son of Man sayings are from the lips of Jesus about himself in all canonical Gospels, and since they allude to the

---

266. See Reynolds, *Apocalyptic Son*, 67–68.
267. Vermes, *Jesus the Jew*, 180.
268. Witherington, *Gospel of Mark*, 132.
269. Witherington, 132; see also *Jesus the Sage*, 168.

everlasting authority or dominion of son of man of Daniel 7, the term "the Son of Man" in 2:28 is "a reference to the authority of Jesus and not a circumlocution for humanity in general." Thus, "the authority of Jesus as the Son of Man extends over the Sabbath itself,"[270] because as briefly pointed out earlier, this indicates that the old categories of tradition and the law are inadequate to express and judge the newness brought by Jesus.

3.5.2.3.3.2. The suffering, death and resurrection of the Son of Man
As noted previously, while Matthew emphasized the judgmental role of the Son of Man and Luke placed a great emphasis on his role in salvation, the second evangelist in his narrative starkly and purposefully emphasizes the rejection and suffering of Jesus as the Son of Man. The majority of Mark's references in the heart of his Gospel to the passion predictions of Jesus refer to the Son of Man.[271]

The first of the passion predictions with which Jesus begins his new teaching comes in Mark 8:31 which follows Peter's confession of Jesus as the Christ. Thus, Jesus's prediction of his rejection, suffering and death could be seen as "his response to Peter's confession of faith" and "a moment of revelation and insight."[272] In other words, even though Peter's confession is not a full understanding of Jesus's true identity which includes his suffering, it could be considered as a "semi-insight." Hence, Mark begins to remind his readers that they failed to understand the new teaching of Jesus, concerning his (Jesus's) divine identity and his mission, as a corrective to Peter's confession in Mark 8:27–31. Therefore, it is important to understand that Mark 8:31 "is . . . the beginning of a new phase of teaching" focusing on the Son of Man who will suffer, die and raise again.[273]

In Mark 8, Jesus does not merely replace "the Christ" with the "Son of Man" because the phrase "the Son of Man" in Mark has already been used earlier in 2:10, 28 where Jesus describes himself as the unique Son of Man with unique authority to forgive sins and to regulate the Sabbath. Then, in the midsection of his Gospel, even though Peter and the first followers of

---

270. Edwards, *Gospel According to Mark*, 97.
271. For example, see Mark 8:31; 9:9, 12, 31; 10:33, 45; 14:21 [2x], 41.
272. Lane, *Gospel of Mark*, 292–293.
273. Painter, *Mark's Gospel*, 124.

Jesus did not realize the necessity of Jesus's suffering, Mark clearly expounds this, focusing on the passion narrative in the second half of his book. Thus, the readers understand that by teaching about the Son of Man, Jesus is affirming his own suffering as the divine purpose which is written in the Scriptures (Mark 9: 12–13, 31; 14: 62) "and the same thought underlies this and Jesus' other predictions of his passion."[274] In other words, as he responds to Peter's confession, the Markan Jesus, from Mark 8:31 onwards, gives a new orientation to his followers regarding his true identity which necessarily involves his rejection and suffering.[275] Unlike other gospels, in Mark's central section, particularly in the three repeated passion predictions (8:31; 9:31; 10:33) Mark points out the new teaching of Jesus's journey which began at Caesarea Philippi (Mark 8:27) through Capernaum in Galilee (Mark 9:30–33) and ends up in Jerusalem, where his suffering and death was accomplished as the fulfilment of his messianic destiny.

Regarding the Danielic background of the son of man's suffering, Thielman thinks that Jesus, as the Son of Man in Mark, followed the pattern laid out for the "one like a son of man" in Daniel 7:13 including his suffering and death.[276] Nevertheless, Bock says that "while the context does have the saints rejected and vindicated, it is not clear that Daniel's Son of Man suffers other than in his solidarity with the Saints of the Most High."[277] In this context, Marshall suggests that "in Dan 7 the Son of Man is seen as the representative of 'the Saints of the Most High' who suffers defeat and oppression at the hands of their enemies (Dan 7:21, 25)."[278]

In this regard, it is possible to argue that Jesus himself exploited the ambiguity which the phrase possessed already in Daniel 7. In Daniel 7, "one like a son of man" comes on the clouds (not to earth) before the Ancient of Days (God) and is invested with an everlasting kingdom which entails an exercise of God's sovereignty over all the peoples and kingdoms of the earth. This shows that the Danielic son of man is the glorious figure with everlasting power and dominion over all things and kingdoms rather than

---

274. France, *Gospel of Mark*, 334.
275. See Lane, *Gospel of Mark*, 292.
276. Thielman, *Theology of the New Testament*, 71.
277. Bock, "Son of Man," 898.
278. Marshall, "Son of Man," 776.

the suffering one. But at the end of the chapter, it is clear that this "son of man" is a kind of representative or corporate figure, as it is the "Saints of the Most High" who are invested with an everlasting kingdom. Thus, according to Mark's gospel, it is possible to see that this kingdom comes to the Son of Man only by means of suffering. So when Jesus says that "the Son of Man" must suffer many things (Mark 8:31) or that the Son of Man gives his life as a ransom for many in (Mark 10:45) or that the Son of Man will go just as it is written about him (Mark 9:12–13), it is appropriate to think that he is appealing to this tradition.

France believes Jesus's emphasis on his suffering as his Father's purpose for him must happen because he believed the scriptures. In his passion predictions (Mark 9:12; 14:21, 49) "Jesus finds the patterns for what is to happen to him." He also believes that the human figure of Daniel 7:13 is presented later in the chapter to represent the holy people of God who have been oppressed by the worldly empires and their rulers before the final judgment takes place which will be in their favour but will lead to the destruction of their enemies (Dan 7:17, 22). However, France strongly argues that "it is not in their suffering and defeat but in their victory that they are represented in Daniel's dream by the human figure."[279] Put simply, for France, even though the suffering of Jesus as the Son of Man is the scriptural truth which must happen, and though he was described representing the holy people of God, he represented them not in their suffering and defeat but in sharing his eternal authority with them; thus, he is a victorious, not a suffering figure.

Furthermore, Seccombe also argues that "though he [the Danielic son of man] shares humanity with those he comes to save, he is depicted as a glorious figure whose destiny is power and dominion."[280] In other words, it is true that in Daniel 7 son of man is described as the victorious king with universal dominion or authority, not a suffering figure. Nevertheless, it is appropriate to argue that while he remains a glorious figure for ever, he is able to identify himself, willingly, with the oppressed or afflicted humanity (people of God) not simply for the sake of sharing their sufferings but also with the purpose of saving them from their afflictions with his eternal

---

279. France, *Gospel of Mark*, 334; cf. 179–183.
280. Seccombe, *King of God's Kingdom*, 442.

purpose of sharing his dominion and authority with them. Further, similar to the function of the "one like a son of man" in Daniel 7:25, the idea of Jesus's being handed over by the Jewish authorities in Mark 9:31; 10:33 and by Judas Iscariot in Mark 14:10, 20–21, which would be fulfilled according to the scriptures (Mark 14: 49) shows divine purpose to the point of giving Jesus's life as the ransom to save many (Mark 10:45) and his unique self-identification to help those who are in need, even at the margins of life.

3.5.2.3.3.3. Judgment and eschatological coming of the Son of Man
Mark's Jesus speaks of the eschatological coming of the Son of Man in his Father's glory accompanied by the holy angels (see Mark 8:38; cf.13:26; 14:62). As referred by Reynolds, this indicates the future coming of Jesus, as the Son of Man and his judgmental role since he comes "in clouds with great power and glory" and sends his angels to gather his elect or, according to Ezra, the righteous.[281]

In the language of being ashamed of those who were ashamed of him (Jesus), Mark 8:38 also denotes his role of eschatological judgment. In other words, although Mark's Son of Man is not explicitly described as being involved in judgment, his coming in clouds with great power and glory (Mark 13:26) and being seated on the right hand of the power in Mark 14:62 suggests this role. Also, even though the Danielic "one like a son of man" in Daniel 7:13–14 is not explicitly presented as a judge, it reminds Mark's readers of the Danielic son of man's coming with the clouds of heaven to judge, precisely because he is seen receiving kingly authority from the Ancient of Days. One of a king's major roles is to oversee the judgments in his kingdom. Similarly, while commenting on Mark 13:26, Bruce says that "the Son of Man coming in clouds harks back to the 'one like a son of man' who, in Daniel's vision of the day of judgment comes 'with the clouds of heaven' to be presented before the Ancient of Days and to receive universal dominion from him (Dan 7:13–14)." Bruce goes further to explain that Jesus's response to the high priest's question – "I am, and you will see the Son of Man seated at the right hand of Power, and coming with clouds of heaven" – indicates "an emphasis of the judgment motif by the fusion of

---

281. Reynolds, *Apocalyptic Son*, 68; see also *4 Ezra* 13: 12, 27.

Dan 7:13f and Psalms 110:1 where the one called 'my Lord' is asked to be seated until the Lord's enemies are completely subdued."[282]

Furthermore, in the overall context of chapter seven in which the judgment of the beasts (worldly rulers) and vindication of the holy people of God occurred, one can see "the court sat in judgment" in Daniel 7:10 which indicates the Danielic son of man's judgment role.[283] In short, the combination of the OT passages (Dan 7 and Ps 110:1) in Mark 14:62 strongly points out to the judgmental role of the Mark's Son of Man.

3.5.2.4. Conclusion

In conclusion, the term, the "Son of Man" is found in OT and NT canons, implicitly and explicitly, referring to a particular person or to humanity. It is a key image in the Christology of the New Testament. Thus, idiomatically, one can see that pointing out the figure of Daniel 7, Jesus refers it to himself as a unique human being with unique authority, where "one like a son of man" is depicted as a human figure who comes on the clouds of heaven (in glory) to the Ancient of Days (God) to share in divine activities, such as judgment and vindication. In Daniel 7, this figure is described as the victorious conqueror, yet he identified himself with the afflicted people of God with the purpose of not only rescuing them from their present oppression by their enemies but also to share his eternal dominion with them.

Such ideas appear also in Jewish apocalyptic writings, such as *1 Enoch* or the Similitudes and *4 Ezra* which have many similarities to Daniel 7 and the Synoptic Gospels even though there are some fundamental differences. There is no evidence in Jesus's teachings that shows Jesus was using any of these apocryphal texts to explain his Son of Man sayings. Unlike, Jesus's teachings about the Son of Man in the Gospels which involve his rejection and suffering as a crucial part of his identity and destiny, the apocryphal texts do not contain this notion. They only describe their Son of Man as a heavenly, transcendent and exalted figure who judges the wicked people and rescues righteous ones. In other words, the Jewish apocryphal writings do not show their "Son of Man's" life and works such as his suffering and

---

282. Bruce, "Son of Man Sayings," 54.
283. See Bowman, Komoszewski and Bock, *Jesus in His Place*, 246–247.

crucifixion on behalf of others,[284] and his resurrection on the third day which we find about Jesus, the Son of Man, in the Synoptic Gospels.

Finally, in the Synoptic Gospels in general and in the Gospel of Mark in particular the readers can clearly see the God-like authority of Jesus as the Son of Man on earth, able to forgive sins, perform astounding miracles and assuming lordship over the old traditions of the law and regulations. Jesus's self-identification with the suffering, sinful and afflicted people of God whom he came to save rather than righteous ones is indicated in the Son of Man sayings implicitly and explicitly in both OT and NT passages. As noted above, his eschatological and glorious coming to judge the world involves not only his act of vindication to save the lost who have been experiencing suffering but also his eternal power and authority to destroy their enemies.

3.6. Chapter Conclusion

Jesus was described and declared by various human and supernatural sources to have different names and/or titles; among these are the Messiah, Son of David, the Son of God and the Son of Man.

Contrary to those claiming to be Messiahs in the OT and in first and second century Judaism, Jesus of the Gospels, particularly in Mark, redefined and reinterpreted himself and his own messianic role in a unique and unexpected sense. Even though he did not deny it, he did not openly acclaim his messiahship at first precisely because of the connotation the term contained in the minds of his contemporaries. He gave his own redefinition of what it means to be the Messiah, God's chosen king, with a different meaning which involves his own suffering, death and resurrection with the unique purpose of saving or liberating others particularly those who are at the margins of the society, poor and outcast.

Jesus was recognized as being a royal messianic figure by traditional Jews and early Christians. The gospel writers affirm that Jesus is the Son of David precisely because he was a direct descendent of King David. However, according to Mark, he is the one and only Messiah and Son of David because

---

284. This idea is not explicitly stated in Daniel 7 but, as briefly discussed above, Danielic Son of Man identified himself with the oppressed people of God to help.

he is of higher station and authority than David for he is also the Lord of David, the Son of God.[285]

Furthermore, Mark in his narrative clearly emphasizes that Jesus is God's Son. This was repeatedly affirmed by various sources such as God self, demons and finally many people. According to the second evangelist, Jesus was understood and declared as God's Son because the titles above (the Messiah and Son of David) are inadequate to explain the full identity of Jesus for the reasons mentioned above. In addition, throughout the gospel, Jesus's divine identity was revealed and declared by the marginalized and liminal people rather than his first followers who received private training from him precisely because, as I argued above, the right to determine who can see Jesus's true identity and his eternal agenda and who cannot, belongs only to God. In other words, the matter of clearly seeing and hearing the mystery of God's kingdom in Jesus is absolutely under God's control.

Likewise, Jesus whose unique identity must not be separated from his unique destiny was affirmed by himself (Jesus) to be the unique Son of Man with God-like authority explaining his person and ministry in terms of vindication or/and exaltation through suffering in fulfilment of the scripture back in Daniel 7, and his glorious coming to judge the world. Put simply, tracing back to Daniel 7:13–14, Mark tells his readers that while his Jesus has unique authority on earth, he also identified him with the suffering people of God as being their representative. Finally he was vindicated by God and this will be seen when he shares his authority with them on his glorious return.

Finally, the next chapter investigates Jesus's marginality and liminality, and his self-identification with all humanity in general and with those who are marginalized and liminal in particular. His unique death on the cross and subsequent resurrection made him the unique Messiah of God with unique purpose of saving or liberating many others.

---

285. See Kingsbury, *Christology*, 113.

CHAPTER 4

Jesus's Marginality and Liminality

4.1. Introduction

In the previous chapters of this work, it has been shown that from the very beginning of his gospel, Mark introduces Jesus with his divine name and divine activities as the uniquely divine Son of God, and his Yahweh-like coming to the marginalized humanity to help and to save. Mark also teaches that Jesus is the unique Messiah of God with the unique purpose, not simply revealing his divine Sonship to God through miracles, extraordinary teaching and his matchless godly character including forgiving sins of people, but also demonstrating his unique divine messiahship as the suffering, crucified and vindicated Son of Man.

As Elizondo said, "one of the unquestioned constants in the life of Jesus as portrayed in the Gospels was his association with socially despised outsiders and untouchables."[1] The second evangelist also emphasizes that Jesus identified himself with various people who were known as poor and outcast in both Jewish and gentile territories.

Even though Jesus does not exclude dealings with the social elite, Mark emphasizes that Jesus particularly associated himself with the ordinary people; and revealed himself especially to the poor and outcasts. This was in marked distinction to the approach of Jewish religious leaders in Jerusalem as will be discussed below. He revealed himself to the marginalized individuals so that they could not only understand him but also recognize who he is and as a result declare and share the truth that they have grasped with others. It

---

1. Elizondo, *Jesus the Galilean*, 274.

was because, as indicated earlier, since the power of revealing himself to others belongs to Jesus alone, the poor and outcasts sometimes have insights into the truth of God in Jesus that even the expected scholars (religious experts) might miss. In other words, Jesus's divine identity as God's messianic Son was revealed to, and understood and declared by marginalized ones while Jewish religious scholars and his taught disciples missed it.

Furthermore, as Jane Kopas said, "according to the gospel writers, Jesus both allowed the marginalized to speak their truth, and also he experienced that truth by being marginalized himself,"[2] similar to other Galileans, Jesus willingly became a marginalized Galilean Jew in several ways.

This chapter seeks to discuss not only Jesus's association with the poor and outcasts, as already emphasized, but it investigates the marginality and liminality of Jesus himself, for the sake of others. In doing so, some questions need to be answered: how and in what ways Jesus became marginalized? Who or what made him marginalized and liminal? What do the gospels in general and Mark in particular say in this regard? What was or is the major purpose of Jesus's liminality and marginalized death on the cross?

4.2. Jesus's Voluntarily Marginalization as Galilean Jew

4.2.1. Jesus the Galilean Jew

"Almost the entire career of Jesus of Nazareth lay within the borders of this tiny region" [Galilee],[3] so that Galilee therefore formed the area in which Jesus conducted most of his earthly work. Clark goes on to say that "all the rest of the gospel account, prior to the passion narrative, is in the setting of the sea of Galilee."[4] Readers must first understand that Jesus was marginalized himself by becoming a marginalized Galilean Jew by birth and beginning his public ministry in and around the Sea of Galilee.[5]

---

2. For this perspective, consult http://www.theway.org.uk/Back/33Koas (see also Kopas, *Outsiders*, 117).

3. Clark, "Galilee," 347.

4. Clark, 347.

5. It is true that Jesus did not become a Galilean Jew at this point but he returned from Judean desert to Galilee (Mark 1:14), however, by saying he became a Galilean Jew, I

Further, the second evangelist also tells us that Jesus, the divine Son of God has come, in a human form, to proclaim the kingly rule of God around the Sea of Galilee. He was not just Jesus, but Jesus of Nazareth,[6] culturally situated as despised and socially conditioned as poor by time and place.[7] Based on this, Kopas describes Jesus as "marginal as regards his origins in national and world history."[8] It is useful to invoke Duling's understanding of self-imposed marginalization here. He defined "*voluntary marginality*" using three criteria; "the individuals and groups who *choose* 'outsider-hood,' that is, to not live according to commonly accepted norms, beliefs, and behaviours of the larger society."[9] This fits the marginality of Jesus himself since he willingly and initially came to Galilee (see Mark 1:14). In addition, as Lee noticed "from historical studies that Galileans were very much a liminal and marginalized people,"[10] Jesus the divine Son of God, voluntarily, became a marginalized and liminal Galilean beginning his public ministry primarily among marginalized Galileans. Furthermore, according to Elizondo, Jesus who is described to be "a craftsman in an insignificant village and son of Mary, . . . becomes one of the rejects and marginalized of society, . . . who suffer exclusion, segregation, and rejection simply because of ethnicity or origin."[11] Thus the gospels indicate that Jesus nationally became a marginalized Jew in Galilee. Meier also profoundly explains that Jesus was marginalized and liminal in various ways, physically, socially, politically, economically and religiously; he willingly presented himself not just as a

---

am referring to his divine origin since according to Mark, Jesus is God's Son.

6. It is true that the Gospels tell us that Jesus was born not in Nazareth but in Bethlehem. However, he stayed in Bethlehem only for a short time or just for weeks; thus canonical gospels claim that he is known as Jesus of Nazareth, not Jesus of Bethlehem precisely because, from his childhood, he grew up in Nazareth.

7. See Costas, "Evangelism," 51–59.

8. Kopas, *Outsiders*, 118.

9. Two other definitions of marginality by Duling are, *involuntary marginality*, the most familiar meaning of marginality, which included not only artisans, the poor and dispossessed, and the unclean, but also those at *any* level of the social structure who . . . were denied the opportunity to participate in roles expected of them . . .; [and] *"Marginal Man,"* an individual who, because of birth, migration, or conquest is "doomed" to live between two or more competing normative schemes . . . (Duling, "Matthew as Marginal Scribe," 521). See also Turner, *Dramas*, 133.

10. Lee, *From a Liminal Place*, 4.

11. Elizondo, *Jesus the Galilean*, 274.

generic human being, a Greek or a Roman, or even as someone from elite family in Judea but as a marginal Galilean Jew who lived with his ordinary family as a village craftsman in a village located on the periphery of all the structures of the powers of the world.[12]

In other words, Jesus went on to become a homeless marginalized Galilean Jew. Meier goes to explains that Jesus left home and his family to lead his purposefully marginalized life.[13] Therefore the reader understands that Jesus not only became marginalized as a Galilean Jew but that he also became homeless and an itinerant preacher of the kingdom of God. Furthermore, as he did to himself, Jesus attracted his first followers to separate themselves from their location and asked them to leave their households without promising a new household to enter. Regarding the main purpose of Jesus's leaving home, Lee suggests that "Jesus left home in order to appropriate the Galilean liminality as his own personal reality. Leaving home for Jesus was an act of owning his Galilean liminality." Put simply, as Lee goes on to say, "identity does not exist apart from a person's households, kinship relations, and village,"[14] Jesus purposefully went out of his social structure and separated himself from the location that had given him his identity. He willingly entered his liminal situation and became a liminal Galilean in order to bring about on earth the reign of God.

However, who were Galileans among whom Jesus became marginalized and liminal? And what was their geographical, racial, social, political and economic situations which distinguish them from others in the Palestinian regions during Jesus's days?

4.2.2. Jesus and Galilee

It is true that, according to the first three gospels, Galilee was the original place and the primary locus of Jesus's earthly ministry in the northernmost part of Palestine at the time of the Second Temple. However, the question of who the "Galileans" certainly were, during those days, is still an unresolved issue.

---

12. See Meier, *Marginal Jew*, vol. 1, 6–9.
13. See Meier, 407.
14. Lee, *From a Liminal Place*, 63–66.

Nevertheless, some, such as Paul Flesher, believe that, in ancient Israel long before the time of Jesus, the tribes of Zebulon, Naphtali, Issachar and Ascher settled in Galilee; later on it belonged to David's kingdom and then, after the separation of Israel from Judah, to the northern nation of Israel until the Assyrian empire conquered northern Israel in 733–722 BC. Much of the population was then evacuated out of Galilee and replaced with others. In other words, Galilee was emptied of its population at the time following the Assyrian invasions and remained largely uninhabited until the beginning of the first century BC, for more than half a millennium.

However, new archaeological evidence shows that at the beginning of the first century BC, over a period of a couple of decades, new villages started to appear. The rapid increase in the numbers in the Hasmonean kingdom in Jerusalem caused great need for land; thus Judean Jews were forced to migrate from the south into Galilee in the north.[15] Archaeological research indicates that this new growing number of inhabitants in Galilee were transplanted Judeans. Some reasons for this direction of migration was that, like the Judeans in the South, Galileans avoided non-Jewish money and also used the coins made by the Hasmonean rulers of Jerusalem. Second, Galileans had similar interest in using ritual pools to purify themselves according to the Judaism of the period. Third, Galileans used stone drinking vessels to protect themselves from impurity. Fourth, Galileans followed Judean diet (food laws) in that they totally avoided eating pork. The absence of pork bones in the garbage of the time also reveals that inhabitants of Galilee were Jews.[16] Finally, as other ancient people, the Galileans used oil lamps to provide light in their houses, either manufactured by themselves or imported from Jerusalem or collected from Jerusalem when they returned from their pilgrimage to the temple. All these and other factors identify the first century Galileans in all likelihood as religiously devout Jews who had strong connection with the temple services in Jerusalem. Therefore, it is appropriate to say that the Galilean population of Jesus's time were descendants of Judean immigrants of a century or so earlier.[17]

---

15. See Matthew 2:22–23; see also Mordechai, "Hasmonean Dynasty's Activities," 41–50.

16. See Reed, *Archaeology*, 27–28.

17. See Clark, "Galilee," 344–345; Reed, *Archaeology*, 49–53. For further information, consult Flesher, "Why Did Joseph Live in Galilee?" http://enrichmentjournal.ag.org

However, it is difficult to conclude that the whole Palestine was entailed one and a unified nation living together harmoniously and doing everything in common since there were some significant differences between groups. Galilean Jews in the north and the Judean Jews in the south had a number of important differences. Vermes argues that "not only did it [Galilee] have its own peculiar past, but its political, social and economic organization also contributed to distinguish it from the rest of Palestine."[18] The term "Galilean" has a variety of ways to explain in those days. "To some it just might mean an outsider, or someone who is not really an old Jew of the traditional sort . . . because [they] had traditionally not been Jewish at the time of the Maccabean Revolt . . . before Jesus."[19]

In this regard, the situation in Galilee corresponded to what pertained among Jewish people in general. France argues that it is a gross distortion of the historical and cultural reality to think that "the Jewish" were an undifferentiated or united community since they live in the Holy Land. Having discussed seven points which distinguished Galileans from the rest of Palestinian Jews, racially, geographically, politically, economically, culturally, linguistically and religiously, France continues to say that "even an impeccably Jewish Galilean in first-century Jerusalem was not among his own people; he was as much a foreigner . . . His accent would immediately mark him out as 'not one of us'."[20] Generally speaking, Galilean people were considered to be despised among Judeans; and it was among them that Jesus was born and took on this marginalized status upon himself.

4.2.3. The Significance of Jesus's Galilean Identity[21]

The point here, in discussing Galilee and Galileans, is not primarily about the historical, archaeological, political or religious understanding of the social world of the region (Galilee) and its inhabitants. It is, rather, about the symbolic-theological meaning of Galilee for the first century Christians and their writings about Jesus of Nazareth.

---

18. Vermes, *Jesus the Jew*, 43.

19. White, "Galilee."

20. France, *Gospel of Matthew*, 5–6.

21. Regarding the significance of Jesus' Galilean identity, consult Rosado, "Significance of Galilee,". http://www.rosado.net

It is important to discuss a few more ways in which the Galilean Jews were distinct from the Judean Jews, and the significance of Jesus's Galilean identity. First of all, geographically and racially Galilean Jews were distinct from Judeans. Galileans lived in the northern part, and Judeans lived in the southern part of Palestine. It is also very important to know that the geographical references in a biblical text are significant and help us understand the main point that the writer is making. Thus, just as Matthew did, Mark also structured his narrative around a geographical framework dividing the north in which Jesus lived and began his popular ministry from the south in which he died and rose again. Thus, the reader understands that Galileans lived in the coast of northern Palestine far away from Jerusalem, the capital City and the centre of religion and theology.

"Galilee was separated from Judea by the non-Jewish territory of Samaria, and from Perea in the southeast by the Hellenistic settlements of Decapolis."[22] Furthermore, having made his home base in Capernaum, it is here, along the fringes of Galilee, that Jesus lived and worked, making several visits into regions of the Decapolis.[23] Likewise, Freyne says, the "Jesus' movement in this 'outer' border regions of essentially Jewish Galilee pointed to his greater sense of freedom with regard to contact with non-Jews than . . . his Galilean co-religionists."[24]

Put differently, even in Galilee, Jesus was seen among non-Jews (or neighbouring Gentiles), particularly, when his movement extended to the coasts of the northern regions of Palestine and Syro-Phoenicia.[25] All this reveals the marginality and liminality of Jesus, the Galilean Jew, not only because he lived and worked among marginalized and liminal Galileans – far away from the holy city of Jerusalem – but also because of his contact with people of other ethnicities and religions moving out into the marginalized gentile[26] regions, as discussed in the earlier, exegetical section of this work.

---

22. France, *Gospel of Matthew*, 6.
23. See Hertig, "Multi-ethnic Journeys," 23–36.
24. Freyne, *Jesus a Jewish Galilean*, 109–110.
25. See Mark 7:1–8:10; see also France, *Gospel of Mark*, 294–309.
26. However, one needs to know that Gentiles living in or around a predominantly Jewish area may have felt "'marginalized'" in relation to the Jewish majority; but in relation to the Roman Empire, it was they who were the mainstream.

As mentioned above, since the resettlement of Galilee in the first century BC, one can see that, racially, Galileans became a mixed population with some conservative Jewish areas such as Nazareth and Capernaum, and largely pagan cities such as Tiberias and Sepphoris.[27] Further, for Jews living in Galilee, their homes were not only surrounded by, but also inhabited by other gentile nationalities such as Phoenicians, Syrians, Greeks, Romans and others.

4.2.4. "Galilee of the Gentiles"

A few passages in the OT (e.g. Josh 20:7, 21: 32; 1 Kgs 9:11; 2 Kgs 15:29 and 1 Chr 6:76) refer to "Galilee," indicating to the location of the region in the northernmost of Palestine. The phrase "Galilee of the nations" or "Galilee of the Gentiles" is uncommon in the ancient literature as well as in the Jewish documents in the Second Temple period and afterwards. As referred by Chancey, even in the Dead Sea Scrolls only the single word "Galilee" is mentioned, not "Galilee of the Gentiles."[28] Josephus, in his works, also mentioned just the single word "Galilee" and then 161 times, but never "Galilee of the Gentiles." He had been commander of the rebel Jewish forces in 66 AD and had fortified many of the cities. It is only in Isaiah 9:1–2 that the phrase "Galilee of the Gentiles" or "Galilee of the nations" is found. Matthew in his gospel (4:15) quotes it as the fulfilment of the OT prophecy precisely because all nations are to be part of salvation through the message of the kingdom of God in Jesus, the Galilean Jew.[29]

The question, then, remains why was the region called "Galilee of the Gentiles" since most of its inhabitants were Jews? According to Freyne, the name "Galilee" came to mean "circle" or "district" indicating that the region was surrounded by gentile areas, such as the coastal plain to the west and the Jordan rift to the east, Esdraelon to the south, and the mountains in the north.[30] As Clark also argued, the name "'Galilee of nations' or 'of Gentiles' reflected a reputation for racial variety and mixture,"[31] Galileans were con-

---

27. See France, *Gospel of Matthew*, 6.
28. Chancey, *Myth of a Gentile*, 170–173; see 4Q522, 4Q Prophecy of Joshuah.
29. See also Chancey, 173.
30. See Freyne, *World of the New*, 3–9.
31. Clark, "Galilee," 345.

sidered to be a mixture of all nations' community, not only racially but also culturally. Further, racially, Galileans were despised by Judean Jews because "they were considered not only ignorant of the law but also impure because of their regular contacts with the Gentiles who lived all around them."[32]

Second, culturally and socially, Galilean Jews were rejected and despised by their southern neighbours, the Judeans, because of this very reputation that they were a racially and culturally mixed people. In other words, they were considered as impure Israelites due to their openness to the Hellenistic influence. This multiracial and multicultural background caused Galileans, to become objects or targets of Judean cruel humour, when they speak in incorrect Aramaic in a distinctive and jarring accent which was strange and hard to understand to Jews from Judea and elsewhere. Vermes states, "the distinction between the various gutturals almost completely disappeared in Galilean Aramaic; the weaker guttural sounds, in fact, ceased even to be audible."[33] Further, the readers of Mark and Matthew discover that Galileans's particular accent betrayed them; for instance, Peter was recognized as the follower of Jesus, the Galilean Jew, due to his unique Galilean accent; thus, he was told, "You are also one of them, for your accent betrayed you" (Mark 14:70).

Moreover, culturally and socially, Galileans were considered as ignorant, uneducated and outcasts by their orthodox Judean fellows. For instance, the terms "peasants" and *am ha-arez*[34] indicate or apply to the stigma of a religiously uneducated or uncivilized person. Later, in the first and second century AD, Pharisees's and rabbis's attitude towards Galileans was hardly complimentary. Using an anonymous source, Vermes quotes, "no man may marry the daughter of the 'am ha-arez', for they are like unclean animals, and their wives like reptiles, and it is concerning their daughters that scripture says: 'cursed be he who lies with any kind of beast' (Deut 27:21, RSV)."[35]

---

32. Freyne, *Jesus and the Gospels*, 216–217.
33. Vermes, *Jesus the Jew*, 52–53.
34. The term *am ha-arez* in Talmud applies "the people of the land" to uneducated Jews, who were deemed likely to be negligent in their observance of the commandments due to their ignorance, and the term combines the meanings of "rustic" with those of "boorish, uncivilized, ignorant." For further information, consult "*Am ha'arez*," http://en.wikipedia.org/wiki/Am_ha'aretz.
35. See Vermes, *Jesus the Jew*, 54–55.

Not only in the rabbinic writings but also in the Gospel of John, as in other gospels in the New Testament, the difference between Galileans and Judeans is clearly indicated since the Messiah, Jesus, was not expected to come from Galilee (see John 7:41, 45–52). In addition, Vermes goes on to explain that "Jesus could have been found guilty of the charge of religious impropriety levelled at the Galileans in general" as he was surrounded by outcasts and accepted the hospitality of the marginalized people. So according to the OT Levitical system, Jesus was considered as impure, by the religious.[36] For instance, according to the second evangelist, Galilee was the place where Jesus found Mary Magdalene and healed her of demon possession (Mark 15:40–41; 16:9; see also Luke 8:2). Therefore, one can see Jesus the marginalized Galilean Jew, willingly, associating himself with those who are marginalized and liminal, socially as well as culturally, in order to liberate them from the plights they were in. Jesus recognized that people only associate with those they feel a bond with.

Third, politically, Galilee was ruled by Herod Antipas, a son of Herod the great, during the time of Jesus. This meant there was a further distancing from Rome, the centre of law and government. Judea and Samaria had however come under the direct rule of Roman governors. In those days, Callahan says, Galilee was "known for being a hotbed of political activity and some of it violent."[37] He goes on to explain that the mixed nature of Galilean Jews in the northern Palestine, with collective consciousness, caused unusual political turmoil in the area of Galilee.[38]

Galilee was also known as a centre of revolutionary movements against the Roman government. It was the original home of Judas the Galilean, son of Ezekias, and the founder of Zealot movement, who attempted to overthrow the Roman rule in 6 AD. It was Judas the Galilean, one of the famous characters of the day, who made the region unsafe and gained possession of the weapons stored in the royal arsenal in Sepphoris, after Herod's death. However, eventually, the Roman governors captured and crucified him and

---

36. See Vermes, 55–56.

37. However, it is true that the extent of political fervour and violence in Galilee in Jesus's time is disputed.

38. See Callahan, "Galilee: A Portrait," http://www.pbs.org/wgbh/pages/frontline/shows/relegion/portrait/galilee.html.

two thousand other Jews and destroyed Sepphoris and sold its inhabitants into slavery.[39] In other words, the word "Galilean" is associated with Judas the Galilean, and rebellion or banditry was common in Galilee and as an area associated with a negative political connotation. Likewise, since the term "Galilean" has a sense of being insurrectionist who resisted the Roman rulers (e.g. Herod and his sons), the term in itself may at time be not only a geographical indication but may also mean something political.

From the Gospels it becomes clear that Jesus was regarded by the Romans as being suspect. "Jesus became a political suspect in the eyes of the rulers of Jerusalem because he was a Galilean."[40] During Pontus Pilate's governorship, some of Jesus's enemies attempted to associate Jesus and his followers with the Galilean extremists. Thus at Jesus's crucifixion, there hung the sign "the King of Jews" (Mark 15:26) above his head. This suggests the underlying fear the authorities had of Galilean rebellion movements and their desire to snuff out any potential rebellion. Put differently, Galilee was considered the land of despised, the outcasts and marginalized people, and this included Jesus; it was also the place to which troublemakers wanted to escape and there hide themselves from their Judean enemies. In a nutshell, Jesus the Galilean Jew willingly became one of these marginalized and excluded people, even being painted as a political suspect by some.

Fourth, debate continues among scholars with different points of view regarding the effects of the socioeconomic background of Galilee during Jesus's time, and its impact on his message and ministry. For example, some believe that the Galilee in which Jesus was born and raised as a Galilean Jew was poor, and consequently his first followers were poor and his audience was made up of the masses of the poor.[41] However others think that Galilee was, economically, a prosperous society.[42]

Vermes has concluded that "the Galilee of Jesus was populous and relatively wealthy . . . [and] the reason for its economic well-being was the

---

39. See Schurer, *History of the Jewish*, 332; cf. 275; see also Chancey, *Myth of a Gentile*, 50–51.

40. Vermes, *Jesus the Jew*, 57.

41. For further explanation consult http://www.pbs.org/wgbh/pages/frontline/shows/religion//jesus/socialclass.html.

42. See Fiensy and Hawkins, *Galilean Economy*, 41–44.

extraordinary fertility of the land."[43] France adds, "Galilee offered better agricultural and fishing resources than the more mountainous territory of Judea, making the wealth of some Galileans the envy of their southern neighbours."[44] That was the reason why Josephus described it as "so rich in soil and pasturage and produces such variety of trees, that even the most indolent are tempted by these facilities to devote themselves to agriculture."[45] Therefore, it is possible to think that Galilee was rich not only in farming or agriculture but also in fishing and industry; in other words, in manufacturing various products and trade as well.

However, the problem is that even though the region was rich and fertile, in the context of the gospels, particularly Mark's gospel, the vast majority of the people mentioned were ordinary and poor. The major reason for this was that "the community would have been obliged to participate in the economic system of its rulers, whether through taxation, tithing and trade."[46] In other words, taxation, not only to the secular government (Herodian regime and Roman tribute), but also tithes to the religious institutions (e.g. the temple officials and/or high-priestly families) was a great burden on the poor. As indicated earlier, the ruling elite among whom most of Jesus's opponents came from, and their retainers, controlled the lives of most people, particularly the common people, the poor, the destitute and the outcast. Some of them lost their lands either by force, as a result of their failure to pay taxes, or by heavy taxation from the state. Jesus of Nazareth could be understood as a marginalized Galilean Jew among these economically poor and oppressed people. These would include peasants, tenant farmers, day labourers, slaves, and the various landless groups that included fishermen, artisans, and other craftsmen.[47]

Finally, Galileans were a marginalized people precisely because, even though they celebrated their Jewishness and were loyal to the Jewish nationality, they were ridiculed by their neighbours, and were considered as

---

43. Vermes, *Jesus the Jew*, 45–46.
44. France, *Gospel of Matthew*, 6.
45. See also Vermes, *Jesus the Jew*, 45–46.
46. Rohrbaugh, "Social Location," 141.
47. See Rohrbaugh, 151.

not only foreigners, but also outcasts in their own country, particularly by Judean Jews in and around Jerusalem.

4.2.5. Jesus of Nazareth

Jesus was born in Bethlehem in Judea, but he was not known as Jesus of Bethlehem nor Jesus of Jerusalem, but Jesus of Nazareth in Galilee. Further, even in Galilee, he was not from the capital city, Sepphoris, a major center of political activity of the region, but from Nazareth, a small peasant village. It "was a home to fewer than four hundred people, almost all farmers."[48] However Nazareth was not completely isolated as it was within about four or five miles from Sepphoris.

It is also said that there is no mention of Nazareth prior to the Gospels and that there is minimal information about it. It was not mentioned either in the Old Testament or in Josephus's works or in the rabbinic literature of the Mishnah. "All four [Gospels] regard the village [Nazareth] as the hometown of Jesus, and John suggests that it was not a notable town."[49] That was the reason why Nathaniel expressed a common opinion at the time, asking, "Can anything good come out of Nazareth?" (John 1:46), which indicates that even in Galilee, Nazareth did not have good reputation. So the reason why Jesus was called Jesus of Nazareth is because he grew up and spent most time doing his entire career in and around Nazareth of Galilee.

4.3. Jesus's Marginalized Occupation

In addition to his social location at the time, Jesus is to be seen as a marginalized and liminal Galilean Jew as regards his occupation. In most translations, Matthew[50] and Mark report that Jesus, along with his physical family, was a manual worker or carpenter (see Mark 6:3; Matt 13:55). The Greek term τέκτων (*tekton*) seems to be "a rather vague term that would mean he [Jesus] worked in either wood or stone,"[51] but nevertheless indicated an occupation

---

48. Bauckham, *Jesus*, 27.

49. Chancey, *Myth of a Gentile*, 83; cf. Matt 4:13; 13:54; 21:11; Mark 1:9; 6:1; Luke 4:16; John 1:45.

50. Whereas Mark shows that Jesus was a carpenter, Matthew reports that it is a trade of Joseph; thus, maybe Jesus learned it from Joseph, his physical father which was not an uncommon practice in ancient times.

51. Bauckham, *Jesus*, 27.

at the lower end of the peasant class. Put differently, the term *tekton* shows that Jesus's occupation of carpentry made him more marginalized than a peasant, since peasants were ones who either owned a piece of land or belonged to a family that had lost their lands due to their failure to pay taxes to the state (the Roman government). Jesus seems to be a rural peasant farmer in Nazareth because most of his parables and sayings during his teachings were firmly rooted in peasant society (e.g. the sower or sowing seed Mark 4:4–5 and the tenants and vineyard Mark 12:1–2);[52] however, since he used other images and parables (e.g. land owners, masters and their servants as well as slaves and their owners Mark 12:4, 9), it must be concluded that Jesus was "a rural artisan working often within typical peasant context."[53] It was also argued that Jesus and his family were village artisans even "below peasants on the socioeconomic scale. Moreover, the small minority who were village artisans would have been especially marginalized."[54] In other words, Jesus must be understood as a liminal and marginalized Jew on the lower social scale of the society, and economically, poor from the unwanted small village, originally. Further, Jesus is to be understood as the one who relied on the good will and economic support of his followers and thus "became marginal in the eyes of ordinary working Jews in Palestine, while remaining very much a Palestinian Jew himself."[55]

Likewise, Jesus attracted his first disciples, marginalized and liminal people from among his fellow Jews in Galilee, except Judas Iscariot (see Mark 3:13–19; also Matt 10:2–4; Luke 6:13–16). Put simply, whereas the other first apostles of Jesus were known as Galilean Jews, Judas Iscariot, the traitor or the man who was known for his betrayal of Jesus, was from Judea.[56]

In addition, unlike the other disciples who were fishermen, Matthew (Levi in Mark 2:14) was a tax collector. Although the tax collectors collected

---

52. Nevertheless, surely, Jesus could have been familiar with the way his social world worked generally – we cannot make too narrow a conclusion about his social position from his parables alone.

53. Oakman, *Jesus and the Peasants*, 31.

54. Rohrbaugh, "Social Location," 156; cf. Rohrbaugh, *New Testament*.

55. Meier, *Marginal Jew*, vol. 1, 8.

56. Even though the exact locality of Judas's original place is a bit doubtful, his second name, Iscariot indicates that Judas was a native of Kerioth (Josh 15:25) probably in southern Judea. For further information consult Kerr, "Judas Iscariot" at http://classic.net.bible.org/dictionary.phb?word=JUDAS.

"public money" and hence were known as publicans, they were a despised group among the religious Jews in particular. They were considered to be "quislings" who cooperated and benefited from their association with the occupying Romans. When Jesus invited Matthew to be one of his chosen disciples he further antagonized the local Pharisees because he was associating with "tax collectors and sinners"; in other words, in doing so, he was fraternising with the riffraff of society which further marginalized him from "good society."

Finally, except for Judas Iscariot who was from Judea – the region of the ruling elites and religious leaders – Jesus the Galilean Jew selected his other disciples for his eternal purpose from among Galileans. As noted earlier, Galilee was a land of rejected rebels and outcasts, where people wanted to flee to in order to escape from their enemies.

4.4. Jesus Became Marginalized as Regards His Unique Style of Teaching

Jesus was a marginalized and liminal Galilean Jew as regards his non-traditional source of teaching. "As a poor rural Galilean, he [Jesus] had never attended any scribal school or studied under a noted teacher";[57] he did not have any human teacher/rabbi to help him understand the Scriptures or to assist others during his earthly life and ministry.[58]

It is also true that even though

> from his childhood visits to the Temple to his death on the cross, . . . Jesus loved his Jewish religion with its unwavering hope in the God who saves . . ., however, . . . he does not seem to have been limited by an overly strict religious interpretation

---

57. Meier, *Marginal Jew*, vol. 1, 8.

58. In this regard, in response to my question, "Did not Jesus have any human teacher/rabbi to help him . . .?" during our private email discussion, John P. Meier's answer was, "I think what can be said is that, in his pronouncements on the Mosaic Law and *halakha*, Jesus shows not only knowledge of Scripture but also of sophisticated modes of interpretation (e.g. his teaching on the two commandments of love, which reflects what rabbis will later call the *gezara shawa*). So I think we can infer that somewhere, somehow, Jesus obtained a certain amount of training in reading and interpreting the Scriptures; how that happened we do not know." Meier, email discussion, 6 November 2015.

of the *Sabbath*, and the code of purity/impurity and exclusion that seems to have been common in his time.[59]

Put differently, Hooker says that "throughout his gospel, Mark depicts Jesus as a faithful upholder of the Torah (1:44; 3:4; 7:8–13; 10:3–9; 12:29–31, etc.) who attacks not the Torah itself, but the interpretation given . . . by the religious authorities of his day."[60] Furthermore, as will be discussed shortly, the Jewish religious leaders (Pharisees) and scholars (Scribes) pushed Jesus and his teachings to the margins of Judaism and thus marginalized him precisely because they misunderstood the source of his teaching authority. Thus, one can clearly see that there is a great difference between the teachings of the Jewish religious authorities and Jesus's unique teaching with astounding authority. For instance, Mark in 7:1–13 shows us that whereas the teachings of the religious groups of Jesus's day are derived from the "traditions of the elders" or the fathers of Judaism, Jesus's authority derives directly from his Father in heaven. Also, whereas the teaching authority of the Jewish leaders depended on the traditions of their religious fathers and their interpretation of the Torah, Jesus's teaching authority resided in himself. Put simply, regardless of his severe marginality and liminality by his opponents and their traditional teachings and practices, Jesus "proclaimed his own teachings with a sovereign authority whose basis was by no means clear to his opponents."[61]

In other words, it is true that Jesus believed in and had great respect for the Jewish religion of his time since it is based on the Scriptures. Nevertheless, he was not limited by the traditional interpretation of them as found in various religious practices (e.g. Sabbath, food laws and/or codes of purity and impurity) focusing on the rules and regulations of the fathers of Judaism. Rather, Jesus had his own exceptional plan emphasizing the kingdom-of-God movement. He taught that God looks at people's hearts and not their outward behaviour, or respectability. He taught that any person, including

---

59. Elizondo, *Jesus the Galilean*, 262. Visit also http://www.virgilioelizondo.com/1/docs/JESUS.

60. Hooker, *According to St. Mark*, 106.

61. Meier, *Marginal Jew*, vol. 1, 8.

especially the oppressed and poor – those who were left out by the human religious leaders, their teachings and practices – can be admitted into God's kingdom.

Finally, as Elizondo said, "Jesus became a man at once distant from all power centers of domination and at the crossroads where various people encounter one another." Thus, it is possible to see that in becoming a marginalized and liminal Galilean Jew and, living and working among marginalized Galilean inhabitants, Jesus's major purpose and goal is to uplift the downtrodden and to invite everyone to the kingly rule of God from all nations beginning with Israel. Further, Elizondo goes on explaining that the aim of Jesus's marginality as a Galilean Jew is to show that "he goes to the very depths of the tradition to bring out its farthest reaching implication."[62] Thus, his Galilean experience must be understood as his reparation to create a new humanity in which the rejected and excluded ones can find new possibility by Jesus through whom the newness was brought. The next section will show, in addition to self-marginalization, how and who caused Jesus's marginalization and liminality, and also the main purpose of his marginality and liminality.

4.5. Who Made Him Marginalized and Liminal?

In addition to his own voluntary marginality and liminality as a Galilean Jew in a marginalized region, Jesus became marginalized and liminal due to his own family and even his closest disciples, as we shall see. The remarkable fact is that although Jesus's enemies, such as the Jewish religious authorities (e.g. Pharisees, Sadducees, scribes, high priest and elders) and politicians (e.g. Herodians, the Roman governors) wanted to permanently marginalize Jesus by having him killed, Jesus knew that this was what was about to happen yet still set his face to go to Jerusalem in a determined way. He knew that his fate was to be crucified and that his crucifixion was essential in order both to fulfil the Jewish (OT) prophecies and to save many people, even by experiencing abandonment by God his Father on the cross. The next section will briefly describe Jesus's marginality not only by his religious

---

62. Elizondo, *Jesus the Galilean*, 273.

and political opponents, but also by his family and close friends as well as his loving Father.

His family and relatives: It was not only the religious authorities who opposed Jesus and his mission, but also Mark's readers knew that Jesus's family and friends were not sympathetic to him from the outset (Mark 3:21, 31–35). They misunderstood him, particularly his claim to be able to forgive sin (Mark 2:7) and other activities saying, "He is out of his mind" (Mark 3:22). In other words, "the religious authorities are not alone in their mistaken apprehensions of Jesus";[63] Jesus's relatives were no better than the scribes since both were blind to see the source of Jesus's power and his divine nature.

Jesus's family wanted to restrain him because they thought that he became mad. Since the verb κρατέω is a violent one, it indicates an analogous attitude on the side of Jesus's family to seize him or to arrest him, in a similar way to religious authorities in the gospel (see also Mark 6:17; 12:12). In other words, whereas the scribes from Jerusalem regarded Jesus as Beelzebub, the prince of demons (i.e. Satan, v. 22), Jesus's family perceived him as losing his mind or becoming possessed "since madness was often regarded due to possession by a demon."[64]

So Jesus was pushed to the margins not only by outsiders around Galilee (religious and political leaders) but by his own family and close friends through misunderstanding. However, the attempt of Jesus's family to restrain him for his own sake and for the reputation of his family was unsuccessful since "their places of privilege are taken by those who follow Jesus and whose concern, like his, is to do God's will."[65]

His first followers: Jesus also was marginalized not only by his own family and the religious and political leaders of his day in and around Galilee, Judea and Jerusalem, but also by his own close followers, the disciples, who were loved and invited by him and were privileged to receive his teachings privately as well as corporately. Peter was a spokesman or representative of the first followers and disciples of Jesus. In the beginning of the second half of Mark's gospel (e.g. Mark 8:31–33), he demonstrated his disagreement or

---

63. Edwards, *Gospel According to Mark*, 119.
64. Hooker, *According to St. Mark*, 115.
65. Hooker, 114.

opposition to God's eternal plan, attempting to avert him from his suffering and death. This prospect was unthinkable to Peter but inevitable for Jesus. As Edwards argues, "a near-truth is more dangerous than an obvious error, since a partial-truth is more believable."[66] So when Peter said, "You are the Messiah" (Mark 8:29), the readers can see that this is true. However, his rebuke of Jesus not to suffer and die must be understood as his opposition against the goal of Jesus's mission. When Jesus said, "the Son of Man must undergo great suffering, . . . and be killed . . . and rise again" (8:31), the term *must* indicates that Jesus's "suffering and death were *necessary*, predicted in the Scriptures and an expression of the will and purpose of God."[67] This would be fulfilled "in the shame of crucifixion as well as in the triumph of the resurrection."[68] To oppose this death and the resultant salvation of many people was to oppose God's eternal plan.

In addition, since Peter was seen as the spokesman or representative of all the disciples of Jesus and there is no record of any disagreement, they were probably all mistaken in their attitudes towards Jesus's mission, particularly, his shameful death on a Romans cross. When Jesus sharply rebuked Peter for opposing his plan to die and rise from the dead, as the Son of Man, Jesus first turns and looks at his disciples before rebuking Peter as the spokesman for the disciples (8:33). Thus it is likely that all the disciples thought in the same way as Peter; they had not clearly understood who Jesus was and his purpose for coming to earth (see also Mark 9:32–41; 10:32–45).

Jesus was later pushed to the margins by Peter, the leader of the apostles, when he followed Jesus at a distance in Mark 14:54. This foreshadowed Peter's denial of Jesus in the courtyard of the high priest (Mark 14:66–72). Likewise, Mark mentioned that all Jesus's disciples forsook their promises to die with Jesus (14:31), but instead left him alone and fled (14:50). In 14:66, 69–71, Peter denied Jesus three times (v. 49) as foretold by Jesus himself (14:30). Further, when denying Jesus, Mark records Peter as saying, "I do not know or understand what you are talking about" (14:68). Edwards suggests that two Greek terms for "know" are significant; "the first (*oida*) [οἶδα] tends to denote theoretical knowledge, and the second (*epistamai*)

---

66. Edwards, *Gospel According to Mark*, 255.
67. Painter, *Mark's Gospel*, 125.
68. Lane, *Gospel of Mark*, 301.

[ἐπίσταμαι] practical knowledge; Peter's denial is thus a total denial – in theory and practice!"[69]

In addition to the misunderstanding of Jesus's disciples in general and Peter's open denial of Jesus, Mark's readers discover that one of them, Judas Iscariot, betrayed Jesus secretly (Mark 14:43–46). Mark describes the arrest of Jesus as being instigated by the Jewish authorities, with three groups (e.g. chief priest, teachers of the law, and the elders) authorizing the arrest of Jesus (see Mark 14:43). The second evangelist also reports that Judas, "one of the twelve" whose name is mentioned earlier in Mark 3:19 and 14:10 is identified playing the major role as the antagonist of Jesus and "the betrayer" (v. 44). Moreover, although it is an act of love and respect to their great ones, Judas's kiss of Jesus, as part of irony in Mark, must be seen as "the first example of the *mockery* of Jesus, which will play a key role in the crucifixion narrative of chapter 15."[70] Thus, the readers realize that along with the Jewish religious leaders who counted Jesus as a bandit or rebel, Jesus was betrayed and arrested by someone from among his trusted followers whom he also taught.

Thus, even though it was happening as the fulfilment of the Scriptures and divine will of God, Jesus was pushed to the margins of death not only by various groups of people from both religious and political circles but also by his own family, his close friends, and even the disciples in his inner circle, who were expected to be sympathetic to him and help him in his mission.

Pharisees: Meier states that "the dirty little secret of NT studies is that no one really knows who the Pharisees were."[71] However, what is clear is that the name "Pharisee" is from the Greek term Φαρισαῖοιν or "*Pharisaios*," probably denoting a group of people who strictly avoided anything that might bring impurity. Even though the origin of the historical Pharisees is uncertain, as discussed by Beit Emanuel, there are enough material in the Gospels in which the term refers to the idea of their separation not simply from the influence of the culture of foreigners (Greek and Roman) who invaded their land but also from the usual practices of the common Jewish

---

69. Edwards, *Gospel According to Mark*, 450.
70. See Edwards, 438.
71. Meier, *Marginal Jew*, vol. 3, 311.

people in the land. The Pharisees were the most influential Jewish religious sect or party during Jesus's earthly career and were portrayed in the Gospels as the principal enemies of Jesus. This movement is thought to have originated in the third century BC, in days preceding the Maccabean wars, which were the result of Jews' reaction against Greek domination when they were forced to accept Greek culture with its unacceptable religious customs.[72]

The Pharisees have been considered the most meticulous and rigid observers not only of the Mosaic laws but also of the oral traditions handed down by their predecessors (see also Mark 7:1–13; Luke 18:10–12). Their concern was the strict observance of certain regulations such as the Sabbath rest, temple practice (e.g. purity rituals), tithing of agricultural produce, and food laws based on both the OT scriptures and their traditions.[73] They had developed a large body of literature on the interpretation and application of the law which was passed on as oral traditions that they considered to be as binding as the written law itself – oral and written law alike were regarded as having God's authority as they were extensions of the Mosaic Law.

The Pharisees were well respected by the ordinary people who were interested in their interpretation of the Torah. They trained scribes and disciples (Mark 2:16, 18 respectively, see also Matt 22:16; Luke 5:33). Further, they are said to have "a reputation for being the most exact or precise interpreters of the law (though this does not mean they always gave it the most rigorous interpretation)."[74] They were not theologically conservative with their belief in the resurrection of the dead (see particularly Acts 23:1–8), in a future judgment, and in hierarchies of angels and demons; they were open to new ideas, although strict on legal requirements.

It is also obvious that in Mark's gospel the Pharisees were the foremost opponents of Jesus who had been trying to trap and destroy him (Mark 2:24; 3:6; 8:11; 10:2). Their opposition against Jesus occurred not only while he had been undertaking his mission in the Galilean phase of his ministry but

---

72. For further explanation consult Beit Emanuel, "The Pharisees – Jewish Leaders in the First Century AD" http://www.bible-history.com/Pharisees/PHARISEES.

73. For further information, consult Just, 2001. "Jewish Groups at the Time of Jesus" [Online]. Available: http://catholic-resource.org/Bible/jewish_Groups.htm.

74. Bauckham, *Jesus*, 24.

also as he continued his activities in Judaea and Jerusalem.[75] Mark did not mention Pharisees in his passion narrative; however, the conspiracy between some Pharisees and Herodians to destroy Jesus, described in the early chapters of Mark, is an indication of Jesus's approaching passion. This involves Pharisees in those final events, even though their participation was not clearly stated in Mark.[76] In their strong antagonism against Jesus and his mission, the Pharisees tried to join together several groups, such as Sadducees, scribes (2:16; 7:1, 5), Herodians (3:6; 8:15; 12:13) and other Jews (7:3), not simply to make Jesus uncomfortable during his earthly ministry but also to push him towards death.

Herodians: Herodians were a small group of people that supported the government of the Herodian family during the time of Herod Antipas, the ruler of Galilee and Perea at the time of Jesus and John the Baptist. They were a party who are described in the Gospels; first, during Jesus's early days in Galilee (Mark 3:6) and then in Jerusalem (12:13–17; see also Matt 22:16; Luke 13:31–32). The second evangelist, particularly, mentioned them as opponents of Jesus on various occasions, each time with Pharisees, plotting together against Jesus and his mission on earth. Mark reports that the Pharisees drew the Herodians into their secret plan against Jesus's action of healing on the Sabbath day (Mark 3:6). Put simply, the Herodians along with Pharisees planned to destroy Jesus, particularly in the light of his apparent disdain for the Sabbath. In Mark 8:15 Jesus himself identified the dangerous association between the Herodians and Pharisees who wanted to kill him. Likewise, Herodians joined some Pharisees in sending some delegates to challenge Jesus's teaching in the temple in Jerusalem. At first, it seems that they were appreciating the contents of Jesus's teachings but in reality, they were trying to trap him with a question about his attitude towards paying taxes to Caesar. In asking those questions, they certainly wanted Jesus to entangle himself in an inescapable snare. Nevertheless, the Herodians were finally impressed by Jesus's reply to their tricky question and marvelled at him (Mark 12:17). To summarize, Jesus was marginalized by these combined groups of people, "a remarkable combination of religious

---

75. See Seccombe, *King of God's Kingdom*, 358.
76. See Sanders, *Judaism*, 290–293.

and political leaders – Pharisees and Herodians" starting already at the very beginning of his ministry.[77]

Sadducees: even though its origin is not well understood, the name "Sadducees" comes from the Hebrew "*tsaddiqim*" ("righteous ones") which is indicative of the righteous lives that they wished to live. Since many of them were priests, it is thought that the idea comes from Zadok, the high priest mentioned in 1 Kings 1:26. Most of them were from wealthy priestly and aristocratic families who interpreted the law more literally than Pharisees. Like the Pharisees they were another major religious group of people in Palestine; "probably no more than a few hundred members of wealthy aristocratic families."[78]

However, whereas the Pharisees were more respected by the people as a whole, the Sadducees were more political; and lacked popular support among the ordinary people. On the whole they were conciliatory with the Roman authorities, eager to preserve the political status quo in which they enjoyed considerable power and wealth. Put differently, whereas the Pharisees were known for their great influence on the masses, as referred by Sanders, "even when they speak against a king or high priest . . . (*Antiq.* 13.288) . . . the Sadducees [have] the confidence of the wealth alone but no following among the populace."[79]

Further, although the Pharisees held to the oral traditions of their fathers, the Sadducees held only, and followed to the letter, the written laws of Moses in five books (the Torah) in the Hebrew Bible. Nevertheless, it is not only the Pharisees but also according to Meier, "the Sadducees themselves had to develop their own set of traditions not explicitly found in Scripture, notably in questions of cult and purity." For instance, they "enforced the relatively new lunar calendar for temple feasts as opposed to the older solar calendar preserved and championed by the Quarantines";[80] and they became more conservative against the common beliefs of Judaism in which Jesus and Pharisees agreed.

---

77. Hooker, *According to St. Mark*, 106.
78. Bauckham, *Jesus*, 26.
79. Sanders, *Judaism*, 389.
80. Meier, *Marginal Jew*, vol. 3, 637.

However, in the whole of ancient literature and even in their own literature, the Sadducees are not described positively nor are their cases defended in their own voices; even in the Gospels, in Josephus's works, and Rabbinic literature, Sadducees were described negatively by their opponents.[81] Nevertheless, one significant point in which we can clearly see Sadducees disputing with Jesus is over general resurrection of the dead in Mark 12.

In contrast to the Pharisees, they did not believe in life after death (Mark 12:18–27; see also Luke 20:27). In this regard, unlike Pharisees who added the oral traditions to the laws of Moses, the Sadducees' problem was a wrong interpretation of the Scriptures about life after death and resurrection. For instance, they argued that "belief in resurrection contradicts the law about levirate marriage in Deut 25:5–6,"[82] however, Jesus rejected their wrong understanding of resurrection indicating their failure to understand the power of God to restore life, as even their Scriptures taught (see Mark 12:24). Jesus, in the heart of Mark's gospel (e.g. in three passion predictions), repeatedly and clearly affirmed that he would rise again, that there is a resurrection to come (see also Mark 8:31; 9:31; 10:33–34).

Even though they were smaller in number, the Sadducees were a more influential priestly group than the Pharisees, precisely because they were among wealthy ruling elites concentrated in and around Jerusalem. They were the ones who "dominated the Jewish government of Judea under the superior authority of the Roman governor."[83] Put simply, notwithstanding their relative small size as religious group, they were the party of power and of the wealth, especially among the leading priestly families, and thus had great influence in the political circle of the Roman government.

Although the Sadducees were religious as well as political rivals of the Pharisees in the Synoptic gospels, they are portrayed as both having had in common a desire to attack a common enemy, namely Jesus and his teaching mission. Mark thus portrays them as the major opponents of Jesus (Mark 12:18–27; see also Matt 16:1–12), who pushed him to his death (in cooperation with other religious and political groups).

---

81. See Meier, 390.
82. Donahue and Harrington, *Gospel of Mark*, 353.
83. Bauckham, *Jesus*, 26.

Scribes: The scribes were another influential religious group of Jewish men who were trained in writing, interpreting and teaching of the law. They did not have their own formally organized party but they belonged to other parties such as Pharisees (e.g. the scribes of Pharisees, Mark 2:16); in other words, "they were Pharisees or led by Pharisees."[84] They were mainly in charge of writing or drafting legal documents, copying Scriptures, recording achievements and teaching people. Thus, their "reputation was honoured by the title 'rabbi,' meaning 'my great one.'" Furthermore, they were known as experts in the Torah and "capable of issuing binding decisions on its interpretation." Edwards also goes on to say, "the first seats in the synagogues were reserved for scribes, and people rose to their feet when they entered a room."[85] A scribe also was translated as "lawyer" (νομικός) "*nomikos*" (Luke 7:30; 10:25), whereas Matthew and Mark described them as "scribes" (γραμματεῖς) "*grammateis*." It is possible to argue that most of scribes and other elite groups in Jesus's days were opponents of Jesus and the kingdom of God.

However, some members of the elite groups may have been followers of Jesus: ". . . the scribe, who is 'not far from the kingdom' (12:34), Joseph of Arimathea (15:43), and Jairus (5:21–43) . . . these examples prevent us from excluding members of the elite from Jesus' community."[86] It is therefore not appropriate to categorize all religious elites, including the scribes, as being far away from the kingdom of God; some indeed may have been followers of Jesus.

Hence, one can argue that even though Jesus appreciated or praised a few scribes in Mark (12:28–34), many of them were described as antagonists against Jesus who were actively engaged in the secret plan to put an end to Jesus (see Mark 2:6, 16; 9:14; 12:38). Mark mentioned them as the major opponents of Jesus along with Pharisees (7:1, 5), with chief priests (Mark 8:31; 10:33; 11:18, 27) and with the elders (8:31; 11:27).

In addition, the high priests, chief priests and priests whose roots were from the tribe of Levi in ancient Israel, were in charge of the temple services and its sacrifices. They were also the religious as well as social leaders of the

---

84. Sanders, *Judaism*, 388.
85. Edwards, *Gospel According to Mark*, 54.
86. Rohrbaugh, "Social Location," 148; see also Malbon, "Jewish Leaders," 275–276.

Jewish people. For instance, Mark reports that priests offer the sacrifices and they are responsible for the ritual concerns in the temple (Mark 1:44).

Further, the Greek term τῶν πρεσβυτέροι, "the elders," refers to older men in the community who were members of official councils of the ruling elites. They were well respected by others and looked up to as role models. However, the Gospels in general and Mark in particular portray the chief priests, along with scribes and elders as groups of people among ruling authorities who strongly opposed Jesus and his mission, trying to expose him as a false teacher before the people, to arrest him; and they eventually had him killed, in cooperation with the Roman governor (see Mark 8:31; 11:27).

Sanhedrin: The Sanhedrin is a council of seventy or seventy-one senior Jewish men, who advised the high priest on internal national affairs, eventually functioning as the Supreme Court in Jerusalem under the Roman rule. As discussed by Twelftree, the Hebrew term "Sanhedrin" was taken from the Greek word συνέδριον meaning literally a "sitting together" or a council.[87] Moreover, the συνέδριον was described as the supreme Jewish religious, political and legal-council in the Gospels referring to the Jerusalem council (see Mark 15:1; Matt 26:59; John 11:47; Acts 5:27). It was also called the Great Sanhedrin, or simply the Sanhedrin in Jerusalem as distinct from local gatherings.

Some attempted to trace this governing body back to Moses and his seventy elders in Numbers 11:16, but "apart from a supreme law court in Jerusalem (Deut 17:8–13; 19:15–21) and the occasional mention of 'elders' (Exod 3:16; Deut 5:23), there is no hint of the existence of such an institution as the Sanhedrin in this period."[88]

In modern studies, the presence and exact role of a Judean formal council in the first century is debated; however, since all of the Gospels and the book of Acts have Jesus tried in front of such a council, made up of chief priests, elders and scribes, it is difficult to argue cogently against its existence in this period. It is more likely, as some commentators nowadays suggest, that there was a formal council (known as the Sanhedrin), presided over by high

---

87. Twelftree, "Sanhedrin," 836.
88. Twelftree, 837.

priest, and charged with a range of legislative, judicial and administrative matters with restricted powers.[89]

Although there is no clear evidence supporting the notion that the Sanhedrin was a formal ruling assembly that met in the house of the high priest, scholars have suggested that on occasions, when important matters were discussed the high priest met with influential laymen. The composition varied according to the specific matter being addressed.[90] Historians of Judaea have suggested that there was no fixed council known as the Sanhedrin in the Roman period. Rather, like a Roman senator and his concilium, the high priest simply called associates to his house to make a decision about important matters.[91] The evidence from Josephus also seems to suggest that it was more of an ad hoc arrangement, with the high priest simply calling on whatever other aristocrats were competent to judge a case.

Therefore, it is possible to argue that Jesus was not heard by a formal council with fixed membership after his arrest, but was probably taken to the high priest's palace where Caiaphas summoned a relatively small group of chief priests and influential aristocrats with the specific purpose of hearing the prisoner and determining his fate.

Mark describes a formal Jewish council in his narrative in which Jesus's trial in front of the Sanhedrin took place, and further, how Jesus was marginalized by the dominant clique and that which he "endured throughout his ministry reached its extreme point in his crucifixion."[92]

In summary, it is clear from the narrative that Jesus stood trial before a formal council. He is led to the high priest in 14:53 (presumably to his palace), where "all the chief priests, the elders, and the scribes were assembled." In 14:55, the chief priests and all the council seek testimony against him, in 14:60 the high priest acts alone, but in 15:1, in a particularly laboured sentence, we are told that the chief priests with the elders and scribes and all the council were summoned again before having Jesus bound and sent

---

89. See Schurer, *History of the Jewish*, 199–226; Hooker, *According to St. Mark*, 353–355; Grabbe, "Sanhedrin," 1–19.
90. See MacLaren, *Power and Politics*, 88–101; Sanders, *Judaism*, 472–488.
91. See Goodman, *Ruling Class*, 113–118; Goodblatt, *Monarchic Principle*, 77–130.
92. Lee, *Liminal Place*, 80.

to Pilate.[93] Witnesses were called, a verdict was reached, and a sentence was passed. Finally, Meier states that,

> the ultimate margin, is death, especially death by torture as a punishment meted out by the state for gross criminality. In Roman eyes, Jesus died the ghastly death of slaves and rebels; in Jewish eyes, he fell under the structure of Deut 21:23: "The one hanged [on a tree] is accursed by God." To both groups Jesus' trail and execution made him marginal in a terrifying and disgusting way. Jesus was a Jew living in a Jewish Palestine directly or indirectly controlled by Romans. In one sense, he belonged to both worlds; in the end, he was rejected from both.[94]

Thus, the readers understand that Mark is showing them that Jesus was extremely marginalized and liminal by the measure or all branches of Jewish religious and political groups of opponents who finally pushed him to be killed in a most shameful and brutal way.

In other words, "he who was committed to the marginalized of his society became marginalized himself and was executed."[95] Jesus is to be understood as the marginalized and liminal Galilean Jew since of his own will he came to the region, lived and worked among them and faced many challenges from various fronts and finally ended up with shameful death on a cross.

God, his Father: In the exegetical section of this work, above, Jesus is described as being marginalized and liminal not only by associating himself with the poor and outcasts during his earthly ministry in the first part of Mark's gospel but also rejected by his family, by trusted disciples as well as various groups of people in Galilee and Judea and Jerusalem. The striking fact is that he experienced forsakenness or abandonment by God his own heavenly Father during his horrible death (Mark 15:33–39). Hooker also said, "deserted and betrayed by his disciples, rejected and condemned by the nation's leaders, taunted by passers-by and fellow-victims, Jesus now experiences utter desolation: even God has forsaken him!"[96] Jesus who was

---

93. Regarding the formality of the Mark's Jewish council, see Grabbe, "Sanhedrin," 1–19.
94. Meier, *Marginal Jew*, vol. 1, 8.
95. Blomberg, *Jesus*, 213.
96. Hooker, *According to St. Mark*, 375.

rejected and pushed to the margins of society and ultimately to death by different groups of human beings, finally felt that he was separated from God his Father, in spite of his having declared that he loved him (Mark 1:11; 9:7). This happened not by accident but in fulfilment of the words in Psalm 22:1, "My God, my God, why have you forsaken me?" These words were originally written by the psalmist in Hebrew but Jesus spoke them in his native Aramaic, making them utterly his own.[97]

Put simply, the readers of Mark's gospel understand that Jesus was utterly marginalized even by his Father. He was left alone in the darkness and experienced forsakenness at the gate of death crying this out loudly. It was through this unique death of the marginalized Jesus on the cross that his unique identity as the divine Son of God was revealed. Such extraordinary love was witnessed by a wide group of people and was faithfully recorded by the unexpected humanity for all to hear. Therefore, it is now important to discuss the major purpose of Jesus's marginality and liminality up to the point of death, even being abandoned by God, his Father.

4.6. The Purpose of Jesus's Liminality and Marginalized Death

It was briefly noted above, that Jesus's major reason in becoming a marginalized Galilean Jew and ministering in Galilee among the most despised and rejected Galileans was to uplift the downtrodden or outcasts. He went down into the depths in order to identify himself with them. Jesus also was marginalized by the unjust religious and political authorities in and around Galilee and Jerusalem in order to contradict their human-made teachings which focused on human traditions rather than the commandments of God. Instead he determined to create a new community for God through himself. He recognized that because of who he was and the sacrificial atoning death he was to endure, that the newness was available for all people.

Jesus, who had been marginalized and made liminal by various groups of people in different regions, was pushed to the margins of death and then reached the climax of his own marginality by being forsaken by God his Father. This rejection by his heavenly Father was depicted by darkness.

---

97. See Bauckham, *Jesus*, 103–104.

Jesus endured all this as this was the only way of liberating people from the consequences of their sin (Mark 10: 45). It has been said, "even this final agony was not private, but his final act of self-giving for others."[98] The major purpose of Jesus's suffering and godforsaken death in Mark's narrative is the climax of his self-revelation to humanity who are in darkness, experiencing God's absence (Mark 15:33, 39). By entering the terrible situation of humanity at the deepest level of the human plight – in the darkness, through his unique death on the cross – Jesus revealed himself to the godforsaken world and was declared by unexpected humanity as God's divine Son.[99] To put it succinctly, as a result of Jesus's shameful death, his divine identity was revealed to the whole of humanity in order to save those who recognize and declare that Jesus is the Son of God.

4.7. Conclusion

Jesus who was described in the first half of Mark's gospel as having the unique supreme authority as the divine Son of God, by his own initiative and voluntarily, came to the region and became involved in the lives of marginalized Galilean Jews. He was marginalized by being born in Galilee and brought up as a Galilean Jew, and through his occupation as a poor village artisan, by his non-traditional style of teaching and finally by his unique death on the Roman cross.

He was further rejected by his own family and by his close disciples. This was compounded when he was rejected by both Jewish religious authorities who tried to mix up the commandments of God with their human traditions and the Roman political governor. They all pushed him to the shameful death. Finally, Jesus experienced abandonment by his loving Father. He cried out in distress when he experienced God's absence, depicted by the darkness and he died the death of outcasts on the cross.

In doing so, Jesus's main purpose as the divine Son of God was, in the second half of Mark, to reveal himself to the whole marginalized world, as the divine messianic Son of Man and to be confessed as the divine Son of

---

98. Bauckham, 104.

99. See Bauckham, *God of Israel*, 266–267; see also Edwards, *Gospel According to Mark*, 481.

God by living as the perfect human being. In a nutshell, the major purpose of Jesus's death was to reveal himself to the whole world and to save those who confess him God's Son.

CHAPTER 5

Conclusion

Through the course of our investigation of the messianic identity in Mark's gospel, an attempt has been made to examine the idea of Jesus's unique divine identity, emphasizing his self-identification with the marginalized and liminal individuals and groups to help and to save. It has been demonstrated that the central theme of Mark's whole narrative is that Jesus is revealed and proclaimed as the divine Son of God and the vindicated Son of Man, or the uniquely divine King-Messiah in a very unique sense. Yet he associated himself with the poor and outcasts rather than the more privileged. Nevertheless, the second evangelist recorded this idea of Jesus's messiahship in a different way which might have caused some ambiguity among his readers. After divine miracles and other activities during his earthly ministry, Jesus avoided the open proclamation of his messianic title, "the Messiah," particularly, in the first half of his gospel. Put simply, even though his messianic role is implicitly recorded throughout Mark's narrative, Jesus is not recorded as openly claiming to be the divine Messiah. Rather, unlike other evangelists, Mark's Jesus ordered demons, the supernatural beings and other human beings not to proclaim who he was publicly.

Some scholars, such as Wrede and his supporters, have suggested that in Mark's narrative Jesus neither thought of himself as the divine Messiah nor identified himself as such before his resurrection. Rather, according to Wrede, the Gospel of Mark is not a reliable source about Jesus's life, and the idea of Jesus's messiahship is an invention of the second evangelist and the early church for their own theological agenda. Likewise, others, such as Weeden and his followers, argued that Jesus's divine messiahship or God's Sonship in Mark's gospel is a false belief of Jesus's first followers. Thus, correcting their wrong understanding of his messiahship, Jesus was himself rejecting this idea; and affirmed that his divine identity was that of the suffering Son of Man who died and rose again.

Thus, I have argued that this is a false dichotomy or an unnecessary dividing line between the first and the second halves of Mark's gospel, since it is a unified message of the second evangelist which contained the glory and suffering as well as the divine identity and destiny of the same Jesus in both halves of the gospel.

5.1. Unified Work of Mark's Narrative

This work emphasized that the Gospel of Mark is a unified work of the second evangelist for several reasons. For instance, it has been shown that Jesus did not completely avoid an open proclamation of his messianic activities since in the first part of Mark's narrative he commanded a healed leper to go and show himself to the priest to confirm his healing (see Mark 1:44). Another place where Jesus tells the healed gentile demoniac to go and tell "what the Lord has done for you" is Mark 5:19. This could be taken as an indication that Jesus's motivation for keeping his identity a secret is political since the political risk (as John 11 indicates) is in the threat of an uprising among Jews. But one suspects that Mark is interested in the incident because the demoniac goes and announces in all the Decapolis "what the Lord had done for him" as "what Jesus had done for him." In other words, it corresponds to the wider theme of Gentiles seeing most clearly who Jesus is, climatically with the statement of the centurion at the cross (Mark 15:39) and grasping his mission (the Syro-Phoenician woman in Mark 7:36–37).

Jesus's messianic activities continued to be demonstrated in the second half of Mark's gospel, particularly, when Jesus rid a boy of an evil spirit (Mark 9:14–29), when he healed the blind beggar Bartimaues (Mark 10:46–52) and when he cursed a fig tree (Mark 11:12–14, 20–22). Thus, unlike Wrede's view above, I would argue that Jesus's divine messianic activities were publicly demonstrated and declared among people both before and after his resurrection in both Jewish and gentile territories.

The reason why Jesus avoided public proclamation of his messiahship, particularly in Mark's first half, is not because he did not think that he was the divine Messiah, or because his messiahship was a creation of the second evangelist or of the early church. But rather, the readers of his gospel can see that in the first half, while Jesus was in Galilee, the political danger was low but his concern to conceal his messianic identity was high. When the political danger was high, in the second half, his concern to conceal his identity was low.

It has been demonstrated that Jesus suppressed his messianic identity, mainly among Jews in Mark's first half because, first, he did not want his teaching ministry to be disturbed or hindered by too early revealing and proclaiming of his messianic identity. He wanted to wait until the time intended by himself when his suffering, shameful death and resurrection occurred (as indicated in Mark 9:9; 15:39; 16:6–7). Second, it was to demonstrate that he was indeed the divine Son of God and so the unique Messiah, different from all other so-called messiahs of those days. His messiahship is not explicitly recorded by the second evangelist but implicitly mentioned in a totally unique and redefined fashion by Jesus himself. Thus I would argue that Jesus's divine messiahship is revealed. It is also understood and declared in unexpected ways, or from unexpected sources (the marginalized and liminal people) rather than his close family members and even his first followers who were chosen and taught by Jesus himself. Finally, as the uniquely divine Messiah of God, it has been shown that Jesus associated himself not with those who were on the top of the society such as the elite and their retainers but mainly with the ordinary people, the poor or destitute as well as the outcasts of society to liberate them from their plights, physically and socially.

5.2. Jesus's Self-Identification with the Marginalized and Liminal

It has been shown further that Jesus is proclaimed the divine Son of God, first of all by God his Father, and then by others who are known as poor and outcasts. In chapter 2 of this work, I demonstrated that it was not only his Father who declared him to be his uniquely beloved Son in Mark 1:11 and 9:7, but it was also the demon-possessed and outcasts or marginalized (Mark 3:11–12; 5:1–20) in both Jewish and gentile territories that recognized Jesus and proclaimed him to be the divine Son of God or the divine Messiah.

Second, Jesus was understood and confessed by the blind beggar in his royal messianic title as the son of David (Mark 10:47–48); thus, even though the blind beggar does not call Jesus the Lord of David, Mark's readers understand him as the Lord of David (Mark 12:35–37). It occurred by the road, not in the synagogue or in any religious institution in and around Galilee (the main place for his miraculous ministry). It also happened unexpectedly on the way to Jerusalem while Jesus was heading towards his destiny to die a shameful death on a Roman cross.

Third, I have also attempted to show that apart from two moments of revelation and declaration of Jesus by his loving Father as his uniquely beloved Son during his baptism and transfiguration (Mark 1:11; 9:7), and by demons (the supernatural beings in Mark 3:7–12; 5:1–20), his climactic revelation came through a human being, the gentile centurion in Mark 15:39. It occurred again not through Jesus's Jewish friends and family members or religious leaders but through a gentile soldier who probably had no Jewish religious background or experience. Jesus's divine Sonship to God was unexpectedly revealed and proclaimed by the gentile centurion not in a religious or political arena, similar to other messiahs of the day. Nor did it happen while Jesus was doing miraculous activities or works of power including forgiving sins of others but unexpectedly at the cross while he was dying a shameful death. Finally, rather than his trained apostles, who were expected to do more, it was some women who were culturally neglected ones, so marginalized and liminal, as the discoverers of his victory over death. Jesus chose the women to be the living witnesses of the gospel's decisive events (his death, resurrection and empty tomb); they went beyond serving him and others around him like the other disciples.

All this reveals the sovereignty of God who revealed his Son in such an unexpectedly unique way, not to save himself from his death on the cross or to liberate a special group of people (e.g. Israel) from their surrounding enemies, but to help and save many (the whole marginalized and liminal humanity, Mark 10:45), particularly those who recognize and confess his true Sonship to God.

In chapter 3 I have attempted to discuss certain christological titles (among many) by which Jesus was recognized and declared from various sources explicitly and implicitly. Through these four titles or names (the

Messiah, Son of David, the Son of God, and the Son of Man), Mark's Jesus is to be understood as a unique figure, therefore different from the OT and popular expectations of the first-century messiahs and son(s) of God. For instance, first, I have pointed out that Mark's Jesus is the unique divine Messiah of God. Even though the term "messiah" is not explicitly stated in the OT as well as in the first-century writings, its meaning is "Anointed One" and its significance is clearly shown as the fulfilment of the Davidic Messiah through whom God would establish his everlasting kingdom. He is also a unique Messiah who redefined his messiahship and messianic role, not as all-conquering king similar to his contemporaries who defeated the enemies of Israel, but unexpectedly in terms of his own suffering and crucifixion, associating himself with the marginalized and liminal ones to liberate them (Mark 10:45).

Second, I argued that Mark's Jesus is described as the Son of David precisely because in fulfilling the OT prophecies, he came from King David's line (Rom 1:3). This description also appeared in the *Psalms of Solomon* (17:23) where the Lord's anointed one is a conquering king who would defeat the enemies of Israel as a military messiah. Jewish contemporary expectations at Jesus's time were similar. Even in the Synoptic Gospels, Jesus was understood as such by his first followers who did not understand his real messianic mission, and by scribes, the experts of the law who questioned him, "how can he be his [David's] son?" (Mark 12:37). Therefore, I have suggested that Mark's Jesus is unique by revealing himself using his royal messianic title "Son of David," and identifying himself with the unexpected poor beggar in unexpected location. Jesus not only gave the beggar physical sight but also spiritual insight to recognize him and follow him along the road that led to the place of his execution (Mark 10:47–48, 52).[1] Furthermore, I showed that the Messiah is the Son of David because he is the physical descendant of King David; however, he is also much more than that, since he is the Lord of David, thus "he is of higher station and authority than David."[2]

Third, I have also reasoned that Mark's Jesus is the divine Son of God with unique supreme power and authority over natural elements, over sickness,

---

1. However, Mark's readers know that Bartimaeus does not reach a higher understanding of Jesus than "Son of David."

2. Kingsbury, *Christology*, 113.

over evil spirits and even over death itself. However, his Sonship to God is totally different from all other so-called son(s) of God (gods) in the OT, in first-century religious writings and Roman traditions, because he did not fulfil the expectations of the people in the ways they expected. Further, it was shown that in the OT, in contemporary Judaism, and in the Hellenistic traditions about God, nowhere did God say "my beloved Son" to any of those so-called son(s) of gods, and nobody addressed God as "Abba" or "my Father" except Jesus.

Jesus is truly the Son of God as seen in his shameful death. I attempted to demonstrate that his divine messianic identity was declared not merely by his divine activities in and around Galilee in the first half of Mark's gospel. He was also ultimately proclaimed in an unexpected way as the suffering, dying, resurrected and so vindicated Son of God by marginalized humanity in the second half of Mark. In short, Jesus's divine identity was revealed and declared not simply through his works of power in political or religious circles but unexpectedly in his horrible death on the Roman cross in total commitment to his Father's will for the salvation of the marginalized world through him.

As already noticed previously, the marginalized gentile centurion who ultimately declared Jesus's divine Sonship in a unique manner (during crucifixion), represents all of godforsaken humanity by Jesus's self-identification with them. Bauckham is correct in arguing that "Jesus' filial relationship to God and his filial mission from God are interrelated, and the uniqueness of his Sonship is to be found in this interrelation."[3] In other words, I argued that Jesus is the unique, divine Son of God whose mission is to liberate and save marginalized humanity through his unique death on the cross and subsequent resurrection.

I have, finally, shown that the title Son of Man is mentioned in both OT and NT canons explicitly and implicitly with a uniquely great significance. Unlike other titles such as "the Son of God," "the Messiah," "the Christ," and "the King," in all the canonical gospels in general, and in Mark's gospel in particular, the "Son of Man" exclusively appeared on Jesus's own lips as his favorite self-designation in Mark. He is referring to himself as a mere

---

3. Bauckham, "Sonship," 113.

ordinary human being. In other words, Jesus was subtle by using this title because he did not explicitly say "I am the Son of God" or "I am the divine Messiah," but rather he referred to himself with an ordinary phrase, "Son of Man," emphasizing his humanity. In addition, he preferred this title for himself as a more manageable designation in order to avoid the politicized distortion of his identity since the other titles could cause a hindrance or disturbance to his mission. Put simply, Jesus was concerned not to be misunderstood in terms of current Jewish expectations. He wanted to define his role for himself, rather than be slotted into a ready-made role. All of the Gospels rather carefully preserve Jesus's ways of speaking about himself and do not attribute to him titles or descriptions that were commonly used in the early church. Thus, he never calls himself Messiah.

It was also emphasized that unlike the Son-of-Man sayings in the Jewish Apocryphal books such as *1 Enoch* or the Similitudes and *4 Ezra*, Mark used Daniel 7:13–14, as his key OT source, where we see this unique human figure was not only given everlasting dominion from God but also shared it with the oppressed people of God. Thus, even though there are some similarities between the idea of the Son of Man in Daniel 7 and the Gospels, it also appears in some apocryphal books though we cannot be fully confident of those apocryphal sources for some significant reasons.

First, since there is no clear evidence showing that Jesus used the apocryphal writings to describe himself in this title, we cannot depend on any of these writings to explain the Son of Man idea and its significance. Second, whereas the second half of Mark's narrative describes the crucial part of Jesus's identity and destiny as the suffering, dying and vindicated Son of Man, there is no idea of the suffering Son of Man in the Similitudes and *4 Ezra*, that we can see in Daniel 7 and in the Synoptic Gospels. Third, in contrast to the Son of Man of the Jewish apocryphal books where he is portrayed as the pre-existent, heavenly and exalted one who is expected to destroy wicked sinners and rescue the righteous ones, the Son of Man of Mark's gospel is described as the rejected, suffered, and crucified and resurrected one identifying himself with the afflicted saints of God. Therefore, in using this title Jesus is not to be understood as the one whose mission on earth is to be proclaimed as a great figure of the day and consequently to be served by others, but as one who came to serve and save many (Mark

10:45), identifying himself with the people he came to save. Furthermore, Mark's Jesus is the one who associated himself with the lost sinners through forgiveness, not only to rescue them from their afflictions but also to share his final glory and victory with them when he returns as the final judge of the world (see Dan 7:13–14; Mark 14:62).

I have thus far attempted to argue that regardless of his supreme power and universal authority, in Mark's gospel Jesus associated himself with the marginalized and liminal people to help liberate them from different sorts of plights physically, socially, culturally and spiritually. Further, in chapter 4, I argued that it was not only Jesus's identification of himself with the poor and outcast, but also the extreme marginality and liminality of Jesus himself for the sake of others.

Regardless of his Yahweh-like power and authority over all things, Jesus became a marginalized Galilean Jew by being brought up in Galilee as a village artisan in a small and insignificant town (Nazareth) rather than the capital of the region, Sepphoris. His independent and unique style of teaching with sovereign and at times startling authority also put him in the margins of Judaism of his day. His opponents' misunderstanding of the source of his teaching given in the Scriptures rather than human traditions, and their wrong interpretation of the Scriptures, further contributed to his marginalization. Jesus was also pushed to his death not only by the religious authorities of Judaism, the Pharisees and Sadducees, the scribes, high priest, chief priests, priests and elders, but also by the politicians such as Herodians and the Roman governors. Jesus was neglected by his own family members and his close friends, the disciples, who were expected to be sympathetic to him. Finally, I emphasized that Jesus's marginality reached its climax when he experienced God's absence when he died on a Roman cross.

5.3. Jesus's Unique Death and the Revelation of Divine Identity

I have so far attempted to argue that the suffering and godforsaken death of Jesus, the Son of God and the vindicated Son of Man, is a very important issue in Mark's narrative. It was correctly noted, "This is the point toward which everything has been moving since Jesus' prediction of his death in 2:20, and, by Jesus own testimony in 10:45, is a major reason for his coming."[4] Therefore I have pointed out that Jesus's unique death was indicated not only in the three passion predictions in the second half but also in the first half of Mark's gospel.

It is also noticed that God the Father declared that Jesus is God's uniquely beloved Son (Mark 1:11) who must be listened to and obeyed (9:7) by his followers. As mentioned above, Jesus's followers must listen and obey his teaching about the path of his cross. In other words, the divine voice, "This is my beloved Son; listen to him" to Jesus's disciples and all the subsequent readers was not merely about listening to Jesus's verbal teachings in general and obeying them but it is about his whole life and ministry, especially his teachings concerning his passion, his path to crucifixion and glorious resurrection.[5] Finally since God his Father left Jesus, the beloved Son, to die (15:33–39), the readers are to believe that Jesus's beloved Sonship to God, paradoxically, led him to his horrible and forsaken death, but also resurrection so that all Mark's readers should listen to and obey his teachings in the same way.

Furthermore, Jesus's unique Sonship to God required his unique death, unlike any human being. Even two great prophets of the OT (Elijah and Moses) appeared with Jesus during his transfiguration in Mark 9. It is true that, similar to Jesus, these two great figures of the OT faced opposition or persecution during their ministries long ago. However, unlike Jesus, neither of them were led to such a horrible death, since Moses died peacefully and honored at his old age and Elijah was taken up to heaven in a chariot. Put differently, even though Moses and Elijah faced suffering and rejection in their times, God did not let them suffer such a fate;[6] but he allowed his uniquely beloved Son to die the death of outcasts.

It is also important to note that there is a similarity between the stories of Jesus's baptism in Mark 1:10–11 and Jesus's death in Mark 15:38. In the story of Jesus's baptism, leaving the usual terminology "opened," Mark uses the phrase "the heavens torn apart." In the Bible when visions occur the heavens were opened, not torn apart. For instance, Matthew and Luke

---

4. Thielman, *New Testament*, 62.
5. See Stein, *Mark*, 418–419; cf. Gundry, *Mark*, 461–462.
6. See Bauckham, *God of Israel*, 263–264.

in their accounts of Jesus's baptism (Matt 3:16; Luke 3:21) used the word "opened" ἀnoίgw to describe it; but, Mark has this very unique image of the sky torn apart. This verb itself "being torn apart" σχιζομένους is used only twice in Mark (1:10; 15:38) out of eleven times in the NT. In Mark 15:38 he uses the same verb to describe the unusual event that occurred in the temple at the time of Jesus's death: the veil was torn in two. Thus, the readers understand that this is surely a deliberate echo, a verbal indication of a connection between the two events of Jesus's revelation to be God's Son by God himself as well as by humanity.[7]

In short, Mark's gospel is from first to last a gospel of God breaking through and breaking into human affairs and human lives. It begins with the ripping open the heavens and a voice declaring Jesus to be God's Son and ends with the ripping of the temple veil. It shows us that the God of Mark's gospel is a God whom neither heaven nor the temple can contain; he is breaking through all that separates us (humanity) from God.

In other words, the whole of Mark's story is the divine revelation from God: a revelation of Jesus's uniquely beloved Sonship to God (Mark 1:11), a revelation from God the Father to Jesus's first followers (Mark 9:7), and finally a revelation not only to the gentile centurion and other people in Mark's story, but also to us, all the subsequent readers of Mark's story. It is Mark's story of revelation to us who recognize that Jesus is truly the Son of God through his extremely shameful death on the cross.

Further, it was during this unique death of Jesus that the way to the presence of God was opened, and his true Sonship to God was recognized and proclaimed by the unexpected marginalized humanity. This is also the reason why I argued that the revelation of his divine identity and the mystery of God's kingdom belongs to God alone. Put simply, God revealed this truth in Jesus to those who have eyes to see and is proclaimed by the unexpected outcasts rather than those who were expected ones.

Finally, it is argued that the purpose and goal of Jesus's marginality and liminality as a Galilean Jew in and around Galilee and finally in Jerusalem was to identify himself with the poor and outcasts in order to lift them up by going to the depths of the tradition to the point of death on the cross in

---

7. See Stein, *Mark*, 56–57, 719; see also Bauckham, *God of Israel*, 267.

order to create a new humanity out of the excluded ones. Put another way, it was to reveal his divine identity in an unexpected place (on the cross), in an unexpected manner (crucifixion), and to marginalized humanity through his own unique and forsaken death. In doing so, it was to save or atone marginalized humanity, particularly those who recognize and confess that Jesus is truly the Son of God.

Bibliography

Achtemeier, P. J. "'And He Followed': Miracles and Discipleship in Mark 10:46–52." *Semeia* 11 (1978): 115–145.
———. *Mark*. Proclamation Commentaries: The New Testament Witnesses for Preaching. Philadelphia: Fortress, 1975.
Amoss, G. "Introduction to the Christology of Mark's Gospel." (1979). Accessed 26 June 2015. http://www.qis.net/~daruma.mark-c.html.
Anderson, H. *The Gospel of Mark*. The New Century Bible Commentary. London: Marshall, Morgan & Scott, 1976.
Andres, T. "Jesus the Son of Man in Mark." (2014). Accessed 10 November 2014. http://digitalcommons.fui.edu.
Bauckham, R. "The Gospels as Histories: What Sort of History Are They?" (2011). Accessed 4 September 2013. http://thebiblicalworld.blogspot.co.za/2011/02/gospels-as-histories-richard-bauckham.html.
———. *Jesus and the God of Israel*. Grand Rapids: Eerdmans, 2008.
———. *Jesus: A Very Short Introduction*. New York: Oxford University Press, 2011.
———. "Salome the Sister of Jesus, Salome the Disciple of Jesus, and the Secret Gospel of Mark." *Novum Testamentum* 33 (1991): 245–275.
Bauckham, R. "The Sonship of the Historical Jesus in Christology." *Scottish Journal of Theology* 31 (1978): 104–114.
Bauer, D. R. "Son of God." In *Dictionary of Jesus and the Gospels*, edited by Joel B. Green, Scot McKnight, and Marshall I. Howard, 769–775. Downers Grove: InterVarsity, 1992.
Beasley-Murray, G. R. *Jesus and the Kingdom of God*. Grand Rapids: Eerdmans, 1986.
Beavis, M. A. "From the Margin to the Way: The Story of Bartimaeus." *Journal for the Feminist Study of Religion* 14 (1998): 19–39.
———. *Mark*. Grand Rapids: Baker, 2011.
Best, E. *Following Jesus: Discipleship in the Gospel of Mark*. Sheffield: JSOT, 1981.
———. *The Temptation and the Passion: The Markan Soteriology*. Cambridge: Cambridge University Press, 1965.

Betz, H. D. "Jesus as Divine Man." In *Jesus and the Historian*, edited by E. C. Colwell and F. C. Trotter, 114–133. Philadelphia: Westminster, 1968.

———. *Lukian von Samosata und das Neue Testament*. TU 76. Berlin: Akademie, 1961.

Beyschlag, W. *Die Christologie Des Neuen Testament: Ein biblisch-theologischer Versuch*. Berlin: Rauh, 1866.

Bieler, L. *Theios Aner*, vol. 2. Vienna: Oskar Hofels, 1935–1936.

Bird, M. F. *Are You the One Who Is to Come?: The Historical Jesus and the Messianic Question*. Grand Rapids: Baker, 2009.

Black, D. *Learn to Read New Testament Greek*. Nashville: Broadman & Holman, 2009.

Black, M. "The Son of Man in Recent Research and Debate." *BJRL* 45 (1963): 305–318.

Blomberg, C. L. *Jesus and the Gospels: An Introduction and Survey*. Nashville: Broadman & Holman, 2009.

Bock, D. L. *Blasphemy and Exaltation in Judaism: The Charge Against Jesus in Mark 14:53–65*. Biblical Studies Library. Grand Rapids: Baker Academic, 2000.

———. "Son of Man." In *Dictionary of Jesus and the Gospels*. Downers Grove, IL: InterVarsity, 2013.

———. "The Use of Daniel 7 in Jesus' Trail, with Implications for His Self-Understanding." In *Who Is This Son of Man?: The Latest Scholarship on a Puzzling Expression of the Historical Jesus*, edited by Larry W. Hurtado and Paul L. Owen et al., 78–101. New York: Bloomsbury; T & T Clark, 2011.

Bolt, P. G. *Jesus' Defeat of Death: Persuading Mark's Early Readers*. Cambridge: Cambridge University Press, 2003.

Borg, M. *Conflict, Holiness, and Politics in the Teachings of Jesus*. Harrisburg, PA: Trinity, 1998.

———. "A Portrait of Jesus: From Galilean Jew to the Face of God." (1997–2015). Accessed 10 May 2015. http://www.aportraitofjesus.org/borg.shtml.

Bornkamm, G. *Jesus von Nazareth*. Stuttgart: Kohlahammer, 1956; [*Jesus of Nazareth*. Translated by Irene and Fraser McLuskey. New York: Harper & Row, 1960].

Bowker, J. W. "Son of Man." *Journal of Theological Studies* 28 (1977): 19–48.

Bowman, Komoszewski, and D. L. Bock. *Putting Jesus in His Place: The Case for the Deity of Christ*. Grand Rapids, MI: Kregel, 2007.

Branscomb, B. H. *The Gospel of Mark*. London: Hodder & Stoughton, 1937.

Brooks, J. A. *Mark*. New American Commentary 23. Nashville: Broadman, 1991.

Brown, R. A. *The Death of the Messiah: From Gethsemane to the Grave*, vol. 2. New York: Doubleday, 1994.

Bruce, F. F. "The Background to the Son of Man Sayings." In *Christ the Lord: Studies in Christology Presented to Donald Guthrie*, edited by Harold H. Rowdon, 50–70. Downers Grove, IL: InterVarsity, 1982.

———. *This Is That: The NT Development of Some OT Themes*. Exeter: Paternoster, 1968.

Bryan, S. Class Lecture New Testament One. Addis Ababa: Evangelical Theological College, 2003.

Bultmann, R. *The History of the Synoptic Tradition*. Translated by John Marsh. New York: Harper & Row, 1963.

———. *The History of the Synoptic Tradition*, 2nd revised edition. Translated by J. Marsh. New York: Harper & Row, 1968.

———. *The History of the Synoptic Tradition*, revised edition. Translated by J. Marsh. Oxford: Basil Blackwell, 1972.

———. *Jesus Christ and Mythology*. New York: Scribner, 1968.

———. *Theology of the New Testament*. New York: Scribner, 1951–1955.

Bultmann, R., and K. Kundin. *Form Criticism: Two Essays on New Testament Research*. Translated by Frederick C. Grant. New York: Harper & Brothers, 1962.

Burger, C. "Jesus als Davidssohn: Eine traditionsgeschichtliche Untersuchung." In *Forschungen zur Religion und Literatur des Alten und Neuen Testaments* 98 (1970). Gottingen: Vandenhoeck & Ruprecht.

Burkett, D. *The Son of Man Debate: A History and an Evaluation*. Society for New Testament Studies Monograph Series 107. Cambridge: Cambridge University Press, 1999.

Burkill, T. A. *Mysterious Revelation: An Examination of the Philosophy of Mark's Gospel*. Ithaca, NY: Cornell, 1963.

Byung-mu, Ahn. "Jesus and the Minjung in the Gospel of Mark." In *Minjung Theology: People as the Subjects of History*, 138–152. Maryknoll, NY: Orbis, 1981.

Callahan, A. D. "Galilee: A Portrait of Jesus' World." (1995–2014). Accessed 10 March 2015. http://www.pbs.org/wgbh/pages/frontline/shows/religion/portrait/galilee.html.

Campbell, J. Y. "The Kingdom of God Has Come." *Expository Times* 48, (1936–37): 91–94.

———. "The Origin and the Meaning of the Term 'Son of Man.'" *JTS* 48 (1947): 144–155.

Caragonis, C. C. "The Son of Man: Vision and Interpretation." *Wissenshaftliche Untersuchungen zum Neuen Testament* 38 (1986). Tübingen: J. C. B. Mohr.

Carl, H. B. "Crucifixion Darkness." (2015). Accessed 8 September 2015. http://en.wikipedia.org/wiki/Crucifixion_darknes also; http://en.wikipedia.org/wiki/Hasmonean_dynasty#Roman-Intervention.

Carter, C. W. "Son of Man." In *Zondervan's Pictorial Encyclopaedia*, edited by M. C. Tenney, 485. Grand Rapids: Zondervan, 1975.

Casey, M. *Aramaic Source of Mark's Gospel*. Society of New Testament Studies Monograph Series 102. Cambridge: Cambridge University Press, 1998.

———. *The Solution to the "Son of Man" Problem*. LNTS. Edinburgh: T & T Clark, 2009.

———. *Son of Man: The Interpretation and Influence of Daniel 7*. London: SPCK, 1979.

Catchpole, D. R. "The Angelic Son of Man in Luke 12:8." *NovT* 24, no. 3 (1982): 255–265.

Chancey, M. A. *The Myth of a Gentile Galilee*. Cambridge: Cambridge Press, 2002.

Charles, R. H. "The Damascus Document." In *The Apocryphal and Pseudepigrapha*, vol. 2. Oxford: Clarendon, 1913.

———. "The Testaments of the Twelve Patriarchs." In *The Apocryphal and Pseudepigrapha*, vol. 2. Oxford: Clarendon, 1913.

Charlesworth, J. H. "The Concept of the Messiah in the Pseudepigrapha." *ANRW* 19, no. 1 (1979): 188–218. [Part 2, Principat, 19.1; (ed.) W. Hasse, Berlin: Walter de Gruyter].

———, ed. *The Old Testament Pseudepigrapha*, vol. 2. Garden City, NY: Doubleday, 1983, 1985.

Chester, A. *Messiah and Exaltation: Jewish Messianic and Visionary Traditions, New Testament Christology*. Tübingen: Mohr Siebeck, 2007.

Chilton, B. "Jesus ben David: Reflections on the Davidssohnfrage." *Journal for the Study of the New Testament* 14 (1982): 88–112.

Chronis, H. L. "To Reveal and to Cancel: A Literary-Critical Perspective on 'the Son of Man' in Mark." *NTS* 51 (2005): 459–481.

———. "The Torn Veil: Cultus and Christology in Mark 15:37–39." *JBL* 101 (1982): 97–144.

Clark, K. W. "Galilee." In *The Interpreters' Dictionary of the Bible*. Vol. 2. New York: Abingdon, 1972.

Collins, A. Y., and J. J. Collins. *King and Messiah as Son of God: Divine, Human, and Angelic Messianic Figures in Biblical and Related Literature*. Grand Rapids: Eerdmans, 2008.

Collins, J. J. *The Apocalyptic Imagination: An Introduction to Jewish Apocalyptic Literature*. Grand Rapids: Eerdmans, 1984.

———. *The Apocalyptic Imagination: An Introduction to Jewish Apocalyptic Literature*. 2nd edition. Grand Rapids: Eerdmans, 1998.

———. *The Apocalyptic Vision of the Book of Daniel*. HSM 16. Missoula, MT: Scholars Press, 1977.

———. "'He Shall Not Judge by What His Eyes See': Messianic Authority in the Dead Sea Scrolls." *Dead Sea Discoveries* 2, no. 2 (1995):145–164.

———. *The Sceptres and the Star: The Messiahs of the Dead Sea Scrolls and Other Ancient Literature*. Anchor Bible Reference Library. New York: Doubleday, 1995.

Collins, J. J., and D. C. Harlow. *The Eerdmans Dictionary of Early Judaism*. Grand Rapids: Eerdmans, 2010.

Conzelmann, H. "Gegenwart und Zukunft in der Synoptischen Tradition." *Z. Th. K.* 54 (1957): 277–296.

Costas, O. E. "Evangelism from the Periphery: A Galilean Model." *Apuntes* 2, no. 3 (Fall 1982).

Cranfield, C. *The Gospel According to St Mark: An Introduction and Commentary*. Cambridge Greek Testament Commentaries. Cambridge: Cambridge University Press, 1959.

Crossan, D. J. "Jesus' Many Faces: A Peasant Boy in a Peasant Village." (1995–2014). Accessed 20 February 2015. http://www.pbs.org/wgbh/pages/frontline/shows/religion//jesus/socialclass.html.

Cullmann, O. *The Christology of the New Testament*. Philadelphia: Westminster, 1959.

———. *The Christology of the New Testament*. 2nd edition. Translated by S. C. Guthrie and C. A. M. Hall. London: SCM, 1963.

Dalman, G. *The Words of Jesus Considered in the Light of Post-Biblical Jewish Writings and the Aramaic Language*. Edinburgh: T & T Clark, 1909.

Davis, P. G. "Mark's Christological Paradox." *JSNT* 35 (1989): 3–18.

DePoe, J. "The Messianic Secret in the Gospel of Mark: Historical Development and Value of Wrede's Theory." Accessed 22 August 2013. www.johndepoe.com/Messianic_secret.pdf.

de Jonge, H. J. "The Historical Jesus' View of Himself and of His Mission." In *From Jesus to John: Essays on Jesus and the New Testament Christology in Honour of Marinus de Jonge*, edited by M. C. de Boer, 21–37. Sheffield: JSOT, 1993.

de Jonge, M. *From Jesus to John: Essays on Jesus and New Testament Christology in Honour of Marinus de Jonge*. Sheffield: JSOT, 1993.

———. "Messiah." In *Anchor Bible Dictionary*, vol. 4, edited by D. N. Freedman, 777–778. Anchor Bible Reference Library. New York: Doubleday, 1992.

———. "The Use of the Word 'Anointed' in the Time of Jesus." *Novum Testamentum* 8, (1966): 132–148.

Dibelius, M. *From Tradition to Gospel*. Cambridge: James Clarke, 1971.

Dinkler, E. "Peter's Confession and the Satan Saying: The Problem of Jesus' Messiahship." In *The Future of Our Religious Past: Essays in Honour of Rudolf Bultmann*, edited by J. M. Robinson, 169–202. New York: Harper & Row, 1971.

Dodd, C. H. *According to the Scriptures*. London: Nisbet, 1952.

———. *The Interpretation of the Fourth Gospel*. Cambridge: Cambridge University Press, 1953.

Donahue, J. R., and D. J. Harrington. *The Gospel of Mark*. Sacra Pagina Series. Collegeville: Liturgical Press, 2002.

Duling, D. C. "Matthew as Marginal Scribe in the Advances Agrarian Society." Unpublished paper presented at the International Context Group Meeting, at the University of Pretoria, June 2001.

———. "Solomon, Exorcism, and the Son of David." *Harvard Theological Review* 68 (1975): 235–252.

Dunn, J. D. G. *Christology in the Making*. 2nd edition. London: SCM, 1989.

Eckstein, H. J. "Marcus 10, 46-52 als Schlussel text des Markusevangeliums." *Zeitschriftfurdieneutestamentliche Wissenschaft* 87 (1996): 33–50.

Edwards, J. R. *The Gospel According to Mark*. Pillar New Testament Commentary. Grand Rapids: Eerdmans, 2002.

———. "The Son of God: Its Antecedents in Judaism and Hellenism, and Its Use in the Earliest Gospel." PhD dissertation, Fuller Theological Seminary, 1978.

Elizondo, V. "Jesus the Galilean Jew in Mestizo Theology." *Theological Studies* 70 (2009). Accessed 23 February 2015. http://www.virgilioelizondo.com/1/docs/JESUS.

Elwell, W. A., and R. W. Yarbrough. *Readings from the First-Century World*. Grand Rapids: Baker, 1998.

Emanuel, B. "The Pharisees: Jewish Leaders in the First Century AD." Accessed 5 April 2015. http://www.bible-history.com/Pharisees/PHARISEES.

Evans, C. A. *The Historical Jesus: Jesus Mission, Death and Resurrection*. London & New York: Routledge, 2004.

———. *Mark 8:27–16:20*. World Biblical Commentary 34B. Nashville: Nelson, 2001.

———. "Messianic Hopes and Messianic Figures in Late Antiquity." *Journal of Greco-Roman Christianity and Judaism* 3 (2006): 9–40.

Feneberg, W. "Der Markusprolog: Studien zur Formbestimmung des Evangeliums." *Studien zum Alten und Neuen Testament* 36 (1974). München: Kosel-Verlag.

Fiensy, D. *The Social History of Palestine in the Herodian Period: The Land Is Mine*. Studies in the Bible and Early Christianity 20. Lewiston, NY: Mellen, 1991.

Fiensy, D., and R. Hawkins, eds. *The Galilean Economy in the Time of Jesus.* Atlanta: SBL, 2013.

Fiorenza, E. *In Memory of Her: A Feminist Theological Reconstruction of Christian Origins.* New York: Crossroad, 1985.

Flesher, P. "Religion Today: Why Did Joseph Live in Galilee?" (2015). Accessed 27 November 2015. http://religion-today.blogspot.com.

———. "Why Did Joseph Live in Galilee?" (2014). Accessed 23 September 2015. http://enrichmentjournal.ag.org.

Fowler, H. W., and F. G. Fowler. *Concise Oxford Dictionary.* 5th edition. Oxford: Oxford Clarendon, 1964.

Fowler, R. M. "Who Is 'the Reader' of Mark's Gospel?" Edited by K. H. Richards. *SBL, Seminar Papers* (1983): 31–53.

France, R. T. *Divine Government.* London: SPCK, 1990.

———. *The Gospel of Mark.* The New International Greek Testament Commentary. Grand Rapids: Eerdmans, 2002.

———. *The Gospel of Matthew.* The New International Commentary on the New Testament. Grand Rapids: Eerdmans, 2007.

Freyne, S. *Galilee, Jesus and the Gospels: Literary Approaches and Historical Investigations.* Philadelphia: Fortress, 1988.

———. *Jesus a Jewish Galilean: A New Reading of the Jesus Story.* Edinburgh: T & T Clark, 2005.

———. *The World of the New Testament.* Wilmington, DE: Michael Glazier, 1980.

Fuller, R. H. *The Foundation of New Testament Christology.* New York: Scribner, 1965.

———. *The Mission and Achievement of Jesus: An Examination of the Presuppositions of New Testament Christology.* Studies in Biblical Theology 12. London: SCM, 1954.

Funk, R. W. *The Gospel of Mark: Red Letter Edition.* Sonoma, CA: Polebridge, 1991.

Gnilka, J. "Das Evangeliumnach Markus (Mk 1-8, 26)." *Evangelisch-Katholischer Kommentarzum Neuen Testament* 2, no. 1 (1978). Zurich: Benzinger.

Goldingay, J. "'Holy Ones on High' in Daniel 7:18." *JBL* 107 (1988): 495–499.

Goodblatt, D. *The Monarchic Principle: Studies in Jewish Self-Government in Antiquity.* Tübingen: J. C. B. Mohr, 1994.

Goodman, M. *The Ruling Class of Judea: The Origin of the Jewish Revolt against Rome A. D. 66-70.* Cambridge: Cambridge University Press, 1987.

Grabbe, L. L. "Sanhedrin, Sanhedriyyot or Mere Invention?" *JSJ* 39 (2008): 119.

Grant, F. C. *The Gospel of the Kingdom.* The Haskell Lectures. New York: Macmillan, 1940.

Grundmann, W. "Χριστός." In *Theological Dictionary of the New Testament*. Edited by G. Kittel and G. Friedrich. Translated by G. W. Bromiley, 527–580. Grand Rapids: Eerdmans, 1965.

Guelich, R. *Mark 1–8:26*. World Biblical Commentary 34. Dallas: Word, 1989.

Gundry, R. H. *Mark: A Commentary on His Apology for the Cross*. Grand Rapids: Eerdmans, 1993.

Hahn, F. *The Titles of Jesus in Christology: Their History in Early Christianity*. Translated by J. Knight and G. Ogg. New York: World, 1969.

Hare, D. R. A. *The Son of Man Tradition*. Minneapolis: Fortress, 1990.

Harner, P. B. "Qualitative Anarthrous Predicate Nouns: Mark 15:39 and John 1:1." *JBL* 92 (1973): 75–87.

Henderson, S. *Christology and Discipleship in the Gospel of Mark*. Cambridge: Cambridge University Press, 2006.

Hengel, M. *The Son of God*. Translated by J. Bowden. Philadelphia: Fortress, 1976.

Hertig, P. "The Multi-Ethnic Journeys of Jesus in Matthew: Margin-Center Dynamics." *Missiology: An International Review* 31, no. 1 (1998): 23–35.

Hess, R. S., and R. M. D. Carroll. *Israel's Messiah in the Bible and the Dead Sea Scrolls*. Grand Rapids: Baker, 2003.

Higgins, J. B. *Jesus and the Son of Man*. Pennsylvania: Fortress, 1964.

Hindley, J. C. "Towards a Date for the Similitudes of Enoch." *New Testament Studies* 14 (1968): 551–565.

Hobsbawm, E. "Peasants and Politics." *Journal of Peasant Studies* 1 (1973): 3–22.

Hofius, O. "1st Jesus der Messias? Thesen." *JBTH* 8 (1993): 107.

Hooker, M. *The Gospel According to St. Mark*. Black's New Testament Commentary. London: Black, 1991.

———. *Not Ashamed of the Gospel: New Testament Interpretations of the Death of Christ*. Grand Rapids: Eerdmans, 1994.

———. *The Son of Man in Mark: A Study of the Background of the term "Son of Man" and its use in St. Mark's Gospel*. London: SPCK, 1967.

Horbury, W. *Jewish Messianism and the Cult of Christ*. London: SCM, 1998.

Hurst, L. D. "Did Qumran Expect Two Messiahs?" *Bulletin for Biblical Research* 9 (1999): 157–180.

Hurtado, L. W. *Mark*. New International Biblical Commentary. Peabody: Hendrickson, 1983.

———. "Summary and Concluding Observations." In *Who Is This Son of Man?: The Latest Scholarship on a Puzzling Expression of the Historical Jesus*. Edited by Larry W. Hurtado and Paul L. Owen et al., 159–176. New York: Bloomsbury; T & T Clark, 2011.

Ilan, T. *Jewish Women in Greco-Roman Palestine*. Peabody, MA: Hendrickson, 1996.

Jeremias, J. *The Prayers of Jesus*. Translated by John Bowden, Christoph Burchard, and John Reumann. Philadelphia: Fortress, 1978.

Jerome, H. N. Who Is Poor in the New Testament? Online. Accessed 25 March 2015. https://www3.nd.edu/jneyrey1/Attitudes.html.

Johansson, D. "The Identity of Jesus in the Gospel of Mark: Past and Present Proposals." *Current in Biblical Research* 9, no. 3 (2011): 364–393.

Johnson, E. S. "Is Mark 15:39 the Key to Mark's Christology?" *Journal for the Study of the New Testament* 31 (1987): 3–22.

Joy, C. R., and M. Arnold. *The Africa of Albert Schweitzer*. New York: Harper, 1948.

Just, F. "Jewish Groups at the Time of Jesus." (2001). http://catholic-resource.org/Bible/jewish_Groups.htm.

Käsemann, E. "The Problem of the Historical Jesus." In *Essays on New Testament Themes*, translated by W. J. Montague, 37–38. Philadelphia: Fortress, 1982.

Keck, L. E. "The Introduction to Mark's Gospel." *New Testament Studies* 12 (1965): 352–370.

Kelber, W. H. *The Kingdom in Mark: A New Place and a New Time*. Philadelphia: Fortress, 1974.

———. *Mark's Story of Jesus*. Philadelphia: Fortress, 1979.

Kerr, C. M. "Judas Iscariot." Accessed 20 April 2015. http://classic.net.bible.org/dictionary.phb?word=JUDAS.

Kidger, M. *The Star of Bethlehem*. Princeton: Princeton University Press, 1999.

Kingsbury, J. D. *The Christology of Mark's Gospel*. Philadelphia: Fortress, 1983.

———. "The 'Divine Man' as the Key to Mark's Christology – The End of an Era?" *Interpretation* 35 (1981): 243–257.

Kirchhevel, G. D. "The 'Son of Man' Passages in Mark." *BBR* 9 (1999): 181–187.

Kopas, J. "Outsiders in the Gospels: Marginality as a Source of Knowledge." (1993). Accessed 6 February 2014. http://www.theway.org.uk/Back/33Koas.

Kümmel, W. G. *Promise and Fulfilment: The Eschatological Message of Jesus*. Translated by Dorthea M. Barton. SBT 23. London: SCM, 1961.

———. *The Theology of the New Testament According to Its Witnesses: Jesus–Paul–John*. Nashville: Abingdon, 1973.

Lacocque, A. "The Vision of Eagle in 4 Esdras, a Reading of Daniel 7 in the First Century CE." Edited by K. H. Richards. *SBL Seminar Papers* 20 (1981): 237–258.

Ladd, G. E. *A Theology of the New Testament*. Grand Rapids: Eerdmans, 1993.

Lane, W. L. *The Gospel of Mark*. The New International Commentary on the New Testament. Grand Rapids: Eerdmans, 1974.

La Shure, C. "About: What Is Liminality?" (2005). Accessed 18 October 2013. http://www.liminality.org/About/whatisliminality/.

Lee, S. H. *From a Liminal Place: An Asian American Theology*. Minneapolis: Fortress, 2010.
Lendering, J. "Messiah." Accessed 25 September 2014. http://www.livius.org/men-mh/messiah_14.html.
Liefeld, W. "The Hellenistic 'Divine Man' and the Figure of Jesus in the Gospels." *JETS* (1973). http://www.estjets.org/files/JETs-PDFs/16/16-4/16-4.
Lindars, B. *Jesus Son of Man: A Fresh Examination of the Son of Man Sayings in the Gospels*. Grand Rapids: Eerdmans, 1984.
Longenecker, L. R. "'Son of Man' as a Self-Designation of Jesus." *Journal of the Evangelical Theological Society* 12, no. 3 (1969): 153–154.
Lukaszewski, A. L. "Issues Concerning the Aramaic Behind ὁ υἱὸς τοῦ ἀνθρώπου: A Critical Review of Scholarship." In *Who Is This Son of Man?: The Latest Scholarship on a Puzzling Expression of the Historical Jesus*, edited by Larry W. Hurtado and Paul L. Owen et al., 1–26. New York: Bloomsbury; T & T Clark, 2011.
Mack, B. L. *A Myth of Innocence: Mark and Christian Origins*. Philadelphia: Fortress, 1988.
MacLaren, J. S. *Power and Politics in Palestine: The Jew and the Governing of Their Land 100 BC–AD 70*. Sheffield: JOST, 1991.
Malbon, E. "The Jewish Leaders in the Gospel of Mark: A Literary of Marcan Characterization." *JBL* 108 (1989): 259–281.
Malina, B. J. *The New Testament World: Insights from Cultural Anthropology*. Louisville: John Knox, 2001.
Manson, J. *Jesus the Messiah: The Synoptic Tradition of the Revelation of God in Christ, with Special Reference to Form Criticism*. London: Hodder & Stoughton, 1944.
Marcus, J. "Son of Man as Son of Adam." *RB* 110 (2003): 38–61, 370–386.
———. *The Way of the Lord: Christological Exegesis of the Old Testament in the Gospel of Mark*. Louisville: Westminster, 1992.
Marshall, I. H. *The Gospel of Luke: A Commentary on the Greek Text*. NIGTC. Exeter: Paternoster, 1978.
———. *Luke: Historian & Theologian*. Exeter: Paternoster, 1970.
———. *The Origins of New Testament Christology*. Leicester: IVP, 1976.
———. "Son of Man." In *Dictionary of Jesus and the Gospels*, edited by Joel B. Green, Scott McKnight, and I. Howard Marshall, 775–781. Leicester: IVP, 1992.
Marxsen, W. *Mark the Evangelist*. Translated by Roy A. Harrisville et al. Nashville, TN: Abingdon, 1969.
Matera, F. *New Testament Christology*. Louisville, KY: Westminster John Knox, 1999.
———. *What Are They Saying about Mark?* New York; Mahwah: Paulist, 1987.

Meeus, J. "The Maximum Possible Duration of a Total Solar Eclipse." *Journal of the British Astronomical Association* 113, no. 6 (2003): 343–348.

Meier, J. P. Correspondent, email message to author, 6 November 2015.

———. *A Marginal Jew: Rethinking the Historical Jesus*, vol. 1. New York: Doubleday, 1991.

———. *A Marginal Jew: Rethinking the Historical Jesus*, vol. 2. New York: Doubleday, 1994.

———. *A Marginal Jew: Rethinking the Historical Jesus*, vol. 3. New Haven & London: Yale, 2001.

Metzger, B. M. "The Fourth Book of Ezra." In *Apocalyptic Literature and Testaments*, The Old Testament Pseudepigrapha, vol. 1, edited by J. H. Charlesworth, 517–560. New York: Doubleday, 1983.

Michael, O. "The Son of Man." In *The New International Dictionary of New Testament Theology*, vol. 3, edited by Colin Brown, 607–660. Grand Rapids, MI: Zondervan, 1978.

Milik, J. T. *Ten Years of Discovery in the Wilderness of Judea*. Translated by J. Strugnell. London: SCM, 1959.

Miller, S. *Women in Mark's Gospel*. London: T & T Clark, 2004.

Miura, Y. "Son of David." In *Dictionary of Jesus and the Gospels*. Downers Grove, IL: InterVarsity, 2013.

Moltmann, J. *The Crucified God*. London: SCM, 1974.

Moo, D. *The Old Testament in the Gospel Passion Narratives*. Sheffield: Almond, 1983.

Moo, J. "A Messiah Whom 'The Many Do Not Know'? Rereading *4 Ezra* 5:6–7." *JTS* (2007): 525–536.

Mordechai, A. "The Hasmonean Dynasty's Activities in the Galilee." In *Jews, Pagans, and Christians in Galilee*, 41–50. New York: University of Rochester, 2004.

Morrison, G. S. *The Turning Point in the Gospel of Mark: A Study of Markan Christology*. Washington, DC: Catholic University of America, 2008.

Moule, C. *Birth of the New Testament*. London: A & C Black, 1966.

———. *The Gospel According to Mark*. Cambridge: Cambridge University Press, 1965.

———. *The Origin of Christology*. London: Cambridge University Press, 1977.

———. *The Phenomenon of the New Testament: An Inquiry into the Implications of Certain Features of the New Testament*. London: SCM, 1967.

Mowinckel, S. *He That Cometh*. Oxford: Blackwell, 1959.

———. *He That Cometh: The Messiah Concept in the Old Testament & Latter Judaism*. Grand Rapids: Eerdmans, 2005.

Moxnes, H. *Putting Jesus in His Place: A Radical Vision of Household and Kingdom*. Louisville: Westminster John Knox, 2003.

Muller, M. *Der Ausdruck "Menschensohn" in den Evangelien. Voraussetzungen und Bedeutung.* Leiden: Brill, 1984.

———. *The Expression "Son of Man" and the Development of Christology: A History of Interpretation.* Sheffield, UK: Equinox, 2008.

Munro, W. "Women Disciples in Mark." *CBQ* 44 (1982): 225–241.

Myers, C. *Binding the Strong Man: A Political Reading of Mark's Story of Jesus.* Maryknoll, NY: Orbis, 1988.

Neyrey, J. H., and E. Stewart, eds. *The Social World of the New Testament.* Peabody, MA: Hendrickson, 2008.

———. "Who Is Poor in the New Testament?" https://www3.nd.edu/~jneyrey1/Attitudes.html.

Nickelsburg, G. W. E. "Son of Man." *ABD* 6 (1992): 137–150.

Nineham, D. *The Gospel of St. Mark.* London: Adams & Charles, 1963.

Noth, M. "The Holy Ones of the Most High." In *The Laws in the Pentateuch and Other Studies.* Translated by D. R. Ap-Thomas, 215–228. Edinburgh: Oliver & Boyd, 1966.

Oakman, D. E. *Jesus and the Economics Questions of His Day.* Studies in the Bible and Early Christianity, vol. 8. Lewiston, NY: Mellen, 1986.

———. *Jesus and the Peasants.* Eugene: Cascade, 2008.

Olekamma, I. U. *The Healing of Blind Bartimaeus (Mk 10, 46–52) in the Markan Context: Two Ways of Asking.* Frankfurt: Peter Lang, 1999.

Otto, R. *The Kingdom of God and the Son of Man.* London and Redhill: Lutterworth, 1943.

Owen, P. L. "The Son of Man Debate." In *Who Is This Son of Man?: The Latest Scholarship on a Puzzling Expression of the Historical Jesus,* edited by Larry W. Hurtado and Paul L. Owen et al., vii–ix. New York: Bloomsbury; T & T Clark, 2011.

Painter, J. *Mark's Gospel: Worlds in Conflict.* London: Routledge, 1997.

Pannenberg, W. *Jesus: God and Man.* Edited by Lewis Wilkins and Duane A. Priebe. Philadelphia: Westminster, 1968.

———. *Jesus – God and Man.* 2nd edition. Translated by Lewis Wilkins and Duane Priebe. Philadelphia: Westminster, 1977.

Perrin, N. "The Christology of Mark: A Study in Methodology." In *A Modern Pilgrimage in New Testament Christology,* 104–121. Philadelphia: Fortress, 1974.

———. *A Modern Pilgrimage in New Testament Christology.* Philadelphia: Fortress, 1974.

———. *Rediscovering the Teaching of Jesus.* London: SCM, 1967.

Powell, M. A. *What Is Narrative Criticism?* Minneapolis: Fortress, 1990.

Punt, J. "Biblical Hermeneutics, Actualization, and Marginality in the New South Africa." In *African and European Readers of the Bible in Dialogue: In*

Quest of a Shared Meaning, edited by H. de Wit and G. O. West, 387–405. Studies of Religion in Africa: Supplements to the Journal of Religious in Africa, vol. 32. Leiden, Boston: Brill, 2008.

Rabbi, J. S. *"Am ha'aretz."* (2008). Accessed 28 May 2015. http://en.wikipedia.org/wiki/Am_ha'aretz.

Reddish, M. *Apocalyptic Literature: A. Reader*. Peabody: Hendrickson, 1993.

Reed, J. L. *Archaeology and the Galilean Jesus: A Re-examination of the Evidence*. Harrisburg: Trinity, 2000.

Resseguie, J. *Narrative Criticism of the New Testament*. Grand Rapids: Baker, 2005.

Reynolds, B. E. *The Apocalyptic Son of Man in the Gospel of John*. Tübingen: Mohr Siebeck, 2008.

Richardson, A. *An Introduction to the Theology of the NT*. London: SCM, 1958.

Roetzel, C. J. *Paul, a Jew on the Margins*. Louisville; London: Westminster John Knox, 2003.

Rogers, A. "Unveiling Mark's High Christology of Divine 'Inclusion.'" (1999–2013). Accessed 2 July 2013. http://www.answeringislam.org/authors/rogers/mark_inclusio.html.

Rohrbaugh, R. L. *The New Testament in Cross-Cultural Perspective*. Eugene: Cascade, 2006.

———. "Social Location: Jesus' World: The Social Location of the Markan Audience." In *The Social World of the New Testament*, edited by J. H. Neyrey, and E. C. Stewart, 141–162. Peabody: Hendrickson, 2008.

Rosado, C. "The Significance of Galilee to the Mission of the Church." (1995). Accessed 19 January 2015. http://www.rosado.net.

Rowe, R. D. "Is Daniel's Son of Man Messianic?" In *Christ the Lord: Studies in Christology Presented to Donald Guthrie*. Edited by Harold H. Rowden, 71–90. Leicester, UK: IVP, 1982.

Rusty, R. "The Pharisees – Jewish Leaders in the First Century AD: Jesus and the Pharisees." (2001). Accessed 3 May 2015. http://www.bible-history.com/Pharisees/PHARISEES.

Sanday, W. *The Life of Christ in Recent Research*. New York: Oxford, 1907.

Sanders, E. P. *Jesus and Judaism*. London: SCM, 1985.

———. *Judaism: Practice and Belief 63BC–66CE*. Philadelphia: SCM, 1992.

Schmidt, N. "The 'Son of Man' in the Book of Daniel." *JBL* 19 (1900): 22–28.

Schneider, G. "Der Menschensohn in der lukanischen Christologie." In *Jesus und der Menschensohn: Fur Anton Vogtle*, edited by R. Pesch and R. Schnackenburg, 267–282. Freiburg: Herder, 1975.

Schreiner, T. R. *New Testament Theology: Magnifying God in Christ*. Grand Rapids: Baker, 2008.

Schurer, E. *The History of the Jewish People in the Age of Jesus Christ*, vol. 1. Edited by G. Vermes and F. Millar. Edinburgh: T & T Clark, 1973.

———. *The History of the Jewish People in the Age of Jesus Christ*, vol. 2. Edited by G. Vermes, F. Muller and M. Black. London: New York: T & T Clark, 1979.

Schweitzer, A. *The Quest of the Historical Jesus*. Translated by W. Montgomery. New York: Macmillan; London: Black, 1961.

Schweizer, E. *Jesus*. Translated by D. E. Green. London: SCM, 1971.

———. "The Son of Man." *JBL* 79, no. 2 (1960): 119–129.

———. "The Son of Man Again." *New Testament Studies* 9 (1963): 256–261.

Seccombe, D. *The King of God's Kingdom*. London: Paternoster, 2002.

Sidebottom, E. M. *The Christ of the Fourth Gospel in the Light of First-Century Thought*. London: SPCK, 1961.

Silberman, L. H. "The Two 'Messiahs' of the Manual Discipline." Leiden: Brill, 1955.

Stalker, J. "Son of Man." In *The International Standard Bible Encyclopaedia*. Edited by James Orr, 2829. Chicago: Howard-Severance, 1915.

Stegemann, W., B. Malina, and G. Theissen. *The Social Setting of Jesus and the Gospels*. Minneapolis, MN: Fortress, 2002.

Stein, R. H. *Mark*. Baker Exegetical Commentary on the New Testament. Grand Rapids: Eerdmans, 2008.

———. *The Method and Message of Jesus' Teachings*. Louisville: Westminster John Knox, 1978.

Stone, M. E. *Features of the Eschatology of IV Ezra*. HSS. Atlanta: Scholars, 1989.

Straton, H. H. "The Son of Man and The Messianic Secret." *Journal of Religious Thought* 24 (1967–68).

Sweetland, D. *Our Journey with Jesus: Discipleship According to Mark*. Wilmington: Michael Glazier, 1978.

Swidler, L. *Biblical Affirmations of Women*. Philadelphia: Westminster, 1979.

Talbert, C. "The Concept of Immortals in Mediterranean Antiquity." *JBL* 94, no. 3 (1975): 419–436.

Taylor, V. *The Gospel According to St. Mark: The Greek Text with Introduction, Notes, and Indexes*. London: Macmillan, 1952.

———. *The Person of Christ in New Testament Teaching*. London: Macmillan, 1959.

Theisohn, J. "Der auserwahlte Richter." *SUNT* 12. Gottingen: Vandenhoeck & Ruprecht, 1975.

Theissen, G. *The Miracle Stories of the Early Christian Tradition*. Translated by F. MacDonagh. Philadelphia: Fortress, 1983.

Tejada-Lalinde, A. A. "Jesus as the Son of Man in Mark." *FIU Electronic Theses and Dissertations*. Paper 1175, 2014. Consult also, http://digitalcommons.fui.edu.

Telford, W. R., ed. *The Interpretation of Mark*. Edenburgh: T & T Clark, 1995.

Thielman, F. *Theology of the New Testament: A Canonical and Synthetic Approach*. Grand Rapids: Zondervan, 2005.

Thomassen, B. "The Uses and Meanings of Liminality." *International Political Anthropology* 2, no. 1 (2009): 5–28.

Thompson, G. H. P. "The Son of Man: The Evidence of the Dead Sea Scrolls." *E.T.* 72 (1961): 125.

Tödt, H. E. *The Son of Man in the Synoptic Tradition*. London: SCM, 1965.

Tuckett, C. M. "The Lucan Son of Man." In *Luke's Literary Achievement: Collected Essays*, JSNT Supplement Series 116, edited by C. M. Tuckett, 198–217. Sheffield: Sheffield, 1995.

Turnage, M. "First-Century Galilee: Contextualizing Jesus." (2015). Accessed 13 June 2015. http://enrichmentjournal.ag.org.

Turner, C. H. "OUIOSMOUOAGAPHTOS." *Journal of Theological Studies* 27 (1926): 113–129.

Turner, V. W. *Dramas, Fields, and Metaphors: Symbolic Action in Human Society*. Ithaca & London: Cornell University Press, 1974.

———. *Ritual Process: Structure and Anti-Structure*. Chicago: Aldine, 1969.

Twelftree, G. H. *Jesus the Exorcist: A Contribution to the Study of the Historical Jesus*. Tübingen: Mohr, 1993.

———. "Sanhedrin." In *Dictionary of Jesus and the Gospels*. Downers Grove, IL: InterVarsity, 2013.

Van Gennep, A. *The Rites of Passage*. London: Routledge & Kegan Paul, 1967.

———. *The Rites of Passage*. London: Routledge & Kegan Paul, 1977.

Van Iersel, B. V. *Reading Mark*. Edinburgh: T & T Clark, 1989.

Vermes, G. *The Complete Dead Sea Scrolls in English*. London: Penguin, 2004.

———. *Jesus the Jew: A Historian's Reading of the Gospels*. Pennsylvania: Fortress, 1973.

Via, D. O. Jr. *The Ethics of Mark's Gospel – In the Middle of Time*. Philadelphia: Fortress, 1985.

Vielhauer, P. "Erwagungen zur Christologie des Markusevangeliums." In *Aufsatze zum Neuen Testament*, 199–214. TBu 31. Munich: Chr. Kaiser, 1965.

Waetjen, H. C. *A Reordering of Power: A Socio-Political Reading of Mark's Gospel*. Minneapolis: Fortress, 1989.

Watts, R. E. *Isaiah's New Exodus and Mark*. Tübingen: Mohr Siebck, 1997.

Weeden, T. *Mark: Tradition in Conflict*. Philadelphia: Fortress, 1971.

White, M. "Galilee." (1995–2014). Accessed 14 February 2015. http://www.pbs.org.

Williams, P. J. "Expressing Definiteness in Aramaic: A Response to Casey's Theory Concerning the Son of Man Sayings." In *'Who Is This Son of Man?': The Latest Scholarship on a Puzzling Expression of the Historical Jesus*, edited by Larry W. Hurtado and Paul L. Owen et al., 61–77. New York: Bloomsbury; T & T Clark, 2011.

Wilson, A. *When Will These Things Happen? A Study of Jesus as Judge in Matthew 21–25*. PBTM. Carlisle: Paternoster, 2004.

Winn, A. "Son of God." In *Dictionary of Jesus and the Gospels*, 886–893. Downers Grove, IL: InterVarsity, 2013.

Wise, M. O., and J. Tabor. "Messiah at Qumran." *Biblical Archaeology Review* 18, no. 6 (1992): 60–65.

Witherington, B. III. *The Acts of Apostles: A Socio-Rhetorical Commentary*. Grand Rapids: Eerdmans, 1997.

———. *Christology of Jesus*. Minneapolis: Fortress, 1990.

———. *The Gospel of Mark: A Socio-Rhetorical Commentary*. Grand Rapids: Eerdmans, 2001.

———. *Jesus the Sage: The Pilgrimage of Wisdom*. Minneapolis: Fortress, 1994.

Wrede, W. *The Messianic Secret*. Translated by J. C. G. Grieg. Greenwood, NC: Attic, 1971.

Wright, N. T. *The Challenge of Jesus*. London: SPCK, 2000.

———. "Christ Is Risen from the Dead, the First Fruits of Those Who Have Died." Unpublished paper delivered at the Conference of Italian Bishops "Jesus, Our Contemporary." Rome, February, 2012.

———. *Jesus and the Victory of God*. Christian Origins and the Question of God, vol. 2. Minneapolis: Fortress, 1996.

———. *Mark for Everyone*. London: SPCK, 2001.

———. *The New Testament and the People of God*. Christian Origins and the Question of God, vol. 1. Minneapolis: Fortress, 1992.

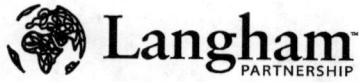

Langham Literature and its imprints are a ministry of Langham Partnership.

Langham Partnership is a global fellowship working in pursuit of the vision God entrusted to its founder John Stott –

> *to facilitate the growth of the church in maturity and Christ-likeness through raising the standards of biblical preaching and teaching.*

Our vision is to see churches in the majority world equipped for mission and growing to maturity in Christ through the ministry of pastors and leaders who believe, teach and live by the Word of God.

Our mission is to strengthen the ministry of the Word of God through:
- nurturing national movements for biblical preaching
- fostering the creation and distribution of evangelical literature
- enhancing evangelical theological education

especially in countries where churches are under-resourced.

Our ministry

Langham Preaching partners with national leaders to nurture indigenous biblical preaching movements for pastors and lay preachers all around the world. With the support of a team of trainers from many countries, a multi-level programme of seminars provides practical training, and is followed by a programme for training local facilitators. Local preachers' groups and national and regional networks ensure continuity and ongoing development, seeking to build vigorous movements committed to Bible exposition.

Langham Literature provides majority world preachers, scholars and seminary libraries with evangelical books and electronic resources through publishing and distribution, grants and discounts. The programme also fosters the creation of indigenous evangelical books in many languages, through writer's grants, strengthening local evangelical publishing houses, and investment in major regional literature projects, such as one volume Bible commentaries like *The Africa Bible Commentary* and *The South Asia Bible Commentary*.

Langham Scholars provides financial support for evangelical doctoral students from the majority world so that, when they return home, they may train pastors and other Christian leaders with sound, biblical and theological teaching. This programme equips those who equip others. Langham Scholars also works in partnership with majority world seminaries in strengthening evangelical theological education. A growing number of Langham Scholars study in high quality doctoral programmes in the majority world itself. As well as teaching the next generation of pastors, graduated Langham Scholars exercise significant influence through their writing and leadership.

To learn more about Langham Partnership and the work we do visit **langham.org**

www.ingramcontent.com/pod-product-compliance
Lightning Source LLC
Chambersburg PA
CBHW051539230426
43669CB00015B/2660

Bekele Deboch Anshiso engages many of the most perennially challenging issues in the interpretation of Mark's gospel. He brings fresh insight to Mark's presentation of the divine messianic identity of Jesus by focusing on the way in which the revelation of Jesus as the divine Messiah in his crucifixion is anticipated and mirrored by his interaction with marginal and liminal characters in the gospel. Just as the rejected and outcast see who Jesus really is, so too, who he really is, is revealed most clearly as he is rejected and outcast. His identification with the demonized and downcast, with the sinful and excluded, reveals the nature of his mission, the nature of the people he will form, and ultimately his own nature as the revelation of God himself. The book holds many unexpected delights on Mark's unexpected Messiah.

Steven M. Bryan, PhD
Professor of New Testament, Trinity Evangelical Divinity School,
Deerfield, IL, USA

Bekele Deboch Anshiso's close reading of Mark's gospel highlights Jesus's messianic identity as his self-identification with marginalized and liminal people. He convincingly shows how Mark's narrative enigmatically portrays the Son of God as the suffering and vindicated Son of Man, associating with disowned and disregarded people. With careful attention, Anshiso also shows how Jesus's extreme self-marginalization and identification with liminals informs his own identity, and the identity of his followers, past and present.

Jeremy Punt, DTh
Professor of New Testament, Faculty of Theology,
Stellenbosch University, South Africa

At our first discussion over coffee in Muizenberg I failed to see the importance of Bekele Deboch's new ideas about Mark. This was because I was reading Mark with the eyes of a later Christian. It appeared obvious to me that the Messiah would associate with the marginalized. But how might it have struck someone without that background? My excitement about his thesis grew, especially in later discussions when we explored how strange it must have seemed to the first readers of Mark that a king (God no less) should associate so freely with the despised and unimportant members of his society. Was there any precedent for it?

Bekele Deboch is a remarkable person, deeply touched by God, and used by him to spread the message of Jesus among some of the poorest elements of Ethiopian society. I warmly commend this study about Jesus and the marginalized in the Gospel of Mark.

David Seccombe, PhD
Author and Speaker
Research Fellow, George Whitefield College, Cape Town, South Africa